9780520015159
AF576883

IXIL COUNTRY

IXIL COUNTRY

A Plural Society in Highland Guatemala

BENJAMIN N. COLBY
PIERRE L. VAN DEN BERGHE

University of California Press
Berkeley 1969

University of California Press
Berkeley and Los Angeles, California
University of California Press, Ltd.
London, England

Library of Congress Catalog Card Number: 68-16740
Printed in the United States of America

To the memory of
JACKSON STEWARD LINCOLN
who died during his
pioneer ethnographic work
among the Ixil

PREFACE

The central aim of this monograph is to study the structure and dynamics of a plural society in the northwest highlands of Guatemala. We call a society pluralistic to the extent that it is divided into socially, and in most cases culturally, distinct groups, with a compartmentalized institutional structure of *duplicatory* (as distinguished from functionally differentiated) sectors. Thus a society is pluralistic if it consists of several interacting ethnic, "racial," or caste groups linked through a set of economic and political ties, each group having its own set of kinship institutions, religious and cosmological systems, voluntary associations, child-rearing practices, and so on.

Of course, the Ixil region is not a complete independent society, but rather a segment of the larger national society of Guatemala. The autonomy of the Ixil zone is limited by the political hegemony of the central government, the economic integration with the rest of the country, and the linguistic, religious, kinship, and other ties of its inhabitants with the larger society. While we relate the Ixil region to the larger society at various points, the main scope of the monograph is geographically circumscribed to an area of approximately 2,300 km^2, with a biethnic population of around 50,000, only one percent of the national total. Our regional approach is closely similar to that adopted by the Mexican anthropologists of the Instituto Nacional Indigenista, notably by Gonzalo Aguirre Beltran and Julio de la Fuente. The entire population of the region is our unit of analysis, rather than a single ethnic group as defined by certain linguistic and other cultural characteristics.

This book is decidedly not a general ethnography of the Ixil. The focus is on the relations *between* two ethnic groups, not on the culture or social structure of either group. Nor have we attempted to describe Ixil culture "from the inside," that is from the perspective of the Ixil world view. Finally, we have not been concerned here with the range of individual variation exhibited by the users of any given culture. This last task, to which Colby intends to devote his next several years of field work, requires much more ethnographic information than we have collected so far.

Local ladino (non-Indian) culture departs in only relatively minor ways from the dominant hispanic culture in other parts of Mesoamerica, and can thus be largely taken as "known" for purposes of this work. The same cannot be said of Ixil culture, of which there is no comprehensive published account. Consequently, we have found it necessary to include in summary form some material that would normally be found in a general ethnography. This is especially the case for the religious, political, and economic institutions which are the main areas of contact between the two ethnic groups. In order to understand the interplay between two institutional structures, or two ethnic groups, the reader must be given some idea of the cultural content of the entities in presence.

If this book had to be classified into any existing genre, it would probably best fit in the category of monographs on "ethnic relations." However, unlike many such studies which have dealt with their subject as a special and isolated aspect of social relations (e.g., as a special case of social stratification), our study has approached ethnic relations from the more holistic perspective of pluralism. That is, we have treated the interplay of institutional structures belonging to different cultures and the network of relations between members of distinct ethnic groups as "total social phenomena" with ramifications in the entire society. Pluralism is a basic property of the social system under study here, and, indeed, of most of the world's national societies. So important and general is pluralism as a dimension of both social analysis and empirical reality that its neglect limits the validity of studies which treat "cultures" as approximations to closed systems. Instead of treating culture contact and "intergroup relations" as phenomena peripheral to the study of internally integrated cultures, we reverse the emphasis by suggesting that contact, cooperation, and conflict between ethnic groups, and the coexistence of culturally diverse and only partially integrated institutional structures characterize most contemporary societies, and are among the most important sources of social change.

Chapter I puts the Ixil region in the larger context of contemporary Guatemala, and gives the geographical and ecological setting of Ixil country. Since the late nineteenth century, the development of cash crops, the consolidation of the power of the central government, the opening of better means of communication, and other processes of "modernization" have increasingly reduced the economic and political autonomy of the Ixil zone, and drawn it into the life of the national society.

In Chapter II we trace the evolution of the plural society in the Ixil region from the time of the Spanish Conquest. Although there is evidence of extensive trade and other forms of contact between the Ixil and their other Maya neighbors in pre-Conquest times, the arrival of the Spaniards in the 1520's clearly increased the degree of pluralism in the region. Thus, the Conquest marks the beginning of the plural society with which we are concerned here. It is not our aim to give a comprehensive treatment of local history, for that would require further work in archeology and oral tradition; such research falls outside the scope of this monograph. The available evidence prior to the nineteenth century is fragmentary, and conditions prior to that period often have to be inferred from documents dealing with neighboring areas. Nevertheless, we have tried to sketch the broad outline of the region's history of contact in the last four and a half centuries, insofar as available sources have allowed us to reconstruct it, and insofar as an understanding of the past is essential to a treatment of present conditions.

The next three chapters deal with three main aspects of the plural society of the Ixil region. In Chapter III, the analysis is focused at the *group* level; that is, we define the main lines of cleavage between ladinos and Indians, orthodox and syncretistic Catholics, rural and urban inhabitants, and members of different social strata. Chapter IV is devoted to an analysis of the *institutional structure* of the plural society, with special emphasis on the three main areas of interpenetration: politics, economics, and religion. Here the focus is on the set of institutions which define the form and the content of intergroup behavior and thus create the structural backbone of the plural society. In Chapter V, we shift our analysis on the specific forms of behavior between members of the two ethnic groups. That is, we describe how the dual pluralism of the local society in terms of group membership and institutional structure is expressed at the level of individual behavior across ethnic lines.

So far, the analysis has been fairly static. In Chapter VI, however, we turn to the complex process of change in ethnic membership and relations. As much of the change is exogenous to the local region, we must once more broaden our scope to the national society and indeed to Mesoamerica as a whole.

The reader may legitimately ask how we arrived at our conclusions. To state our various sources of evidence in the body of the text would be tedious and repetitive. Therefore, we shall attempt to do so in a general way, in the form of a methodological statement. This study is the product of collaboration between an anthropologist and a sociologist. We have worked together before in a similar study of ethnic relations in Chiapas, Mexico (Colby and van den Berghe, 1961; van den Berghe and Colby, 1961). The present work represents a resumption of this collaboration with a similar division of labor. Colby selected the Ixil area for study on the basis of a brief visit in 1962. Lincoln's field notes on the Ixil (1945) gave us much valuable ethnographic information as well as a time depth seldom achieved in ethnographic work. Thus Lincoln's previous work was an important factor affecting the choice of Ixil country for study. Colby's principal interest in Ixil society was in the culture variation among individuals, and the project supported by the National Science Foundation (Grant G.S. 990) was titled "The Ixil of Guatemala, a Study of Variation in a Complex Society." Van den Berghe was primarily interested in studying a situation of ethnic relations which presented both similarities and differences with neighboring Chiapas.

Colby began his field work in January of 1966. He made several field trips that year, accompanied at one time by his wife, Lore Colby, and children, and another time by a cinematographer. He also brought informants with him to Santa Fe.

In June, 1966, we went into the field together, though we worked together for little more than two weeks. During that time Colby recorded texts, trained some literate Indians to transcribe Ixil, and supervised the pretesting and administration of a 50-item interview schedule (which had been developed together with Lore Colby and Ixil assistants in Santa Fe) to a sample of ninety Ixil, selected partially by assistants and informants. The questions were asked in Ixil, and the answers were recorded verbatim in Ixil. Colby then returned to the United States, while van den Berghe briefly visited Chiapas and returned to Nebaj, where he remained until the end of August. At the same time, Fernando Cruz, a Guatemalan anthropology student, spent several weeks in the field gathering data on the Ixil *cofradías*. Van den Berghe worked mostly among ladinos, using the standard techniques of participant and nonparticipant observation; extended and repeated interviews, mostly unstructured, with a score of key informants; and analysis of the rather scanty municipal and parochial records. Field notes were written every evening from sketchy notations taken during the day. In addition, a 64-item questionnaire was distributed to a selected sample of forty literate ladinos. (For a description of sample characteristics see n. 4, chap. 3.) With both ladinos and Indians, van den Berghe used Spanish as the medium of communication. Except for a short trip to Chiapas, a two-day visit to the plantation of San Francisco, a day's visit to Chajul, another day in Cotzal, and a few days in Guatemala City, the entire period was spent in Nebaj. As field headquarters, we rented a large house owned by a local upper-class ladino and located on the central plaza of Nebaj.

In January, 1967, Colby returned to the field with his wife and children and gathered information mostly from Ixil informants, using both Spanish and Ixil questions and conversing in Spanish or with Spanish-Ixil interpreters. During the time thus far covered in field work, Colby has been mostly in Nebaj, though numerous trips lasting from one day to a week have been made to Chajul and Cotzal. Colby also made various trips on foot to outlying villages and hamlets such as Juil, Kamb'alam, and Peșla. In addition to attending religious ceremonies and rites and observing other Ixil activities, Colby made motion-picture records. In Guatemala City, where Lore Colby was based because of the children's school requirements, life histories, myths, folktales, discussions, and explanatory texts were recorded in Ixil by informants who stayed with the Colbys. These were then transcribed with the help of native assistants. The results of the Ixil interview schedules were coded and sent to Cambridge Computer Associates, who ran the data on Harvard's IBM 7094 with the Multivariate Statistical Analyzer program. Colby gathered additional data from the Archivo Nacional; the Archivo Eclesiástico de Guatemala; the parochial records of Nebaj, Cotzal, and Chajul; and the Guatemalan Census Office. Throughout the two periods of field work the authors exchanged ideas, field notes, and chapter drafts.

Rapport presented no serious problems at any time in our study except in the Chajul area, which has many characteristics of the more conservative pueblos in the southwestern United States, where traditional religious information is guarded closely from outsiders. Most ladinos and Indians received us with great courtesy and hospitality and graciously gave us the information we requested. The usual amount of gossip and rumors surrounded our stay. In the beginning we were frequently ascribed a religious role. In Nebaj some thought us to be Protestant missionaries because we were "gringos," as were also the three Protestant missionary families in town. The role was also imputed to us because our field headquarters had previously been rented to a Protestant denomination which used the house as a chapel. In Chajul, Colby was thought to be a Catholic priest because he once spent a week living in the convent, and because the Land-Rover we drove was of similar color and model as that used by the two resident priests in Chajul. At all times, we presented ourselves as being interested in local history and in Ixil culture, and the municipal authorities and many of our respondents apparently accepted our explanations at face value. Because of the cleavage between catechists and "old Catholics," it was important to dissociate ourselves from the Catholic Church. Because of resentment against Protestant missionaries on the part of others, we also tried to avoid being associated with that group.

Understandably, there was at first some reluctance on the part of municipal authorities to let us consult the records. In view of the transfer of power from a military government to a democratically elected one in 1966, and in view of the unsettled political climate which persisted through 1967, a certain amount of official caution was to be expected. After a former mayor of Nebaj vouchsafed for the purity of our intentions, the *municipio* extended to us its most courteous collaboration. Later, when Colby showed some of the films he had taken in the area to the townspeople, there was an increased interest in our work. The films of religious activities were shown at the expressed request of some of our Ixil informants, who wanted their companions to know that their time with us was not spent in witchcraft machinations. As a result of one of the film showings, however, one of our informants was assaulted by a drunken fellow Ixil for "working with the gringos." These cases were minor, however, except for the Chajul area, where some of the people showed the same hostility that Stoll in the last century ascribed to the Nebaj Ixil. Traditional Chajul people would say they would talk to us for a price, which, when quoted, would be exorbitant by local standards. This xenophobia, however, also seems to be shown toward fellow Ixil from the other two dialect areas, except during the main fiesta of Chajul.

Our disproportionate reliance on literate, high-status informants among both ladinos and Indians undoubtedly introduced a class bias in our sources of interview data. However, 36 percent of our Ixil sample were illiterate. Furthermore, the observational data was presumably free of this bias. Our residence in the town of Nebaj also introduced an "urban" bias, insofar as that town can be called "urban." There are some significant differences between the town dwellers and the people living in the more remote *aldeas,* and we interviewed urbanites, mostly but not exclusively. This bias applies somewhat more for ladinos than for Indians. From the beginning of the Ixil project in 1966 to the time this manuscript went to press, Colby has had continuous contact with Ixil informants, even when he was in the United States.

Since this book has gone to press, eight Ixil (a couple with children, a carpenter, a diviner, and a transcribing assistant) have come to the University of California, Irvine, where Colby is teaching. They are training students and building an Ixil house on the campus at the Anthropology Farm. Additional research was done by John and Dorothy Clement, who spent the summer of 1968 in Nebaj studying curing practices, divination an other matters of ethnographic interest. Some of their photographs are included in this book.

ACKNOWLEDGMENTS

Financial support for this study was given by the National Science Foundation (Grant G.S. 990) and by the Graduate School of the University of Washington through a faculty summer research grant, for which we are indebted. Our sponsors have, of course, no responsibility for the views advanced in this work. The alphabetical listing of our names in the title implies equality of seniority and responsibility between us. We each have a debt of gratitude to our wives and children for putting up with absences, discomfort, and other inconveniences of field work. In addition, Lore Colby, who worked with us as linguist for the Ixil project, gave invaluable assistance in the translation and transcription of texts, questionnaires, and interview schedules. She worked with us during and between the various periods of field work from January through August of 1966 and January through June of 1967. Fernando and Gloria Cruz assisted us in the early bibliographic work at the Morley Library for Mesoamerican Research at the Museum of New Mexico. Later Maria del Socorro Velasco Coello gave much valuable assistance in locating relevant historical data in Santa Fe. Fernando Cruz also gathered data on the Ixil *cofradías* of Nebaj and made helpful comments on a draft of this monograph. We are grateful also to the Museum of New Mexico's Research Division for allowing Colby and his wife such long periods of absence from Santa Fe. Mrs. Beulah Reddaway in Seattle and Señora Stella Mendez de Giracca in Guatemala typed much of the field notes and various revisions of the manuscript as they were sent back and forth between Guatemala and Seattle. The Colbys are especially indebted to Friedrun Polster, who came to Guatemala to handle the logistics of feeding the Colby family, the native transcribing assistants as well as numerous informants from Chajul, Nebaj, and Cotzal, who worked with us in Guatemala City when we were not in the field itself. Cambridge Computer Associates arranged to run the results of the ninety Ixil interviews on the computer at Harvard. When red tape threatened to delay the computer work, Philip J. Stone generously loaned us some of his machine time.

Our greatest debt, of course, is to the two or three hundred people of Nebaj, Cotzal, and Chajul who in greater or lesser degree contributed to our study and put up patiently and graciously with two inquisitive "gringos." To name these informants and hosts would result in unwitting omissions; they include alcaldes, municipal councilmen and employees, teachers, priests, merchants, artisans, holders of religious office, farmers, migrant workers, labor contractors, housewives, and even schoolchildren. Both Ixil and ladinos accepted the obtrusive omnipresence of strangers in their midst with courtesy and good humor. They generously offered their collaboration and often extended us their warm hospitality. Anthropological field work frequently becomes an enriching and fondly remembered part of one's life experience. Our stay in Ixil country certainly fits that pattern. Anthropology is a constant reaffirmation of man's fascinating diversity and fundamental oneness.

Lastly, we are grateful to the Republic of Guatemala's Census Bureau, Department of Statistics, National Archives, Ecclesiastical Archives, and the Instituto Indigenista Nacional and its director, Dr. Epaminondas Quintana, for their collaboration and assistance. In these days of political intrigue and Yankee intervention in various parts of the world, it is no small proof of their confidence that they should have accepted us as bona fide scholars.

CONTENTS

Introduction 1

I The National and Geographical Setting 25

II History 39

III Social Cleavages: Ethnicity, Religion, Urbanism, and Social Class 80

IV The Institutional Context of Ethnic Relations: Politics, Economics, and Religion 117

V The Form of Ethnic Relations 144

VI The Sociocultural Dynamics of the Plural Society 169

Appendixes

A: Note on Ixil Phonology 185
B: Glossary of Spanish and Ixil Words 187
C: Statistical Tables 192

Bibliography 197

Index 209

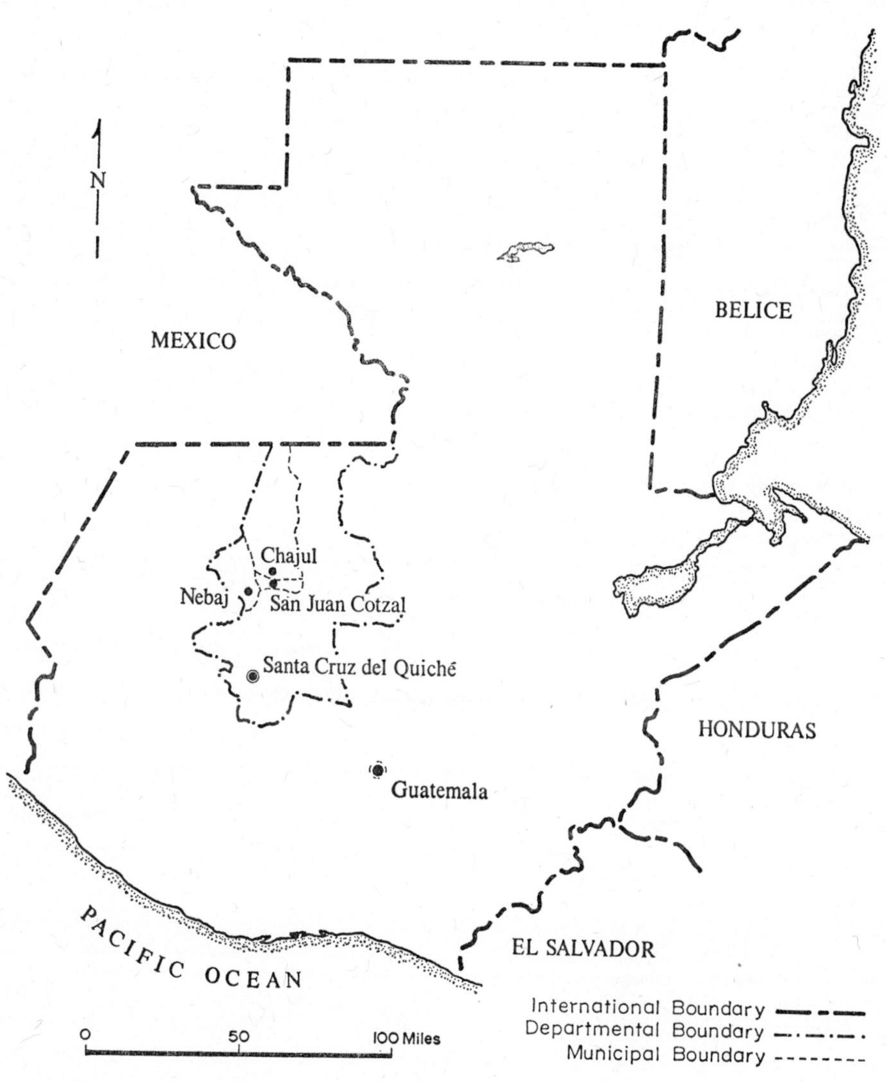

Map 1. Guatemala, showing the three *municipios* of Ixil country

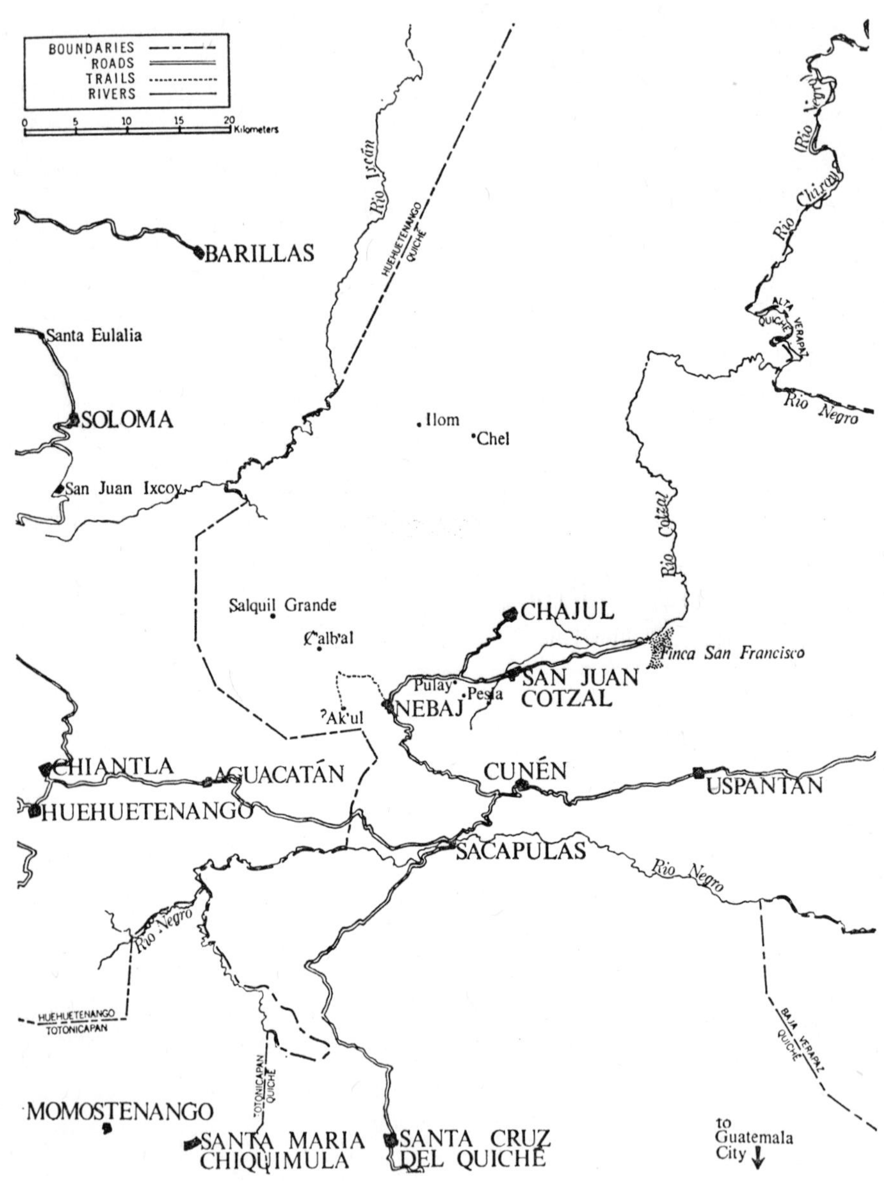

Map 2. Chief towns and outlying communities of Ixil country

INTRODUCTION

THE PRESENT MONOGRAPH constitutes a deliberate attempt to shift the focus of analysis from the "society-culture" treated as a homogeneous, integrated, autonomous whole, to the "plural society" which contains two or more such "cultures." Until the early 1950's, most of French, British, and North American sociology and anthropology adhered to a functionalist view of society and culture as consisting of interacting individuals whose behavior was patterned by a common set of interrelated institutions, values, and norms. The two disciplines differed in their methods, in the scale of the societies they studied, and—at least in the United States—in the respective stress they put on "social structure" as distinguished from the specific cultural forms of interaction. Anthropologists, being more familiar with the wide cultural range of behavior, have been, on the whole, more relativistic, historicist, and reluctant to generalize than sociologists. Nevertheless, both disciplines have built their models largely around the society-culture (or some subunit thereof) treated, if only for analytical purposes, as a closed system.

There are, of course, good heuristic reasons for using the society-culture as basic unit of analysis, and our present approach is meant to complement rather than conflict with the more conventional one. Homogeneity within a group and functional autonomy from other groups are two basic criteria used in the drawing of analytical boundaries between groups, and consequently in the definition of one's unit of analysis. A third criterion is a people's subjective perception of such boundaries. All three criteria are relative, but there are nevertheless certain discontinuities—such as political independence, mutual intelligibility of languages, or economic self-sufficiency—which lend empirical validity to analytical distinctions. For many purposes, it does "make sense" to focus on ethnic groups, to disregard the range of cultural variation within the chosen unit, and to treat the group as a closed system and as an independent "case." Such simplified assumptions, like the recognized fiction of a homogeneous speech community with an autonomous system of internally dynamic forces of change, are sometimes necessary for the exposition of theory.

Our approach does not constitute a rejection of conventional ethnography; it is simply an attempt to demonstrate that a shift in the level of analysis leads one to a new look at old problems of social change, integration, conflict, and many others. Our point of departure is simply the empirical fact that most of the world's societies are culturally and socially pluralistic if the unit of analysis is the independent and centralized polity. Most "cultures," "tribes," "ethnicities," or "castes" are parts of larger social systems which, with the processes of "modernization," become increasingly important. As parts of larger social systems, ethnic groups are so affected politically, economically, and culturally that the validity of treating them as independent systems perpetuating themselves in terms of their own internal dynamics is increasingly restricted.

The above suggestion is, of course, neither profound nor new. The first attempts in anthropology to deal with culture contact and exogenous change date back at least to the 1930's with the development of acculturation theory. Nevertheless, the bulk of ethnographic work until the 1950's retained its traditional focus on the ethnic group as the unit of analysis. Even though nearly all of the microsocieties studied by anthropologists had long been parts of large colonial empires or had been incorporated in modern independent states, the sociological study of colonialism, whether in its overseas or in its internal form, has come in only during colonialism's final phases.[1]

If the shift in emphasis meant nothing more than a change in scale, the study of plural societies would not require a fresh perspective. In fact, while highly pluralistic societies tend to be quite large, so also are some of the world's more homogeneous societies, such as France and the greater part of China. Many anthropologists have studied large-scale societies without being concerned with problems of pluralism. Our contention is that pluralism is an important dimension, or better, a set of dimensions of societies; holding size constant, highly pluralistic countries are significantly different from highly homogeneous ones. Switzerland and Belgium are unlike Denmark or Holland; the United States is unlike the Soviet Union; Guatemala is unlike Costa Rica; and some of their differences are due to their widely varying degrees of pluralism.

We do not claim that there ought to be a special "theory of pluralism." Pluralism is only one of the important sets of dimensions of society. But by making pluralism the focus of analysis, such problems as the balance between endogenous and exogenous change, between cooperation and conflict, between consensus and coercion, between integration and autonomy of parts, between complementarity and duplication of functions, are apt to be answered differently than by placing the focus on the homogeneous ethnic group.[2]

[1] The notion of "internal colonialism" has been used to refer to situations where an independent country has, within its own boundaries, given special legal status to groups that differ culturally from the dominant group, and created a distinct administrative machinery to handle such groups. Marquard (1957) and van den Berghe (1965b) have used the concept in the South African situation, while Pablo Gonzalez Casanova (1964, 1965) has applied it to Mexico.

[2] In a recent article, Marie R. Haug (1967) tested the usefulness of the concept of pluralism in comparative macro-sociology and arrived at very positive results.

More especially, the pluralism approach puts the study of culture change resulting from "culture contact" in a somewhat new perspective. Culture change is regarded as an integral part of the interaction process between groups but *within a single society,* and not as an exogenous source of change impinging, as it were, on the integration of the ethnically defined society-culture. Societies change not only because they are "exposed" to other societies or because they grow in size, complexity, and functional differentiation, but also because their internal heterogeneity, their cleavages, and their partial lack of integration create intrasystemic dynamics of conflict and cooperation, of contradictions and adaptations. At the most general theoretical level, the pluralism approach represents an attempt to bring together within a single analytical framework the "functionalist" and the "conflict" streams of sociological thinking (van den Berghe, 1963).

Two of the earliest analyses of plural societies are those of Max Gluckman (1958) in Zululand and of Robert Redfield (1941) in Yucatán. Both studies were done in the 1930's and both marked significant departures from the conventional ethnographic approach. As a South African influenced by Marx and brought up in a society ridden with racial tensions, Gluckman's basic query was: What makes the South African quasi-colonial regime in Zululand "work"? That is, what is the basis of social integration in Zululand? Instead of social integration being taken for granted, to Gluckman it was problematic. Gluckman's work became influential in Africanist circles, especially in Southern Africa where the impact of the West has been so overwhelming as to make the study of pluralism almost inescapable. Hilda Kuper's work on race relations in Swaziland (1947), Leo Kuper's (1965), van den Berghe's (1964, 1965b), and Philip Mayer's (1961) studies of South Africa, Clyde Mitchell's in Zambia and Rhodesia (1960), M. G. Smith's on Nigeria and the Caribbean

(1965a, 1965b), Burton Benedict's (1961 and 1962) on Mauritius, Adrian Mayer's (1961) on Fiji, and Leo Despres' (1958) on British Guiana all owe something to Gluckman as well as to the studies of Asian colonial societies by Furnivall (1948) and Boeke (1953). Balandier's classic statement on "the colonial situation" (1963) and his studies in west-central Africa are also closely related to the above works.

In the Americas, Redfield's study of Chan Kom in Yucatán was also a significant break from tradition and indeed from his own famous 1926 monograph on Tepoztlán. In *The Folk Culture of Yucatán* (1941), Redfield abandons the "primitive isolate" approach and relates his local community to the whole region of Yucatán and its urban center, Mérida. In the process, he refines his folk-urban dichotomy (which was little more than a reformulation of similar ideal-types propounded by Cooley, Durkheim, and Toennies), and introduces the concept of peasant as an agriculturalist who is economically and culturally incorporated in a partially urban region. In 1956, Redfield clearly stresses the need to relate the "primitive isolate" to the large system, that is, to study plural societies.

"The primitive isolate became connected with the great society while the anthropologist was looking at it; indeed, the anthropologist himself was one of the instruments of this transformation. More and more, anthropologists came to study communities in many and complex relationships with other peoples and with histories known or knowable" (1956: pp. 8–9).

Redfield's influence on subsequent work in Latin America can scarcely be overestimated. Even those who were most critical of him, such as Oscar Lewis (1951) in his restudy of Tepoztlán, owe him a debt. In the applied field, the Instituto Nacional Indigenista of Mexico adopted the framework of regional integration in its program of guided social change. The anthropologists Julio de la Fuente

(1965), A. Villa Rojas, and G. Aguirre Beltrán (1957) are among the most prominent Mexican proponents of the necessity of relating town and country, ladinos and Indians, in Mesoamerican studies. By the 1940's, Gillin (1948, 1951, 1958) and Tumin (1949, 1952) were working on ethnic relations in Guatemala, and Wagley (1953) in Brazil. Recently Wolf (1966) elaborated on Redfield's concept of peasant, stressing political and economic factors.

Closest perhaps to our own concept of pluralism in the Mesoamerican area is the recent statement by Manning Nash (1966):

> This notion takes explicit account of the fact that the unit of study for modernization and development is a political one —a nation or, in looser terms, a country. It turns attention to the horizontal and vertical cleavages within a given country, by stressing the differential scope of command over persons, resources, and symbols, and through accenting the different impulses to change in terms of the opportunities and costs to segments in varying role sets within the social system (1966: p. 126). [He goes on:]
>
> As a social type, the multiple society with plural cultures is marked by the presence of at least two distinct cultural traditions, each significantly different in breadth of integration. The entire population of the national territory is included in a single system of political and economic bonds, but only a part of the population is aware of and identified with a national entity. Only a part of the population participates significantly in the national social and cultural life or has control over resources and communications of nationwide scope or impact. That part of the population which carries the national variety of culture is in fact the national society: it is distributed throughout the national territory; it is the link between the nation and other nations in the world. It is the segment of population in which political control is vested and within which political control is contested. Its decisions have national repercussions in the economy as well as in the polity (1966: pp. 126–127).

Before turning to a more formal treatment of pluralism, we must define two key terms. The definition of what constitutes a *society* is, of course, arbitrary, and the criterion of independent viability is relative. While, for some purposes, a higher or a lower level of analysis may be more appropriate, the social system contained within the boundaries of a sovereign state is probably the most clearly defined unit for macro-sociological analysis. (According to this definition, the subject matter of this monograph is really a sub-society within a total society.) The definition of a *culture* or *culture group* is similarly arbitrary. In many cases the linguistic criterion (i.e., speaking a mutually understandable language) is both fairly clear-cut and significant; however, the subjective perception of cultural differences by the people concerned is sometimes more important than the actual presence or absence of such differences. Adopting these definitions, society and culture are seldom empirically coextensive units. Most of the world's societies are multicultural to a greater or lesser degree, and many ethnic groups are divided among several societies.

Let us now try to specify what we mean by pluralism.[3] Societies are pluralistic insofar as they exhibit, to a greater or lesser degree, the conjunction of two basic features: segmentation into functionally similar corporate groups (whose members frequently, though not necessarily, use different cultures or subcultures); and a social structure compartmentalized into analogous, duplicatory, parallel, noncomplementary, but distinguishable sets of institutions.

These two defining criteria of pluralism distinguish

[3] The following formulation contradicts the position of a number of American and French social scientists. Raymond Aron, William Kornhauser, Seymour M. Lipset, and many others in the tradition of de Tocqueville have defined pluralism primarily in political terms. They have called a polity pluralistic if it contained interest groups competing for power in shifting patterns of alignment and according to commonly accepted rules of the political game. Much of what these authors have meant by pluralism has simply been functional differentiation.

plural societies both from societies with segmentary kinship units (such as lineages, moieties, or clans), and from societies with a high degree of functional differentiation or specialization in their institutional structure. The segmentary, undifferentiated society is divided into clearly defined corporate groups (typically unilineal descent groups), but it has a unitary, homogeneous, institutional structure. On the other hand, the functionally differentiated society has multiple but complementary and interrelated institutions.[4]

Additional characteristics frequently associated with pluralism as we have defined it are the following: relative absence of value consensus; relative presence of cultural heterogeneity;[5] relative presence of conflict between the significant corporate groups; relative autonomy between parts of the social system; relative importance of coercion and economic interdependence as bases of social integration; political domination by one of the corporate groups over the others; and primacy of segmental, utilitarian, nonaffective, and functionally specific relationships *between* corporate groups, and of total, non-utilitarian, affective, diffuse ties *within* such groups.

A further important analytical distinction is that between *social* pluralism and *cultural* pluralism. The latter refers to the degree to which the component groups within a society are culturally heterogeneous. Minimal cultural

[4] Thus, in the United States for example, the fact that labor unions, manufacturers' associations, and religious denominations compete for political power is not an instance of pluralism as we defined the term; these voluntary associations, though multiple, are functionally specific and specialized. On the other hand, the presence in the United States of Protestant, Catholic, and Jewish denominations does constitute an instance of pluralism. So does to an even greater extent the coexistence of Negro and white Baptist groups. The failure of the Tocquevillian concept to distinguish pluralism as we defined it from both segmentation into institutionally identical structures and differentiation into functionally specific ones obfuscates much of the literature on the topic.

[5] In the strictest sense, of course, no culture is completely homogeneous. Each individual uses an idiosyncratic variant of his culture. The magnitude of the variations is obviously an important factor.

without any formal political status to constituent ethnic groups. (Belgium comes close to that model.) Typically in such systems there is a great deal of informal agreement to secure an acceptable ethnic balance in the various organs of government. Or there may be a federal structure wherein political boundaries correspond more or less closely to ethnicity, as in Switzerland or Yugoslavia.

Perhaps the most common type of polity in highly pluralistic societies is the "colonial" one in which the political institutions themselves are pluralistic. There is widespread resort to coercion and a sharp political cleavage based on ethnicity, with one group, often a small minority, exercising control over the others through monopolization of the apparatus of violence and administration. The subject groups often retain a set of clearly distinct political institutions and a certain degree of internal autonomy, but these political sub-systems are firmly subordinated to the central government. Indirect rule typifies such a situation. A special case within the colonial type of polity is that which one of us has called "*Herrenvolk* democracy," that is, a system like that of South Africa until recently, where the dominant group rules itself democratically, but subjects other groups to a colonial tyranny (van den Berghe, 1965b).

Plural societies then are characterized by a common polity wherein political relations are almost invariably specified along ethnic or racial lines, and wherein the constituent groups very frequently have differential relations to the central government. There is a wide range in the degree to which the political institutions themselves are pluralistic, and in the degree to which coercion is resorted to. Generally, the more pluralistic the society as a whole and the political institutions in particular, the more tyrannical the polity tends to be.[6]

[6] This proposition is in conflict with the common assertion that pluralism is conducive to democracy, if indeed it is not a prerequisite there-

2. Pluralistic societies are also held together by ties of economic interdependence between members of different ethnic groups. This is often accompanied by considerable pluralism in the economic institutions themselves—for example, between a subsistence and a money economy, or between a partially monetized, exchange, peasant economy and an urban, market economy. But, even where there is little pluralism in the economic institutions—that is, where there is a single well-integrated, albeit diversified economy—the different ethnic (or racial) groups almost invariably have differential relationships to the system of production and distribution of goods and services. For example, a slave economy based on the monoculture of a cash crop such as sugarcane or cotton exhibits no pluralism in the economic institutions themselves, but extreme differentiation in relationship to the system of production between masters and slaves.

There is, of course, a close interplay between economics and politics as integrative or cohesive factors in plural societies. Both of them together seem to be sufficient conditions to the existence of plural societies, and each of

of. Part of the divergence in the two conceptions of pluralism results from the difference in definition noted above; the rest is attributable to the narrow range of societies studied by the proponents of "democratic pluralism" and by the selective way in which they have examined the evidence in the societies they did study. For example, many theorists extolling the democratic pluralism of the United States have consistently disregarded or underplayed that aspect of the American social structure which was most deeply pluralistic and most thoroughly undemocratic. The racial cleavage makes the United States a "*Herrenvolk* democracy," as much as South Africa, Australia, Canada, and other countries where important segments of the adult population have been debarred from full citizenship rights. Of course, this is not to deny that some highly pluralistic societies have been moderately democratic. India since independence is perhaps the most obvious large-scale example. Belgium and Switzerland could also be advanced, although their degree of pluralism is not nearly as great as that in India. Yugoslavia is also a multinational state which seems to be moving slowly in a more democratic direction. The relationship between pluralism and political institutions is certainly much more complex than has been hitherto supposed, and needs to be explored much more extensively before firm conclusions can be reached.

them seems to be a necessary condition. Economic interdependence between members of different polities (e.g., as in international trade) is too tenuous, segmentary, and functionally specific a system of relationships to justify the use of the term society. Conversely, a common polity without a corresponding network of economic relations would by itself constitute a very brittle foundation for a plural society. Indeed, except for ephemeral conquest states which disintegrated almost as quickly as they came into being, one would be hard put to find any examples of such plural societies; even relatively undifferentiated plural states such as the conquest empires of Mesoamerica and sub-Saharan Africa in precolonial days involved tribute payments, regulation of internal trade, and wealth redistribution. The stabilization of the multiethnic conquest states revolves probably in the first instance around the conqueror's ability to utilize political domination to reduce the conquered peoples to economic dependence, and to use the latter to consolidate political power. (South Africa is a clear illustration of the mutually reinforcing qualities of political oppression and economic exploitation for the maintenance of white supremacy.)

Partial integration of political and economic institutions between the various groups of a plural society thus seems to be a necessary and sufficient condition to the existence of such a society. However, in most cases, these two major institutional areas do not completely exhaust the integrative foci of plural societies. The role of religion in Mesoamerica illustrates such an additional basis of societal cohesion, and this institutional area is in turn related to the political and the economic bases of integration, as we shall see in Chapter IV.

Having given at least a tentative answer to the question of what constitutes the basis of cohesion and integration in plural societies, we must now turn to the problem of conflict in such societies. Conflict, to be sure, is a ubiquitous aspect of social life, but in plural societies, conflict is perhaps even more especially prevalent and conspicuous. From that perspective also the consensus assumption is untenable; many systems are remarkably enduring in spite of considerable conflict and lack of consensus.

First, the very presence of cultural differences and the attempt by one of the groups to impose certain aspects of its culture on the other groups are common sources of conflict in plural societies. This is especially true in the field of religion if one of the faiths engages in proselytism, as Christianity and Islam have typically done. As we shall see, religion is one of the major sources of conflict in the Ixil region, and the conflicts have been intensified in recent years through the rise among the Ixil of a group of recent "re-converts" to Catholicism. Thus, a new line of cleavage was created, beyond the main ethnic division.

In addition to being created by cultural differences themselves, conflict is also generated through the process of interaction in the political and economic spheres. The very institutional areas which are the bases of social integration in a plural society are at the same time frequent sources of conflict. Even in relatively egalitarian and democratic multiethnic countries like modern Belgium or Canada, socioeconomic or class differences between ethnic groups are a major factor in creating mutual animosity. In the political sphere, the maintenance of either ethnic parity or proportional representation is often very delicate and is the result of endless struggles, negotiations, demonstrations, and compromises; even minute changes in the balance of power can unleash violent reactions. Indeed, in the few plural societies which approximate the democratic model, violent conflict is typically aimed at preventing any social, economic, or political change which might alter the ethnic *modus vivendi* and spell the demise of the plural society. Conflict thus acts as a stabilizing factor in such societies, and what conflict occurs frequently assumes a highly predictable, stereotyped, indeed almost ritualized character.

Where, on the other hand, a colonial situation prevails, the sharp disparities of wealth and power between ethnic or social groups make for a revolutionary type of conflict. The subordinate group or groups attempt to overthrow the status quo. The political and economic inequalities which are at the basis of this type of plural society frequently generate a dialectical opposition of interest groups similar in many respects to the classical Marxian paradigm of class conflict. But, at the same time, economic and political inequalities create countervailing ties of mutual dependence. The stablest and most enduring plural societies have been those that have developed paternalistic systems of race or ethnic relations in which dependence has become personalized in some form of master-slave, patron-client, or godfather-godchild relationship. Paternalism is the stablest form of tyranny because it establishes intimate and personal ties of dependence across ethnic or racial lines of cleavage.

The present case study, as we shall see, is especially interesting because it is intermediate between a "colonial" and an "egalitarian" type of plural society. The ethnic balance of power and wealth has been unstable. It first swung for several decades in favor of the ladino (non-Indian) group, which is nationally dominant, but never far enough to make the ladinos a firmly entrenched local ruling class. Today, the situation is slowly being reversed, and the Indians, through a little organization and exercise of their political rights, could at the local level reduce the ladinos to the status of a small, powerless, mercantile, and clerical minority. Land reform and state control over the system of labor recruitment would seriously jeopardize the economic status of the ladino upper and middle class. While there is considerable ethnic interaction in the political and economic spheres, there is neither a well-defined system of paternalistic dependence of Indians on ladinos, nor equality between the two groups. The local system has elements of both, and the outcome is one of approximate group parity in the distribution of wealth and power in the face of great numerical disparity between two groups.

Pluralism is too complicated a phenomenon to be reduced to a single dimension. Rather, it is a set of closely related variables. To mention only a few of them, plural societies can be analyzed demographically (how many groups are present in which proportions and in what geographical concentrations; what are the patterns of internal and external migration, and of relative rates of natural increase), spatially (what are the patterns of residential segregation between groups), ideologically (what ideologies do the various groups hold and how do these ideologies affect relations between groups), or "interactionally" (what actual patterns of interaction prevail between groups).

One of the most important aspects of pluralism, however, is its relationship to stratification. Plural societies range from cases where ethnic cleavages differentiate without stratifying (e.g., in Switzerland), to cases where ethnic and racial cleavages are, first and foremost, a caste-like division between hierarchical groups (e.g., between whites and nonwhites in the United States or South Africa). In most instances, however, an intermediate situation prevails in which ethnic cleavages, while not hierarchical in themselves, are more or less closely linked with certain status characteristics. Often, each ethnic group is itself internally stratified in such a way as to make for a greater or lesser degree of class overlap between ethnic groups; yet, at the same time, modal or mean differences between ethnic groups are sufficiently great that the ethnic groups themselves are ranked in a loose and ill-defined order of prestige.

Frequently this order of prestige is fairly easy for the social scientist to establish, at least from the point of view of the dominant group, because the latter ethnocentrically makes invidious differences between various cultures in terms of a scale of "civilization" or, even more narcissistically, according to the degree to which subordinate groups or individuals are cultural replicas of the dominant group. (The special status of the *évolué* or the *asimilado* in colonial Africa is a case in point.) By and large, however, plural societies are characterized by complex and multidimensional stratification systems for the description of which adequate analytical concepts are still lacking. Plural societies highlight some of the general problems in stratification analysis and bring a few complications of their own.

The first problem concerns whether the analyst chooses "objective" correlates of status such as wealth, income, physical appearance, or power; or whether he describes the stratification system in terms of the participants' own subjective perception of it. The "objective" approach has the advantage that the criteria are often unambiguous, easily ascertainable, and even quantifiable, but even when the resulting classification is valid in the sense that it allows the analyst to make status distinctions and predict behavior, the description of the system frequently has little psychological reality for the people concerned. For example, where two stratified groups are physically distinguishable as well as culturally different, a "racial" description of the system may have high predictive value but little subjective reality if, in fact, the people concerned stratify each other in cultural terms.

The choice of subjective or native criteria, however, is not without its problems, even in culturally homogeneous societies. For example, even in monoethnic societies, the perception and the criteria of social class vary widely at different levels of the hierarchy, a phenomenon which has been little studied. The difficulty is magnified in multicultural societies where each ethnic group may have its own autonomous status system based on idiosyncratic criteria or at least on different rank orders of importance in the criteria. There may even be little consensus about the relative ranking of the ethnic groups themselves, and different rankings may result depending on the criteria chosen. Thus one group may rank higher than another in terms of education but lower in terms of wealth. Or an immigrant mercantile minority (like overseas Chinese or Indian communities) may be politically powerless compared to the much poorer indigenous majority.

The question then becomes: Whose subjective perception of reality is the most important? Often the dominant group's definition of social stratification is more relevant if only because the dominant group has the power to translate its prejudices into economic and political discrimination. But sometimes the viewpoint of subordinate groups is more relevant—for example, in the study of revolutionary ideology.

As the status system of plural societies is even more multidimensional than that of monoethnic societies, any schematic description of it which is valid throughout the society is extremely difficult. More specifically, different components of status are not commensurable. For example, the ascriptive aspects of status such as sex, caste, ethnicity, or "race" are not commensurate with the achieved elements of social class. It is nearly impossible to say, for instance, where an upper-class Negro should be ranked in the general status hierarchy in the United States. Even if being regarded as "upper-class" among United States Negroes meant objectively the same thing as being an upper-class white, the very fact that the color castes themselves are hierarchized would deflate the "total status" of the black in the general society lower than that of his white counterpart. Even that statement would not be true for all Americans, but only for white racists who still constitute a majority of the total population and define to a great extent the "objective" position of Afro-Americans. To attempt a generally valid status ranking of all Americans is futile because such disparate elements as caste, ethnicity, and class are not additive.

Plural societies, then, while often highly stratified, have no single, well-defined status system, but rather a multiplicity of such systems which are only loosely integrated with each other, and which are very differently perceived by members of various groups. Typically, members of one ethnic group are only dimly aware of status differentiation within other ethnic groups. Furthermore, there is seldom complete consensus on the ranking of the ethnic groups themselves, even though subordinate groups are generally aware of the position ascribed to them by the dominant group, and often behave in the way expected of them in intergroup contacts. To complicate matters further, different components of a person's status become activated in different situations involving members of different groups.

The above considerations lead to at least one conclusion, namely, that we must greatly refine our conceptual approach if we are to analyze plural societies adequately. We should like to suggest that the analysis be carried out at three distinct levels, those of the group, the institution, and the individual, as we shall try to do respectively in Chapters III, IV and V of this monograph.

The group level is the most immediately accessible, with readily perceptible lines of cleavage. From this starting point, one then proceeds to determine the finer lines of division and subdivision, the exact criteria of group membership, the form and content of interaction between groups, the relative status, economic and political position of the groups, and their respective attitudes, values, and ideologies. In short, one endeavors to unravel the main dimensions of the group structure of the plural society.

The institutional level overlaps empirically with the group level, yet the analytical distinction is crucial. To the extent that a society is segmented into ethnic groups, its structure is also divided into autonomous and homologous, yet distinct sets of institutions (e.g., religious systems, marriage systems, and so on) which are not shared by the society at large but which are rather specific to one or more groups within it. On the other hand, to the extent that one can speak of a single plural society, certain institutions, particularly in the political and economic spheres, are shared, albeit differentially, by all constituent groups. Basically, the nature of a given plural society is determined at one level by the *structure of intergroup relations,* and at another level by the *overlap and interplay between institutional structures.* Combining these two levels, the differential participation of the various groups in shared institutions constitutes the very core of a plural society. A plural society is not a set of groups or "cultures" living side by side and "borrowing" traits from each other; it is rather *a set of interacting groups which remain distinct by virtue of not sharing all their institutions, and which constitute a single society by virtue of sharing some crucial ones.*

The third level of analysis is that of the individual. For a number of purposes, the individual must be considered apart from his group. This is particularly important in plural societies where there is much horizontal and vertical mobility. A number of persons find it possible to move from one group to another, or to "commute" back and forth between two groups, or to be marginal to all groups. Thus, for example, an Ixil migrant going to work outside his own ethnic area among ladinos and Indians from other groups will often dress and behave in a way which will make him less ethnically identifiable. Over time, he may become fluent enough in Spanish to "pass" as ladino on the coastal plantations. When coming back to visit his relatives in Ixil country, however, he will associate with his Ixil friends and kinsmen and become reincorporated into the Indian group. Or people of mixed parentage in the process of ladinoization may be socially regarded as neither Indians nor ladinos, and in some Guatemalan towns of Alta Verapaz, they are reported as beginning to constitute a "middle group" (Mayers, 1966). In Chinautla, a town near Guatemala City, Ruben Reina reports a group of "Indianized Spaniards" who, though constituting only one percent of the town's population, are locally given a special term, *mengala*. The women of this group dress in brightly colored, colonial-style blouses and wear braids in the Indian manner. These people use Spanish in the home and also speak the Indian language (Pokomam) with ease. *Mengala* families do not hesitate to look for a progressive Indian to be godparent of their children, and the women may marry Indians. The ladinos look down on this group but consider them superior to Indians "because of their stock" (*por su raza*). The ladinos sometimes call them *indianeros*, or "Indian-lovers," because of their willingness to mix freely with Indians (Reina, 1966: pp. 27–29). Though no such group exists in Ixil country, there are ladino individuals who are partly Indianized. For example, a respected and politically active ladino in Chajul sometimes dresses as an Indian. Similar phenomena of marginality or commuting between cultural and social systems have been observed among migrant workers in Southern Africa (Mayer, 1961).

Over the long run, mobility of individuals between groups and between institutional structures will tend to mitigate the cleavages and reduce pluralism in a given society. At any particular time, however, a number of individuals may emancipate themselves, partly or wholly, temporarily or permanently, from the ethnically ascribed pattern of social roles while the society as a whole continues to be highly pluralistic in terms of both group and institutional structure. The Negro American who "passes" does not undermine the racial caste system; he simply uses special circumstances to evade it, and through the clandestine nature of his passing, he indirectly reinforces the system.

At this point we should like to suggest that, since language is a very important special case of culture, the categories found useful in sociolinguistic and psycholinguistic analysis be extended to the study of culture contact and culture change. More specifically, we should analyze culture contact in terms of interaction not only between *ethnic groups,* but also between individual *culture users.* Just as a language can be used beyond its group of native speakers, so are the users of a given culture not coterminous with the community of the people born and socialized into it. In Guatemala, for example, ladino culture is dominant in an analogous way, as Spanish is the lingua franca. There are many more users of ladino culture as a medium of interaction than there are native users of it.

The usefulness of the concept of culture users and of the distinction between native and nonnative users of a culture is that these terms introduce a number of relatively unexplored dimensions into the analysis of culture contact. First, these concepts focus the analysis at the more directly observable level of the dynamics of individual interaction rather than at the more abstract level of acculturation theory. The raw material of culture contact and culture change is *behavior* between persons through the use of a cultural (and, more specifically, a linguistic) medium. Before jumping to the much more abstract level of exchange and reinterpretation of cultural items between "cultures," it might be profitable to look at the underlying behavior from which these abstractions are inferred.

Second, insofar as interaction between a native and a

nonnative user of a culture (or language) gives the former a substantial advantage, the relationship is asymmetrical. It thus becomes essential to introduce the dimensions of power and status into the dynamics of culture contact. "Culture use" no more takes place in a power or status vacuum than any other aspect of human interaction. The manipulation of cultural knowledge and skills for political ends is still a badly neglected, though an obviously central, feature of systems of ethnic relations. We know very little, for example, about the political consequences of cultural differentiation between the ruling class and the masses.

Third, much the same changes happen to a cultural medium used between natives and nonnatives as happen to a language which becomes a lingua franca. Since interaction between ethnic groups is typically segmental and functionally specific, so is the cultural medium through which this interaction takes place. Special-purpose languages and subcultures (such as commercial or technical ones) develop in response to segmentalized interaction. In much the same way as linguae francae often are simplified, impoverished pidgins compared to the language used between native speakers, so we can speak of "pidgin cultures." When native and nonnative users of a culture interact, they typically do so in terms of stereotyped, ethnocentric, and oversimplified views of each other; given the narrowness of the common universe of cultural discourse, interaction is much more limited in scope and complexity than between native users.

Fourth, the concept of culture user rather than culture member or culture participant prepares the way for the development of a more adequate theory of culture. Such a theory should better account for the phenomena of biculturalism and culture commuting with which we have just dealt as well as for a much wider range of human behavior. At a more specific level all individuals are multicultural in some degree. Future studies will have to devote more attention to this multicultural phenomenon which develops out of the interaction between the individual and a complex social environment. The old acculturation framework thus will inevitably have to yield to the more sophisticated approach to cultural dynamics that can be derived from sociolinguistics and the new psycholinguistics.

The above analytical framework has been presented, for the sake of simplicity, in relatively static form. We have suggested concepts for the description of the group and institutional structure of plural societies. It is clear, however, that plural societies, as much if not more so than homogeneous ones, have to be understood dynamically in historical perspective. Plural societies often show rapid and profound structural and cultural changes as heterogeneous groups modify their behavior in interacting with each other, and as economic, political, cultural, and social factors alter relative group position. The concepts used here can, of course, be used diachronically as well as synchronically. The main anthropological model to account for change resulting from contact between different ethnic groups, namely acculturation theory, has had the limitation of focusing the analysis almost exclusively on the cultural content of change. The present approach is at once complementary to and broader than acculturation theory. It shifts the focus of the analysis to change in the total structure of plural societies.

I. THE NATIONAL AND GEOGRAPHICAL SETTING

IN SPITE OF its small size, Guatemala is one of the most heterogeneous countries in the Western Hemisphere. Until a few years ago, a majority of the population did not speak Spanish. (The percentage of Indians declined from 53.6 in 1950 to 43.3 in 1964. See Table 1.)[1] The Indian population is itself divided into a number of related Maya language groups, the four largest of which (Quiché, Mam, Cakchiquel, and Kekchi) number between a hundred thousand and half a million. While Spanish is clearly the dominant and only official language, and while ladinos (non-Indians) are the politically, socially, and economically superordinate group, Guatemala rivals the Peruvian Andes and the upper Amazon drainage as the least hispanicized and Christianized part of the former Spanish American empire. This is particularly true of the northwestern and north central highlands which include the Ixil zone. The Indian population of Guatemala is concentrated in the densely settled western and central highlands where the elevation is highest and the land some of the poorest and most difficult to cultivate except in some areas south of the Ixil that are enriched by volcanic ash. Eight of Guatemala's twenty-two departments include nearly three-fourths (74.3 percent) of the Indian population, and the

[1] Statistical tables can be found in the Appendix. Throughout this book we shall use the metric system of measurement except where local non-metric units are customary. Prices will be quoted in U.S. dollars, but since the quetzal (Q) is on par with the dollar, the figures are in fact the local ones.

department of Quiché, where the Ixil are located, has the second largest Indian population in the Republic. Within this predominantly Indian area, there exists an amazing variability in local patterns of adaptation between Indians and ladinos, ranging from open and occasionally violent conflict to peaceful relations, and from unequivocal ladino supremacy to local Indian dominance in both the political and economic spheres. (Adams, 1957; Bunzel, 1952; Dessaint, 1963; Gillin, 1948, 1951, and 1958; Hoyt, 1955; Lincoln, 1945; Mayers, 1966; McBryde, 1934; Nash, 1955, 1958a; Redfield, 1956a; Reina, 1959, 1960; Roberts, 1948; Silvert, 1954; Tax, 1937, 1942, 1952, and 1953; Termer, 1957; Thomas, 1954; Tumin, 1949, 1950, and 1952; Wagley, 1941, 1949, and 1957; Wisdom, 1940.)

The present monograph deals with the Ixil region located in the Altos Cuchumatanes of west central Guatemala. This area comprises the middle section of a range which starts in Mexico in the northern part of the state of Chiapas, extends south into central Guatemala, and continues eastward, descending finally into the Caribbean (West, 1964: p. 65).

The Ixil inhabit the northern slopes of the range and a middle area between the Cuchumatanes range and a lower range (the Chama Mountains) at the edge of the tropical rain forest further north. Their territory varies in altitude from 3,000 to 700 meters; the terrain is rough, consisting of gorges, valleys, and ridges, some with limestone outcroppings (West, 1964: p. 69). Further north, these mountains gradually diminish to become low folded ranges and hills of about 1,000 meters or less at the edge of the Petén and the Chiapas lowlands.

The Ixil, one of the smaller Maya groups of Guatemala, live in the *municipios* of Nebaj, Cotzal, and Chajul, in the department of Quiché.[2] (Though a few Quiché-speaking

[2] The term *municipio* refers not to an urban community but to a town and its rural hinterland. The closest analog in the United States would be

Indians also live in these municipios, political boundaries correspond rather closely to ethnic ones.) The Ixil number some 45,000 to 50,000 people in an area of 2,314 square kilometers, where they constitute approximately 92 percent of the population. The remaining 8 percent are Spanish-speaking ladinos who belong to the dominant culture of Guatemala.[3] Ixil-speaking Indians and ladinos interact mostly in the political, religious, and economic spheres, and constitute a small, plural sub-society within the Republic.[4]

These three municipios, named for their principal towns, together with fifteen others, constitute the department of Quiché. The capital of the department is Santa Cruz del Quiché. Though El Quiché is only 85 kilometers from Nebaj, it takes some three hours to drive this distance over the unpaved, narrow, winding, and precipitous road. El Quiché is itself some 155 kilometers away from Guatemala City, or about another four hours' drive, the last two over the paved Pan-American highway.

The towns of Nebaj and Chajul are at an elevation of 1,900 meters, while Cotzal is at 1,700 meters. Nebaj is now the principal town, and the largest, with an urban popula-

the county rather than the municipality. Municipios are grouped into the 22 *departamentos* of Guatemala, which correspond to the cognate term in the French administrative structure.

3 The figures are preliminary estimates from the 1964 population census. The total for the republic is 4.3 millions, of whom 43.3 percent are Indians, i.e., persons speaking an indigenous language as their mother tongue and who are regarded as such in their local community. Through the process of ladinoization, there has been a steady decline in the relative proportion of Indians from 64.8 percent in 1921, to 55.7 percent in 1940, to 53.6 percent in 1950. The department of Quiché numbers some 255,000 inhabitants of whom 15.3 percent are ladinos and 84.7 percent Indians. The population of Quiché is 85.1 percent rural. In 1950, the illiteracy rate was 91.7 percent, compared to 72.2 percent for the republic as a whole. This was the second highest rate of the 22 departments in Guatemala after Alta Verapaz (92.5 percent). For more detailed figures on the Ixil zone, see Table 2.

4 For a treatment of the concept of pluralism as we define it here, see the Introduction. See also van den Berghe, 1964 and 1967; and Smith, 1965b.

tion of 5,227. Chajul and Cotzal have populations of 4,172 and 3,609 respectively. The rural populations surrounding these three towns are 18,147, 9,325, and 8,541, respectively. In terms of distance by road and travel time the three towns are about equidistant, some 17 to 23 kilometers or an hour's driving time. In walking distance, Chajul and Cotzal are much closer to each other, about 10 kilometers, than either is to Nebaj.

The abrupt transition from subtropical low country to the high elevations and jagged mountains of the highlands accounts for the weather conditions peculiar to the area. The mountains force the moist trade winds, or "easterlies," to rise and cool rapidly as they sweep over the land from north to south. This releases great quantities of water vapor picked up and carried from the warm surface of the Caribbean, causing unusual amounts of rain. Frequently the area is completely enclosed in clouds and mists. Average relative humidity ranges probably between 70 percent and 90 percent; the mean annual precipitation runs from 2,000 to 3,000 millimeters (Vivo Escoto, 1964: p. 200).

The Ixil region is in an exposed windward position. The winds can be particularly devastating to crops, frequently causing large swaths of corn damage. The rainy season extends from May or June through December. At this time the trade winds reach their maximum instability owing to the rapid ascent and cooling of air masses that converge near the equatorial calms (Vivo Escoto, 1964: p. 192). The dry season begins in January and lasts about five months. The temperature for the three largest population centers, all at about the same elevation, can be cold enough to see breath vapor and can remain at uncomfortably low levels for days on end during periods of extensive cloud cover and rain.

There is considerable variation in vegetation as one moves from the tropical lowlands to the high points in Ixil territory. The dense tropical vegetation in the lower regions gives way to pine, oak, and cypress on the mountain slopes around Nebaj. In abandoned fields and formerly cleared areas, the vegetation tends to be primarily hardwood, brush, or young forest. The paucity of mature forest indicates intensive land use. The few large cypress trees and evergreens that have been preserved at the edges of pastures suggest the beauty of an earlier time when the land was not overtaxed. The Ixil are located in the Usamacinta drainage, which runs north to the Gulf of Mexico. It is the most important in Middle America in terms of discharge (Tamayo and West, 1964: p. 93); the main rivers are the Chajul, Cotzal, and Chixoy.

The rural Ixil are primarily maize farmers. In some of the valley-floor land there is continuous cultivation of maize fields, or *koʔm* in Ixil. In general, however, slash and burn cultivation is practiced. With this method the land is used for two or three years and then another field is cleared for use. The first lies fallow for five or six years, and then it is cleared, burned, and cultivated once more. The yield per *cuerda* (some 500 square meters) can vary from 50 to 200 kilograms.[5]

Work in the maize fields is performed almost exclusively by men. Burning and clearing is done from January through the first part of May, depending on the location. The larger trees that have been cleared off the land are stacked up for firewood, and smaller trees and brush are burned. Axes and machetes are used for the clearing. Maize is planted between March and June. In good soil a large hoe, or *ʔasarón,* is used for furrowing, and the land looks as if it had been plowed. The Ixil do not use their livestock as draft animals. On steep hillsides, furrowing is not done. Planting is usually by groups of men with long digging sticks (four or five feet in length with one end

[5] Monteforte Toledo (1959: p. 445) gives 918.7 kilograms as the mean maize yield per hectare (10,000 square meters). In the subsistence sector alone, the yield per hectare was 716 kilograms.

sharply pointed). After planting, there are periodic weedings.

Since the growing season is unusually long, there is only one harvest per year. This occurs in late autumn and in winter. The harvest is collected in large nets, made in Cotzal, and brought in to the family granaries to be stored. The maize is shelled by hand for seed; otherwise, it is threshed with sticks. Although the maize is usually uniformly yellow in color, more than a dozen different varieties, based mostly on color combinations, are recognized in the language. After the harvest, the maize stalks are used to make fences or, together with the leaves, are used for fertilizer. Animal manure is sometimes employed as additional fertilizer. Maize and beans constitute the major portion of the diet. Tortillas (*le·e·*), tamales or corn dumplings (*sub'*), and various gruels (*ʔuk'aʔ, saq poʔq*) are made from maize. A favorite Ixil tamale is made with a mixture of maize and beans. A popular ceremonial dish called *b'oṣb'oʔl* consists of ground corn wrapped in vine leaves.

Secondary crops are beans, coffee, apples, *guisquiles* (vegetable pears), and potatoes. Beans, peas, squash, and *chilacayotes* are grown on the edges of the maize fields. In addition, many truck vegetables, particularly garlic and onions, come into Nebaj from nearby Aguacatán, which is a major center for irrigated truck gardening in west central Guatemala. Bananas, oranges, chili, and tomatoes are also imported. The Ixil own cattle, horses, donkeys, turkeys, chickens, ducks, geese, sheep, and pigs, though not in large quantities. Meat is a luxury usually eaten no more than once a week. Horses are ridden or more often used for cargo, as are donkeys. Cattle sometimes are used for carrying firewood.

At present, the Ixil area is economically, socially, and politically integrated in the rest of the country, so that we should speak of it as a sub-society within a larger whole. The physical isolation of this mountainous region has been greatly mitigated by the construction of unpaved but passable roads linking the three main Ixil towns and the plantation of San Francisco with each other and with the rest of Guatemala. The one exit road from Ixil country connects Nebaj with Sacapulas, a perilous thirty-seven kilometers and two hours of driving time away. Sacapulas in turn is at the crossroads of the east-west link between Huehuetenango and Cobán, and of the north-south road to El Quiché, Chichicastenango, and the paved Pan-American highway to Mexico and the capital. Nebaj is also linked with the outside world by telegraph, and there is a telephone line between Nebaj, Chajul, and Cotzal. There is a weekly bus service with Huehuetenango, and a biweekly one with El Quiché. In addition, passengers are transported by truck, especially contract laborers going to the coffee, cotton, and sugar plantations of the Pacific coast. There is a movement of 4,000 to 5,000 persons a month in and out of the Ixil zone, labor contracting alone accounting for the majority, and market or fiesta traffic for most of the rest. Mail service takes approximately four days from the capital (240 km away), and two days from El Quiché (85 km away). Mail is delivered in Nebaj three times a week; the flow of incoming mail to Nebaj averages eight hundred to nine hundred pieces a month, about one piece of mail a month per family.

In terms of goods and services, Ixil country exports labor, some livestock (mostly poultry and pigs), fresh produce, which is resold in larger Guatemalan towns, and coffee, which is exported mostly to Germany, Switzerland, and the United States. In addition, the municipio of Cotzal is an important center for the handicraft production of ropes, nets, bags, and other products made from the fiber of a wet-climate agave species. The region imports maize, salt, sugar, canned foods, tobacco, and bottled beverages, both alcoholic and nonalcoholic; machine-made textiles, blankets, hats, and other items of clothing; and a wide array of manufactured and handicraft products such as machetes, kerosene lamps and stoves, earthenware, wooden chests, metal tools, flashlight batteries, toys, patent medicines, radios, motor vehicles and spare parts, furniture, and the like.

A brief summary of Guatemalan agriculture and land tenure is essential here in order to understand the economic system of the Ixil region and its integration into the rest of the country. Agriculture employed 68.1 percent of the economically active population in 1955, compared to only 11.5 percent in manufacturing industries, 9.8 percent in services, and 5.4 percent in commerce (Monteforte Toledo, 1959: p. 472). In terms of gross national product (GNP), agriculture accounted for 56.7 percent of the total (Monteforte Toledo, 1959: p. 583). Basically, Guatemalan agriculture falls into two major sectors; one consists of commercial crops, mostly coffee, cotton, and bananas, with also some sugarcane and a variety of other products, destined principally for export; the other produces staple foods for domestic consumption, principally maize, with some beans, wheat, rice, fruits, and vegetables. This second sector can itself be subdivided between a declining subsistence agriculture and a growing cash agriculture producing staple foods for regional and national consumption. In the 1950's coffee accounted for slightly over 75 percent of Guatemala's exports, and bananas for approximately 10 percent (Monteforte Toledo, 1959: p. 501). These percentages dropped respectively to 58 and 8 between 1960 and 1963, as cotton and nonagricultural exports rose. Maize production alone contributed 13.5 percent of the GNP and covered 77.7 percent of the land under subsistence agriculture during the 1950's. Beans came in second position with 3.7 percent of the GNP and 10.5 percent of the land (Monteforte Toledo, 1959: pp. 501, 583).

The two agricultural sectors interact very closely, yet are clearly differentiated. Their interaction determines in part, and is intimately linked with, the social class and ethnic structure of Guatemala. Commercial crops are grown primarily, though not exclusively, in the low- or medium-altitude coastal areas of the Pacific and the Atlantic where the population is predominantly ladino. Banana plantations in the Atlantic zone are controlled by the United Fruit Company, which uses much Caribbean labor. Most of the land under coffee, cotton, or sugarcane cultivation consists of large or medium-sized fincas ("estates" or "plantations") ; these fincas are almost invariably owned by Guatemalan ladinos or by foreigners, many of whom are absentee landlords. The work is done mostly by Indian wage laborers (*jornaleros*) or tenant-settlers (*colonos*) drawn in good part from the western highlands to which Ixil country belongs. Monteforte Toledo (1959, p. 281) estimated that in the 1950's, some 200,000 migrant workers moved to and from the fincas each year. Today, the migrant population involves some 320,000 persons a year.

The production of staples such as maize and beans represented until the nineteenth century a continuation of Mayan subsistence agriculture. Much of the maize is still grown by Indian subsistence farmers, but now staple foods and livestock are also extensively produced on a commercial basis with wage labor. Not only must the growing urban demand be satisfied; but, as a consequence of population growth, soil erosion, land appropriation and fragmentation, labor exodus, and other factors, the previously self-sufficient Indian highlands now must import food grown on ladino-owned fincas. This food is purchased with wages earned on coffee or other fincas. Food purchased with cash wages allows further population increases in the rural areas; overpopulation and land scarcity forces increasing numbers of subsistence farmers to work on fincas; and the vicious circle becomes inescapable, short of drastic land reform. Thus cash agriculture contributes to the gradual dependence and impoverishment of the subsistence sector. As in many other countries, subsistence agriculture is becoming increasingly "sub-subsistence" as cash crops grow in importance. The peasantry is transformed into a rural sub-proletariat.

If the land were more equitably distributed, the benefits of cash agriculture could be more widespread. But land in Guatemala is still very unevenly shared. The predominantly Indian departments consist overwhelmingly of landless peasants or *minifundia* owners, with a sprinkling of larger ladino *fincas*. Such is the situation in the Ixil area. Conversely, the coastal areas consist predominantly of large or medium-size estates owned by ladinos. In the 1950's, there were some 200,000 landowners who, with their families, represented some 20 percent of the total population and owned a total of some 350,000 fincas. Of the latter, 88.4 percent were less than seven hectares in size; the 47.5 percent of the fincas of less than 1.4 hectares accounted for only 3.2 percent of the total farmland. Conversely, the 22 largest fincas of more than 8,960 hectares covered 13.4 percent of the total area, and the top 3.7 percent of the estates—those of over 22.4 hectares—accounted for 77.1 percent of the land area (Monteforte Toledo, 1959: pp. 418, 419, 424).

Of 317,390 rural families living in Guatemala in 1950, 16.5 percent were landless; 17.8 percent owned properties averaging 0.4 hectares; 56.0 percent owned an average of 2.2 hectares; 7.9 percent owned a mean of 15.1 hectares; another 7.9 percent had land estates averaging 165.5 hectares; while the top 0.1 percent of the families owned a mean of 2,916.5 hectares. The upper one per *thousand* of the rural population owned 40.8 percent of the landed property of the Republic (Anonymous, 1965: p. 145).

To compound the land problem further, most of the land owned by the large *finqueros* is idle. In the twenty-two largest estates, only 5.7 percent of the land was cultivated, compared to 94.7 percent of the area covered by the 165,850 farms of under 1.4 hectares. The Decreto 900, or Law of Agrarian Reform of 1952, attempted to remedy the situation by expropriating idle lands with compensation to the owners. Some 585,000 hectares (or 15.7 percent of the area of the fincas) were expropriated and distributed to some 54,000 peasant families comprising a quarter of a million persons (Monteforte Toledo, 1959: p. 434). But the Arbenz government was overthrown with United States complicity in 1954, and the counterrevolution succeeded in aborting the land reform.

Together with widespread illiteracy, cultural differences, and the low degree of urbanization and industrialization, the distribution and tenure of land in Guatemala is one of the basic causes of underdevelopment and social inequality (Anonymous, 1965: p. 147). Land ownership and tenure is closely related to the ladino-Indian distinction, and the various systems of labor tenancy and contract wage labor determine to a considerable extent the economic life and, indirectly, the political subordination of the Indian areas at the national level. Independently of ethnic affiliation, land ownership is also an important determinant of social class among ladinos. Although ladinos generally deprecate agricultural labor—indeed, any form of manual work—they associate land ownership with upper-class status.

A good, if somewhat schematized and oversimplified, account of social stratification in Guatemala is given by Monteforte Toledo (1959: pp. 251–287, 647, 648). He divides the population into three main classes. A predominantly urban upper class of 1.14 percent composed of large landowners, industrialists, bankers, army officers, professionals, higher civil servants, high clergy, and the like earned a mean per capita annual income of $2,917, or 6 percent of the national income. A middle class of 17 percent of the total population is composed of independent artisans, shopkeepers, small landowners, rentiers, clerks, civil servants, and other salaried people. It earns a mean per capita income of $581 *per annum,* or 55 percent of the national income. Finally, peasants and the urban proletariat constitute 81.9 percent of the people, and earn a per capita income of $84 a year, or 39 percent of the national income. It is interesting to note that, although the upper classes tend to reside disproportionately in the urban areas and to be absentee landowners for much of the year, the stratification system of Guatemala nevertheless cuts across the rural-urban distinction to a greater extent than would be true in a more industrialized country.

The Ixil area is integrated into the national system of ethnic and class stratification in two different ways for Indians and ladinos. The local Indians are part of the politically semiamorphous and economically impoverished peasantry which constitute the broad productive basis of the Guatemalan population and the bottom of the country's social pyramid. The Ixil Indians are, however, a strictly localized segment of the Guatemalan social structure; they have few if any significant ties with groups outside Ixil country, except as transient agricultural laborers. For Indians, ethnicity is not only a factor of political and economic subordination at the national level, but also a factor making for social isolation from other Indian groups, from the labor movement, from the urban working class, from the government, indeed from the national society at large.

For local ladinos, the situation is quite different. As ladinos, they have a nationwide "reference" and "membership" group. They are much more directly involved than Indians in national life and in government. Furthermore, as members of a certain class within the ladino group, they maintain a number of important social and kinship ties with other ladinos elsewhere. This is particularly true of the local upper class, who almost all have relatives, often more financially successful than themselves, who have left the small town for the capital, and can powerfully help their country cousins.

Politically, the three municipios in the Ixil zone are directly dependent on the departmental capital of Santa Cruz del Quiché, where there is a military garrison and a governor representing the central government. In 1964 the department of Quiché included 255,260 persons, or 6.1 percent of Guatemala's population of 4,284,000 and ranked sixth in population among the twenty-two departments in the republic. The town of Quiché with a population of 6,472 is scarcely larger than Nebaj, though its position as capital gives it a much greater importance, particularly in the fields of education and administration. According to the 1950 census, the department of Quiché ranked fourth (out of 22) in the percentage of Indians in its population; fourth in the percentage of its people who went barefoot; second in illiteracy rate among its inhabitants over seven years old; twenty-second in the proportion of people enrolled in schools; and twentieth in the percentage of people living in towns.

Guatemala is a highly centralized country, and although the municipios enjoy some autonomy in the routine administration of their affairs (tax collection, public works, primary education, public health, road maintenance), there is a steady flow of orders and directives from the capital and from Quiché. About one-seventh of the total flow of incoming Nebaj mail consists of official letters (between 100 and 150 pieces a month), and the telegraph is used mostly for government business. Political changes at the national level now have fast repercussions all the way down to the grassroots. The central government is directly represented in Nebaj by a police lieutenant and two constables. Health and school officials come through the area on routine inspection tours, and on occasions, so do other functionaries from Quiché and Guatemala City. After the 1966 national elections, the military government representing the Partido Institucional Democrático (PID) yielded power to a democratically elected civilian government of the victorious Partido Revolucionario. In Nebaj, however, the PID won a slight majority, and municipal government is bipartisan, as we shall see later.

Chichicastenango, located some fifteen kilometers south of Quiché, is the largest town, and its market is the liveliest commercial center in the department. Chichicastenango has also become by far the biggest tourist attraction of the department and receives a steady flow of Guatemalan and foreign visitors. Located only a few kilometers from the paved Pan-American highway, Chichicastenango represents for the Ixil area the nearest southern terminal of significant and direct influences from outside Guatemala. Huehuetenango, an important ladino commercial town to the west of Ixil country, stands in a somewhat analogous position, although its touristic importance is lesser.

Religiously, the three Ixil parishes of Nebaj, Chajul, and Cotzal, which have coterminous boundaries with the municipios, are under the authority of the bishop of Sololá, whose diocesal seat is in the town by that name near Lake Atitlán, some 130 kilometers from Nebaj.

II. HISTORY

THE HISTORICAL ROOTS of contemporary Ixil culture are as deep as those of the Maya civilization out of which it grew. Archeological and linguistic data suggest that ancestors of today's Ixil came into the area from the southwest. During the formative and preclassic periods of Maya prehistory, there is evidence of a substantial population along the Pacific coast, but archeological work conducted by A. L. Smith in the 1940's, by Becquelin in 1964 and 1965, and by Adams in 1965 and 1966 indicates a sparse occupation by pottery-users in Ixil territory during these early periods (i.e., before A.D. 200).

Throughout the Ixil region, carved stone monuments, hieroglyphic writing on pottery, tomb burials, jade artifacts, and other evidence of a wealthy class, and thus of a stratified society have been found. Some of the Nebaj tombs are large chambers with corbeled vaults, and contain alabaster vessels, jadeite beads, plaques and pendants, figurine whistles, and other sumptuary objects made of pottery, pyrite, obsidian, copper, and gold (Smith and Kidder, 1951). Kidder, allowing for a hundred-year lag from the end of the classic period at A.D. 900 in the Petén lowlands, estimated that the classic Nebaj ruins were flourishing concerns from about A.D. 600 to 1000.

Smith and Kidder (1951) think that the Ixil were probably middlemen in the trade between the highlands to the south and the jungle lowlands to the north. The southern highlands exported igneous rocks such as obsidian and pyrite, salt from Sacapulas, and other materials, while the north exported copal, rubber, feathers, skins, cotton, and sea shells. However, Adams does not consider that there was a great deal of trade or other contact between the northern highlands, including Ixil country, and the southern highland centers such as Kaminaljuyu.

The powerful Quiché kingdom was established around the mid-eleventh century; its last capital was Utatlán, close to the present Santa Cruz del Quiché (Recinos, 1947). According to Ximenez (1929: I, 75) the sixth of thirteen Quiché kings, Tepepul Ztayul, enlarged the kingdom to its maximum extent, though Villacorta (1938: pp. 131–132) reports, on the basis of the Quiché traditions at the time of the Conquest, that it was Tepepul Ztayul's successor, Quikap, who conquered the Ixil lands of Nebaj, Cotzal, Chajul, and Ilom, and that his soldiers reached the Lacantun River in the jungle lowlands beyond Ixil country. In the Rabinal Achí, a son of the Quiché king is referred to as Chief of Chajul (Villacorta, 1942b: pp. 352, 354), which was probably the most important Ixil center before the Conquest. Chajul was once a much larger town than Nebaj or Cotzal; it is located closest to the sacred calendar mountain of Juil; and even today it holds a paramount ceremonial position in Ixil country.

Although the Ixil owed allegiance to one of the Quiché ruling families, they were also in frequent contact with non-Quiché peoples in the adjacent lowlands, both before and after the Conquest. Referring to old manuscripts available to him but now lost, Baltazar Balduini said in 1856 that well-kept roads once extended from Ixil country throughout the lowlands as far as Yucatán.[1]

Such was the situation at the time of the Conquest, as far as scanty evidence allows us to reconstruct history. In spite of peace overtures from Guatemala, Cortes dispatched

1 Balduini in the Nebaj church records. The area of Ilom seemed to be a jumping-off place for trips into the lower rain forests, and this was the reason for which the Spaniards decided to force abandonment of Ilom after they had initially established a church there.

from Mexico Pedro de Alvarado with an army of 20,000 Indians, 420 Spaniards (120 of them mounted), and four cannons. In the early part of 1524, Alvarado engaged and conquered in two major battles the main part of the Quiché forces near the present city of Quezaltenango. In the second and more decisive clash, the principal Quiché king, Tecum Umam, was killed, and Spanish paramountcy was established. However, one major part of the highlands, including the Ixil zone, continued to hold out. The military stronghold for this unconquered area was at Uspantán, the capital of a powerful king who was allied with the Ixil, the Quiché of Cunén, and possibly some of the Kekchi to the northeast. As Uspantán had a disquieting influence on the already conquered Quiché immediately to the south, the Spaniards decided to march against the town in the spring of 1529.

Gaspar Arias, the *alcalde ordinario* of Guatemala, set out with three hundred veteran Mexican Indians and sixty Spanish infantrymen. He succeeded in temporarily capturing Nebaj and Chajul on the way to Uspantán (Fuentes y Guzmán, 1933: III, 59), but no sooner had he arrived near his destination than he received news that he had been deposed as alcalde by Francisco de Orduña, the acting governor of Guatemala. Arias returned at once to the capital, leaving his command to Pedro de Olmos who, against the advice of his officers, thought he could carry Uspantán by storm in a frontal assault. The enemy ambushed his troops and attacked from behind. Many of the auxiliaries were killed in battle and many more were sacrificed to the God Exbalamquen; the rest deserted the Spanish and left them to fight their way to Utatlán, the Quiché capital, which they finally reached, exhausted and sick.[2]

The following year, Orduña himself, with Francisco de

[2] The conquest of Nebaj is described in varying detail in Fuentes y Guzmán, 1933: III, 60–64; Juarros, 1936: II, 210–211; Brasseur de Bourbourg, 1857: IV, 700; and Milla, 1882: pp. 218–219. Fuentes y Guzmán is the earliest and most detailed account.

Castellanos and eight Spanish corporals, took 400 Indian auxiliaries, 40 Spanish foot soldiers, and 32 Spanish cavalrymen to redress the previous disaster. When Orduña sent envoys with demands for surrender, they were killed (Fuentes y Guzmán, 1933: III, 61). Orduña then directed Castellanos to begin the campaign. Castellanos' forces crossed the river near Sacapulas, and made a hard and long ascent over a dry and thorny terrain to higher ground, where they encountered "thick woods and rocks of fantastic height" leading to Ixil country; traversing the "unpleasant and extended sierra" near the border and then ascending to a high pass, the Spanish expedition met a squadron of four or five thousand "rebellious and ferocious" Ixil warriors.[3]

When the Spanish cavalry outflanked the Ixil, the latter retreated to Nebaj, which was "isolated by a very deep ravine . . . and defended from all sides." While the main body of the Spanish were confronting the Ixil defenders at the town gate, some of the Indian auxiliary forces got through to the rear of the town and set fire to the houses. At this, many of the Ixil defenders left the entrance to quench the fire, and the Spaniards and their allies were able to enter and capture Nebaj. They made the Ixil prisoners, branded them, and took them slaves. Chajul and other Ixil towns surrendered, but the Cotzal Ixil remained allied with Uspantán, Cunén, and parts of the Sacapulas territory until December, 1530, when Castellanos finally defeated Uspantán. So great was the chagrin and anguish of one of the Indian leaders, Caletohil, that he killed his family and committed suicide on his lance. Castellanos branded and reduced most of the captives to slavery. With the defeat of Uspantán, Cotzal, the last Ixil holdout, also surrendered.

Ixil political organization at the time of the Conquest

[3] This would put the total population as high as 20,000 or 25,000 for the Ixil area in 1530.

probably included a complex system of taxation and theocratic government. Initially, the Spaniards staffed the higher echelons of the hierarchy, but ruled through local native leaders or noblemen who performed administrative and tribute-collecting functions. These nobles were referred to by the Spaniards as *caciques,* a West Indian word that the Spaniards adopted and used in Mexico, and *señores principales.* Some of these nobles were granted special rights, such as carrying firearms or swords, and wearing Spanish clothing (Gibson, 1964: p. 155). Frequently they also adopted Spanish housing and furniture styles. Although we have found no records of this process among the Ixil, the term *principal* is still used today to denote an Ixil who holds or has held an important religious or government office.

At the time of the Conquest, there were at least seven major centers of Ixil political power as well as numerous minor ones. In the Chajul dialect area, there were three major ones: Chajul, Juil, and Ilom, and at least two minor ones, Onkap and Chel. In the Nebaj area, there were also three major centers, Nebaj, Salč'il and ʔAk'ul, and two minor ones, Ajkana and what is now called Magdalena. In Cotzal there were Cotzal and Chichel.[4]

Sometime after the conquest of Nebaj, local tradition of this century (and also of the last, as reported in 1856 by Balduini, a parish priest in Nebaj) maintains that the site of Nebaj was changed from the area now called Salquilito (now one of the outlying *cantones* of the town) to its present site, one kilometer or so away.

Unfortunately, we have found no information about

[4] Major centers are from a list in Remesal (1932: p. 1404) of *caciques* to whom letters were addressed in the matter of founding the convent at Sacapulas, plus a reference to the existence of church ruins in Chichel by Padre Balduini in church records of the past century. Minor centers are from Balduini's and Remesal's list of Ixil villages (1932: pp. 242, 245). Other minor Ixil villages or hamlets which no longer exist (if in fact they were Ixil to begin with) may include Boob, Chaxa, Aguazac, Culchil, Vacaa, Nama, Chicui, Temal, and Caquilax, also from Remesal.

Ixil life or conditions at the time of the Conquest, or about the manner in which the Ixil were ruled. Small Mexican Indian garrisons probably maintained political control under Spanish leadership. The existence of the Nahuatl loan word *tenam,* for town, in the Ixil vocabulary, suggests contact with Mexicans after the fighting.

The impact of the Conquest must have been disastrous for the Ixil. A number of Ixil were killed in combat; more were taken away as slaves; agricultural production was probably disrupted and food scarce; epidemics took a further toll. But even more important were the consequences of tremendous population movements ordered by the Spanish. By the middle of the sixteenth century most of the people scattered in hamlets and villages had been concentrated in larger towns to facilitate Spanish administration and political control. This population transfer was ordered by Pedro Ramirez de Quiñones in 1549 in accordance with a royal cedula issued nine years previously.

The Ixil were probably grouped into four main centers: Nebaj, Chajul, Cotzal, and Ilom.[5] Those Indians who remained away from these centers were regarded as barbarians, rebels, and vagrants (Fuentes y Guzmán, 1933: II, 447).

Such a drastic change must have had a profound effect on the Ixil population, and must have added a great burden to the logistics of corn growing, harvesting, and transporting. (On the other hand, logistic problems may have been alleviated with the drop in population caused by concentrating the people and making them more vulnerable to the devastating epidemics of the period. A reduced population would not have so far to go in the sur-

[5] Remesal (1932: pp. 242, 245) lists a number of Ixil villages which he says were grouped together into towns. He says that the population of Ilom was brought to Chajul. However, this was probably done at a later period, for a church had been built in Ilom. Garcia Pelaez (1951: I, 174) says that Ilom was founded by Pedro Ramirez de Quiñones, which also conflicts with Remesal's account.

rounding countryside to till their fields.) These hardships must have affected the Ixil especially adversely, for Nebaj was singled out as an example of an unviable situation in a complaint to the king several decades after the regrouping of towns and villages was effected. The Ixil were also crushed under the burden of the tribute which each able-bodied adult had to pay annually. Plagued by epidemics and Spanish exactions, the population declined steeply until the mid-eighteenth century. On several occasions, petitions requested a reduction in tribute payments commensurate with the depopulation.[6]

For part of the Cotzal Valley, Adams corroborated this drastic population decline. He found absolutely no trace of colonial pottery in the Cotzal-Chipal junction region (though modern pottery was found), and he concluded that the Middle Cotzal Valley was completely depopulated after the Spanish conquest of the region.[7] While complete depopulation is unlikely, inasmuch as a church was founded in Cotzal in the sixteenth century, there certainly must have been a dramatic decrease in population.

Similar conditions existed elsewhere in Guatemala and Mesoamerica (Aguirre Beltrán, 1946). Of the 20,000 Mexican Indian troops that first came with Alvarado, there were barely a hundred survivors in 1547 (Bancroft, 1883: p. 234). In 1542, Bartolomé de las Casas maintained that in the first fifteen or sixteen years of the Conquest four or five million Guatemalan Indians died (Bancroft, 1883: p.

[6] One document requesting a reduction in tribute payments reported that 402 Chajul Indians, among them 82 tribute-paying adults, had died in the typhoid epidemic of 1798, leaving only 275 tributaries living. In Nebaj there were 227 deaths reported at the same time. The final count after the epidemic was over was 297 dead (among them 50 tributaries) in Nebaj, and 486 dead (101 of them tributaries) in Chajul. This left only 256 tribute-paying survivors and probably less than 1,000 total living of all ages (Document No. A3.16 leg. 242 ex. 4814 Guat. Nat. Arch.). Chajul was also ravaged by epidemics in 1781, 1815, and 1829, which killed respectively 210, 211, and 505 persons.

[7] Richard W. E. Adams, "The Ceramic Chronology of the Southern Maya, Second Preliminary Report: 1966"; and personal communication.

236). This probably was an exaggeration based on an overestimate of the total population, but it reflects the opinion that the population drop was of major proportions. A recent estimate based on tribute lists for neighboring Mexico was a decline from over sixteen million in 1532 to something over one million in 1608 (Cook and Borah, 1960).

As a reward to Spanish settlers, the land and its Indian inhabitants were parceled out in large groupings called *encomiendas,* under a system already applied in Spain to "reconquered" Moorish territories. Indians were placed under the tutelage of an *encomendero,* who was to protect them, direct their work, Christianize them, and collect tribute. These Indians were held by the encomendero and passed on to his heirs. From the very beginning the king was concerned lest the encomenderos become too powerful and autonomous. Several times he abolished the system, but was forced to restore it again, until it was finally abolished for good in 1720. Each encomienda was to have a church. However, if encomiendas existed in the Ixil area as early as during these thirty years of initial political consolidation by the Spaniards, it is doubtful that churches were built before the missionary period somewhat later.

Gibson characterizes the first encomienda generation in the New World as "one of generalized abuse and particular atrocities" (1964: p. 78). Indians were used in all forms of labor, were overworked and overtaxed. The encomenderos ". . . jailed them, killed them, beat them, and set dogs on them. They seized their goods, destroyed their agriculture, and took their women. They used them as beasts of burden. They took tribute from them and sold it back under compulsion at exorbitant profits. Coercion and ill-treatment were the daily practices of their overseers, *calpixque,* and labor bosses. The first *encomenderos,* without known exception, understood Spanish authority as provision for unlimited personal opportunism" (1964: p. 78).

Old documents indicate that there were in fact several encomiendas in Ixil territory. According to one document described by Baltazar Balduini, an encomienda was given to Antonio de Bardarama (or Baldarama) when Francisco Diaz del Castillo was corregidor of Totonicapán. Elsewhere, Balduini again refers to encomiendas, saying that some of the Chajul people still had the pre-Conquest family names of Batz, Pop, Icom, Mo, Etnay, Bob, Uhu, Cah, Bom, Cancab, and Xak, but that Chajul Indians who lived on the encomiendas of the conquistadores and their sons during the reigns of Charles V and Philip II had become hispanicized, not in custom but in family name. He lists these names as Cortes, Laynes, Hernandez, Solano, Lopez, Ramirez, Pacheco, Rivera, Zuñiga, Escobar, Guzmán, Mendoza, Vega, and others. Another document mentions Carlos Vázquez de Coronado as having an encomienda in Chajul.[8]

The encomienda system contributed to a reduction in the authority of native leaders and to the breakdown of the indigenous social class system (Gibson, 1964: p. 80). However, the encomendero's authority had greatly diminished by 1600 in the valley of Mexico (Gibson, 1964: p. 81). This may also have happened in Guatemala, though the *number* of encomiendas continued to increase and the system was not terminated until the eighteenth century.

More important in Ixil history, however, may have been the institution of *corregimiento,* which lasted much longer. The corregimiento represented the highest level of Spanish civil government that was theoretically in direct contact with the Indians. It was a system of local magistrates called *corregidores* and, later, *alcalde mayores.* These magistrates were directly under the audiencia in the au-

[8] The documents are found in the Chajul *Books of Baptisms for 1678–1717;* the Chajul *Book of Marriages for 1856–1867,* p. 4; and Document A1.39 exp. 11737 leg. 1751 fols. 211 and 163, Guat. Nat. Arch.

thority structure. Magistrate positions were salaried in order to avoid the abuses that might otherwise occur if they collected their own tribute, as did the encomenderos. But in actuality the salary proved to be a small part of their total income. The office was used for personal advantage and commercial gain. Corregidores received from the Indians enormous quantities of food and material goods, which were then sold for profit. They also speculated in commodities and controlled markets. Embezzlement of tribute funds earmarked for the king was also common, and Indian labor was commandeered for private interests (Gibson, 1964: pp. 92–94). We have not encountered records of the corregimiento organization for the Ixil during the early period; however, the Ixil seem to have been ruled from Totonicapán, and records indicate that, in the late eighteenth century, the magistrate (alcalde mayor) in Totonicapán was powerful and despotic.

While the exploitation of the Indians was most intense just after the Conquest when the Spaniards were intent on immediate personal profit through tribute and mining, strong control, tribute and corvée or slave labor for agricultural and other activities continued to be imposed. For the Spanish settlers, the sixteenth century was a time of rising economic growth. Cocoa was a principal export, chiefly to Mexico; indigo, though less important, was produced until the middle of the eighteenth century.

Recent scholarship tends to substantiate the exploitative, indeed predatory, nature of Spanish colonialism in the New World. The so-called "black legend" (i.e., the allegedly exaggerated account of Spanish depredations) turns out in fact to be the "black reality." According to Gibson,

> The Black Legend provides a gross but essentially accurate interpretation of relations between Spaniards and Indians. The Legend builds upon the record of deliberate sadism. It flourishes in an atmosphere of indignation, which removes the issue

from the category of objective understanding. It is insufficient in its awareness of the institutions of colonial history. But the substantive content of the Black Legend asserts that Indians were exploited by Spaniards, and in empirical fact they were (1964: p. 403).

In spite of the abuses, there were numerous representatives of the Spanish government and church—for example, Zorita, a judge and member of several audiencias (Keen, 1963), and Las Casas, the great Dominican cleric, who did what they could to put an end to these depredations. In fact from the beginning, when Queen Isabella became angry at Columbus's attempts to set himself up as a slave trader (Bancroft, 1883: p. 255), the Spanish Crown attempted to protect the Indians from the colonists. As Bancroft points out, a study of the royal decrees from Isabella's time onward indicates this desire to protect the Indians, if only in an attempt to curb the power of the Spanish settlers and to halt the depopulation of their realm. For example, a section of Isabella's will enjoins her successors to always insure the fair and kind treatment of the Indians by the colonists.

As early as 1526, the king issued a cedula designed to alleviate conditions of excessive toil in the mines and of lack of food and proper clothing. So many Indians had died that parts of the country were deserted, and many natives had fled to the mountains and forests. The king ordered that at least two members of the church were to accompany future expeditions and were to direct themselves toward obtaining fair treatment for the Indians. Peaceful natives were not to be made slaves, though they might be assigned to Christian Europeans as free servants (Bancroft, 1883: p. 237).

The colonists ignored these decrees, usually disobeying or circumventing them. So bad was the treatment of Indians by some Spaniards that, in 1530, a law was passed ordering the burial of dead Indians who had acted as slaves or servants for Spaniards, rather than permit them to be fed to animals or to be left to rot. By 1536, other laws forbade the overloading of an Indian by more than two arrobas in weight; permitted Indian merchants or those otherwise accustomed to travel to do so; and prohibited Spaniards of any rank from being carried about in a hammock or palanquin (as was the pre-Hispanic custom for important Indian figures). Native villages and settlements were not to be inhabited by Spaniards, Negroes, or mulattoes. A Spaniard when traveling through an Indian village could only remain one night, and Spanish traders three days. Laws were also passed prohibiting Indian *caciques* from selling or bartering their subjects (Bancroft, 1883: p. 238). In 1537, Pope Paul III declared the freedom of Indians, even those who were not Christians (Monteforte Toledo, 1959: p. 139).

Finally, as a result of Las Casas' manuscript of 1542 on the destruction of the Indies, a series of "New Laws" were approved and published. These laws were to some extent a codification of earlier decrees. They contained a large number of articles relating to the enslavement and treatment of the natives. They required the freeing of all Indian slaves unless their owners could establish a legal title to their possession, and from that time in the future no more Indians were to be enslaved. Further, encomiendas were to lapse on the death of the holder. Under reactive pressure from encomenderos and some church quarters, the last provision was revoked, and inheritance of encomiendas was allowed.

The sixteenth century was a period of continual struggle between groups who were intent on exploiting the Indians and those who wished to protect them. In 1549, the Audiencia of the Confines moved to the city of Santiago, and Alonso Lopez Cerrato became its new president. Cerrato proved to be a friend of the Indians, and thus incurred the hostility of the settlers and of Bishop Marroquin. Cerrato felt that the tributes levied were intolerable and told the king that they could not be satisfied even if the Indians were twice as numerous. He also reported to the king that the Indians were still mistreated and enslaved in defiance of the law (Bancroft, 1883: p. 327).

As ruler of Guatemala from 1559 to 1564, Martinez de Landecho undid much of the work of his predecessors, who had been fairer to the Indians. A Dr. Mejia, one of the *oidores,* entrusted the regulation of tribute to the encomenderos and their puppet Indian *caciques.*

Aside from what may have been attempted by the priest who may have accompanied the conquering soldiers, the first missionaries to visit the Ixil were probably Franciscans working out of Sacapulas or Totonicapán. Only one friar, Gonzalo Mendez, was responsible for the vast area of Quiché, Kanjobal, Aguacatec, and the Ixil-speaking peoples. He was occasionally helped by Lorenzo de Salvatierra from Totonicapán (Vasquez, 1937–38: II, 35), but it is unlikely that either friar did much, if any, work among the Ixil. One letter states that Friar Gonzalo visited the mountain villages with difficulty and only occasionally (Remesal, 1932: II, 332).

In 1553, the Dominicans replaced the Franciscans in the region and established a base at Sacapulas. The more conservative Franciscans, who believed in the congruence of religious and lay interests, were thus replaced by the Dominicans, who had greater concern for Indian rights and who believed that local Spanish interests and the welfare of the Indians were basically incompatible. Also, unlike the Franciscans, the Dominicans were opposed to slavery and to forceful conversion.

Ixil oral tradition refers to what might be interpreted as a thirty-year period between the old pre-Conquest order and the new religion. This is six years longer than the interval between the conquest of the Ixil and the establishment of the Dominican convent at Sacapulas; it may well have taken the Sacapulas priests six years to consolidate their position among the nearer Quiché-speaking peoples before they could enter Ixil country on the other side of the high Cuchumatanes range. Indeed, Baltazar Balduini refers to a 1575 manuscript by Pedro Mejia, a Dominican at Sacapulas, stating that the reduction of the Chajul (and also the Olontepeque) Indians took place under Barrio's direction around 1560.[9] Ten years later, the Sacapulas padres built a bridge across the river on the road to Ixil country.

The monastery at Sacapulas was first founded with four friars under the vicarship of Juan de Torres (Remesal, 1932: II, 332–333). By the early 1600's, the convent had eight monks (Remesal, 1932: II, 611), and the areas under the jurisdiction of Sacapulas included, in addition to the three towns of Nebaj, Chajul, and Cotzal, nine non-Ixil towns (Zacualpa, San Andrés, San Bartholomé, Santo Tomás, Santa Cruz, San Pedro, Cunén, and San Miguel); there were still fewer priests than there were towns and churches to attend to.[10]

Though the Ixil had already been regrouped into four main towns, the Dominican missionaries from Sacapulas were probably responsible for giving the Ixil towns their Spanish layout and architecture. Villacorta (1942a: p. 91) describes the way in which the priests planned a typical town of this period. First a site for the church was decided on, the size of the church depending on that of the population. (The biggest Ixil church was thus built in Chajul.) Next to the church was placed the house of the priest, and in front of it was located a large plaza. Across the plaza fac-

[9] Balduini, in a note attached to the book of baptisms for Chajul for the years 1678–1728. The note itself was written in the 1850's.

[10] By 1787, this number may have been reduced to eight: the three Ixil towns of Nebaj, Cotzal, and Chajul and five others: Sacapulas, Uspantán, Cunén, Aguacatán, and Chalchitán, as these were the only ones called on for assistance in rebuilding the Sacapulas bridge (Document A1.24 leg. 6088, ex. 55.138 Guat. Natl. Arch.).

ing the church was the government building with a jail and a community house for visitors. The town was laid out in a grid pattern with broad streets running north-south and east-west. Except for the community house this is exactly the pattern found in Nebaj today and, with some variations, in Chajul and Cotzal.

In addition to churches built in Nebaj, Chajul, and Cotzal, smaller ones were built in Salč'il, Magdalena, ˀAk'ul, Ajkana, Chichel, Ilom, and possibly other villages.[11] Undoubtedly, lesser nobles lived in these villages, and churches or chapels were sited at these native political centers.

It is probable that the methods used by Las Casas in the neighboring Kekchi region were repeated in the Ixil area, except that the priests may not have been able to keep Spaniards from entering the area during the initial pacification period as they were able to do briefly in the Kekchi region. Las Casas' methods of peaceful change met with such success in the Kekchi area that what had been called the "land of war" became known as "land of true peace" (Vera Paz). Even Bishop Marroquin, who was in some respects an opponent of Las Casas, admitted that his methods had been successful. However, Spaniards soon entered the area, imposed tribute, and took seven hundred slaves from the town of Tuzulutlán alone (Bancroft, 1883: p. 355). We do not know how many slaves were taken among the Ixil, nor even whether any were taken at all beyond those branded and carried off at the time of the Conquest.

Interesting comments on the process of Christianizing the Indians during this early period are found here and there in the historical records. Remesal (1932: I, 431) speaks of one of the friars based in Sacapulas, who worked in Cunén, a town near the Ixil border. The priest came to

11 From a list by Balduini in the church records of Nebaj, these being the places where he saw ruins.

baptize a number of Indians and discovered one old man who claimed to have avoided worshipping the Quiché gods even before the coming of the Spaniards. On further inquiry, the Indian explained, "Since I was little I have carried with me two men, one black, dirty, ugly and more disgusting than I can say (so saying, he grimaced and spat some distance) and the other white, handsome, brilliant and marvelously resplendent whom I greatly loved and did whatever he told me. . . ." (pp. 431–434).

Both Indians and Catholic priests recognized, however, that Christianized Indians often behaved worse than the pagans. "He who before baptism did not cheat, swear, kill, lie, or rape, if after baptism did one of these would say, 'I am becoming Christianized' " (Remesal, 1932: I, 431).

The missionary work of the priests was concerned initially with stopping all human sacrifice. At a later period they began establishing *cofradías* (religious brotherhoods or societies) for the saints and they introduced the Catholic calendar to replace the two calendars which formed the core of Ixil religion. Major Ixil ceremonies were probably related to an agricultural calendar of 18 months and 365 days, to which Las Casas must have referred when he spoke of the "large calendar." It must have been used in determining the five or six community-wide ceremonies typically held every year in the Sacapulas and Cobán areas (Las Casas, 1909). For this "large calendar" the Catholic church substituted the fiestas associated with saints' days in the Christian calendar. However, there was no substitute for the small calendar, the special 260-day ritual calendar still used today in a variety of Ixil curing, neighborhood, and town rituals.

Aboriginally, statues were decorated for ceremonies and were carried in processions with the playing of drums, trumpets, and other musical instruments. Some statues were kept in caves or secret places outside the towns where access was difficult. Except for the stone representations still worshipped in Ixil caves, household statues and processions were gradually syncretized with Catholic saints and processions. Religious brotherhoods (*cofradías* and *hermandades*) of the saints were established, each one having one head *mayordomo* and several ranked assistants (perhaps as many as the ten now customary among the Ixil) who collected money from the town to maintain the cofradía, which in turn supported the church by paying for masses and other services.

Local church organization in Nebaj was undoubtedly similar to the general pattern in Guatemala described by Gage (1958). The priest was assisted by a *fiscal,* who carried a white staff topped by a small silver cross. As the priest's clerk and right arm, he represented the church in the priest's absence, and he executed justice under the priest's orders, including the whipping of those who did not attend mass. The fiscal had to be literate, and he was in charge of assembling the young Indians for prayers, sacraments, and the catechism. In Nebaj, there were actually two fiscales, one of them being master of music (*maestro de coro*). The latter would lead the choir and officiate at the mass. In the evening at five, the maestro de coro was in charge of singing prayers called *completas* (complines), and the *salve regina,* a prayer to the Virgin Mary (Gage, 1958: p. 231). The fiscal had more power than the alcalde and his officers. (The fiscal still qualifies for status as *principal* today.) He and other Indians working at the church were exempted from the weekly service due the Spaniards, and from attending travelers and justice officers. They met important visitors or the priest with musical instruments when they came into town; they also decorated the streets with floral arches on these occasions (Gage, p. 231).

According to Gage, a large retinue of servants alternated in performing duty for the priest, presumably in order to have time left for their own work. In a small town, the priest had two cooks as well as several butlers (*chahal*) who were responsible for keeping provisions under lock and key and for issuing the food to the priest's cooks. A number of sacristans were in charge of the vestry and altars for mass; three or four boys ran errands and waited at table. These servants, together with the cooks and butlers, ate in the priest's house and at his expense. A number of old women took turns overseeing six young women who met next to the priest's house to make tortillas, which were brought by the boys to the table (p. 231). According to local Ixil tradition, the priest punished these women by pulling their ears. In addition, the priest had Indian gardeners and stable grooms who only ate at the priest's expense on days when they performed work.

The income of the church derived from a number of sources: charges of two crowns for each mass, offerings brought whenever an Indian spoke to the priest or celebrated a saint's feast, tithes, and a monthly maintenance brought to the priest by the alcaldes or town officials. Occasionally funds were taken from the king's tribute. Income was also derived from a church field cultivated for the priest by the Indians. (Such a field was still maintained in the last century at Chajul, and a hundred nets of maize were delivered to the priest every year.) Indians paid at least a real to receive communion; they also brought money or goods for confession, and bought candles from the priest for as much as a real each (Gage, 1958: p. 236).

There is no evidence on Ixil attitudes toward Christianity and Spanish culture. Between 1560 and 1600, many of the people had still been brought up in the aboriginal religion; pre-Hispanic culture, whether overtly or covertly retained, still existed in the minds of the adult population. That the pressures against the old culture were not as great as elsewhere is suggested by the lack of control by the Spanish government. In a cedula of 1579, King Philip II complained to his officers in Totonicapán (the administrative center controlling the Ixil territory) that no census had been taken of the Chajul Indians and that they did not pay tribute. However, the power of the church, the government, and colonists was increasing in the late sixteenth century. Shortly after the beginning of the missionary period among the Ixil, there were only thirty Dominicans in seven convents in all of Guatemala (Bancroft, 1883: p. 377). By the turn of the century the number of Dominican convents had doubled. In 1587 an act was passed which required each town of 400 tributaries or more to pay 50,000 maravedis for church expenses. Though the initial population of the three major Ixil towns was probably large enough to fall under this law, it may have declined sufficiently by then to escape this tax.

The early seventeenth century is the high-water mark of Spanish power in Guatemala. Though a general economic decline had begun, for many of the Spanish settlers, and for the church, it was a period of continuing affluence. The capital city of Santiago was wealthy and agricultural activities were flourishing. According to Gage, one of his contemporaries retired to the Canary Islands with millions of ducats. Five Spaniards in Santiago had accumulated 500,000 ducats. Back in Spain, the word *americano* was synonymous with rich man. There were large cattle and sheep ranches. Six thousand head of cattle were bought in a single transaction (Gage, 1958: p. 185), and a friend of Gage's had a flock of four thousand sheep. The Dominican cloisters received 30,000 ducats yearly from Indian towns, plantations, and a mine. The Dominicans, Franciscans, and Mercenarians had nearly a hundred friars in each of their palatial cloisters in Santiago, and there were numerous other orders with sizeable memberships.

This opulence in the capital was based on a systematic exploitation of the Indian countryside. Gage (1958: pp. 216–219) describes a system in which Spaniards, for payment of a fee of half-a-real per worker to an official (*juez repartidor*), were entitled to force Indians to work for wages of five reales a week. Indians were frequently whipped, cheated, and mistreated in various ways, being reduced to a virtual slavery. Each married Indian under seventy years of age had to pay an annual tribute of four reales to the Crown, and another four to his encomendero, in addition to arbitrary levies in kind. Whether the Ixil region, through its remoteness from Spanish control, was spared some of these exactions is uncertain.

During the seventeenth century, the impact of the missionaries must have been stronger than before, for the old leaders trained in the pre-Catholic period had died out. Together with religious matters, other aspects of Ixil life began to assume the form in which we know them today or as they were in the nineteenth century. For example, today's Ixil houses are much as Gage describes Pokomam dwellings in the early 1600's: Houses have two rooms (one for cooking and one for sleeping), a yard, and a sweat bath. An open fire occupies the middle of the cooking room and fills the thatch in the rafters with soot. Poorer Indians have only one room for both cooking and sleeping. While many Ixil town houses now have tile roofs, they were earlier of thatch, as Gage describes Pokomam houses, and thatched roofs still predominate throughout the Ixil countryside.

Gage (1958) describes the typical Indian diet of that time, which is nearly identical to that of today's Ixil: beans boiled with chile, bean tamales (dumplings), and the main staple, tortillas. Tortillas as well as tamales were eaten with chile and salt or by dipping in a sauce. Fresh corn was sometimes cooked. Meat was eaten about once a week. Apparently the poorer Indians who had chickens, turkeys, or other fowls could not afford to eat them themselves, but the richer ones did. They also supplemented their diet occasionally with wild deer, porcupine, iguana, or tortoise. (Today there is very little game left.) Atole, chocolate, and alcoholic beverages were also important parts of the Ixil diet. (Today coffee with chile has supplanted chocolate as the principal beverage.)

The early to mid-seventeenth century probably was the period of maximum Spanish control over the Ixil. This was the time when the greatest number of churches were in use in Ixil territory. Later, several of them fell in ruins. Earlier, the Chajul Ixil were described as not paying tribute, and in the late 1600's they are again described as delaying and retarding their tribute payment. When Gage traveled through the Cuchumatanes to the west of Ixil territory during the first quarter of the seventeenth century, he described the Indians as being submissive and under complete Spanish control, and the roads as being open and safe for travel. This is the time when religious beliefs and practices must have solidified in the syncretism of pagan and Christian which still exists today. Knowledge of prohibited pre-Hispanic religious practices was by this time entirely secondhand, and the native leaders had been brought up from childhood under the new system. It is quite possible that priests lived at convents in all three of the main towns, for special maize fields had been set aside to support them.

Priests and ruling *b'o·q'ol*—unofficial Ixil leaders usually more powerful than Ixil incumbents of government office—seem to have worked in close cooperation, and Ixil leaders were often ruthless in exercising the authority delegated to them by the Spaniards. In Nebaj, the alcaldes and the fiscales of the church had the power to whip disobedient Indians. The fiscal taught the catechism with a whip in his hand. The Spaniard was still a powerful person; according to Gage, an entire town would stand in awe of a single Spaniard.

After the Spaniards established their control over the Ixil and other highland Indian groups, their attention began to shift to the lowland rain forests north of Ixil territory whence Lacandons, Chols, Maya-speakers, and possibly other groups continued to raid the areas under Spanish rule. The Itza Maya around the lake of Petén, for example, maintained their independence until 1697, when they were finally subjugated. In the Ixil region, the population of Ilom, which was at the very edge of the unconquered area, was probably removed in the late seventeenth century. Many Ixil had taken refuge beyond the limits of Spanish control, or else had close contact with the free Indians in the north. Part of the Ilom population was moved to Santa Eulalia, where Kanjobal speakers lived, and the other part to Chajul, where to this day one of the two cantones is called Ilom.[12]

Fuentes y Guzmán visited Ixil country in the late seventeenth century and described it as follows (1933: III, 57–58):

> . . . the priory of Sacapulas which contains a larger population [than Uspantán] has under its dominion members of the Nebaj curate of the Ixil nation. The Ixil language is spoken only there and in its subsidiary towns of Cotzal and Chajul. . . . Nebaj is in the peak and dome of the Sacapulas range in the roughest mountains. It lies between two of the deepest ravines whose slopes are brambled and rocky. The temperature of the area is harsh and its climate unwholesome, being extremely cold and misty. . . . There are 95 tribute payers in this town with 380 inhabitants scattered in numerous places: Cuchil, Salquil, Ixil, and others. So also, with its poor parroquial church roofed in *esparto* grass, just as the surrounding structures, and with the same climate and solitude, is Cotzal which is even more populated with 144 tribute payers and 576 inhabitants. Its neighboring town, Chajul, has 240 tribute

[12] According to various notes by Balduini in parish records of the 1850's, however, Ilom was reinstituted in the eighteenth century as a separate tribute-paying village along with Onkap. This is confirmed by 1752 tribute lists for these villages (Document A3.16 leg. 945, exp. 17657, Guat. Natl. Arch.).

payers which brings the number of its people to 960 inhabitants. The people are all rustic and wild, given to laziness and roaming; they like the roughness of the mountains better than the softness of the town and, because of this type of life . . . they delay and retard the payment of their taxes which many a time are lost.

The number of encomiendas and smaller land grants made to Spanish foot soldiers and horsemen throughout Guatemala increased steadily. (The *caballería,* a land unit of 45 hectares, was the standard land grant made to a cavalry soldier.) By 1665, there were seventy-two encomiendas in Guatemala, which together produced 80,000 ducats a year. The Spanish Crown, wishing to further curb the encomenderos whose power derived ultimately from the exploitation of Indians (whose numbers were sharply decreasing), continued in its efforts to gain rights for the Indians. A cédula of 1697 declared Indians equal to Spaniards and *criollos,* and in 1721 the encomiendas were officially abolished. Labor exploitation of the Indians continued, but the power of the encomenderos was curtailed.

Demographic evidence on Ixil country is extremely scanty. From the statement that the Spaniards fought against 4,000 to 5,000 Ixil warriors, we may estimate the Ixil population at 20,000 to 25,000 at the time of the Conquest. However, the number of Ixil warriors may have been exaggerated. Aside from this, the earliest population estimate is 2,000 for the 1670's or 1680's when Fuentes y Guzmán visited the area. He seems to have reached that figure by multiplying by four the number of tributaries in Nebaj, Cotzal, and Chajul.

The figure had dropped further by 1740 when Olaverreta gave the number of tributaries for the three municipios. If we follow the practice of multiplying by four, Chajul had only 352 inhabitants, Nebaj 228, and Cotzal 404. This was probably the low point in the Ixil population, after which it climbed fairly steadily in spite of frequent epidemics. In the 1850's Balduini estimated the total Ixil population at 6,700 by multiplying by twenty the average yearly number of baptisms. That figure is almost certainly an underestimate since it assumes a very high birthrate of fifty per thousand, not to mention the infants who died before being baptized. In fact, Balduini was well aware of the unreliability of his method, which, he writes, "is the least (multiple) used by statisticians to calculate the populations of countries in which the increase in population is held down by the various obstacles that prevent longevity as exist in these mountains because of the climate, the epidemics, lack of medicines, family separations and the humidity of the forest."

Church records for the Ixil territory exist only since the end of the seventeenth century, with a gap during the first part of the eighteenth century. From that time through the middle of the nineteenth century, a serious epidemic occurred every ten to twenty years. In Cotzal, for example, where the most complete records exist, the average number of deaths reported between 1675 and 1775 ranged from 20 to 25 per year. In some years there would be as few as 3 or 4 deaths, but the usual number for non-epidemic years seemed to be around 15 per year. The population during this period increased from a little under 500 to a little under 1,000, which put the death rate in the vicinity of 30 per thousand. Among the numerous epidemics in Cotzal were those of 1693, 1701, and 1733, which killed respectively 81, 90, and 193 persons.

The advent of the eighteenth century marks a continuing decline in Spanish control over the Ixil. During a visit by Olaverreta to Chajul, Nebaj, and Cotzal in 1740, only one priest is mentioned as being present among the Ixil, and he was based in Nebaj. In the same account Chajul is described as being in a valley surrounded by large mountains; it is overcast because of rain during most of the year. Its temperature is cold rather than temperate; the Indians sow much corn; the Indian women are great workers, weaving continually and sending [their cloth] for sale to Guatemala; very devoted, they worship the Divine Cult more than the men; the latter occupy themselves also in making *chiguahuetes* and other things of a thin cane they have. [Chajul is] 22 leagues distant from the *cabecera.* There are many fruit trees. [In Nebaj] there is a convent attended by the priest of the sacred order of *Predicadores* [Dominicans], the Indians are very reasonable, gentlemanly, devoted to the church which they keep well cleaned and adorned. Most attain a comfortable living because they sow good corn fields, have many mules, some cattle and are enterprising. The temperature is cold. The town is pleasantly situated in a broad valley with attractive and orderly streets. There are some houses of tile. It is fifteen leagues from the *cabecera* (Olaverreta: pp. 22–23).

In 1731 there were probably only six cofradías in Nebaj, seven in Chajul, and six in Cotzal.[13] In 1750, church records indicate the founding of the Guadalupe cofradía in the three towns. A new list in the late 1820's indicates a further increase of one new cofradía and one new hermandad for Nebaj (and one former hermandad changed to the category of cofradía), two new cofradías and one new hermandad for Chajul, and one new cofradía and two hermandades for Cotzal (again with one former hermandad changed to a cofradía category).[14] Thus there has been a steady increase, along with population growth, in these religious associations. There are now twelve Ixil cofradías in Nebaj, and ten each in Chajul and Cotzal.

Contact between Indians speaking different languages and dialects was quite frequent, perhaps even more so then

13 *Visitas Pastorales,* M. Juan Gomez de Parada, 1731, 1732 Tomo 5, arch. ecc.

14 From parish records.

than now. In 1752, for example, a tribute list for Chajul (Doc. A3.16 leg. 945. 17657 Guat. Natl. Archives) shows a considerable amount of intermarriage between Chajul and Ilom Indians, who, though of the same dialect, live a hard day's journey from each other. There were also quite a few marriages with Indians from the Nebaj and Cotzal dialect areas. One Indian was married to a woman from Mazatenango near the Pacific coast. In Cotzal also there were many non-Ixil Indians from other towns, as evidenced by the church burial records of the late 1600's and early 1700's which list people from Uspantán, San Sebastián (Huehuetenango), Mazatenango, and Aguacatán. A ladino, Bernardino Albares, is listed as the natural son of one Daniana Albares.

The eighteenth century was a period of declining power for the Spanish colonists and for the various religious orders in Guatemala. But great wealth was still concentrated in some sectors. Before its destruction by an earthquake in 1773, the capital ranked second only to Mexico City among the Spanish cities of the Western Hemisphere. The convents of the Jesuits, Dominicans, Augustinians, and other religious orders had become opulent and lavishly decorated. In 1754, the power of the religious orders was reduced when the missions throughout most of Guatemala were turned over to the secular clergy. However, as the Dominicans were allowed to stay in the provinces of Vera Paz and Quiché for an unknown length of time after that date, the Ixil region may have been secularized as late as 1769.

As Spanish power was gradually eroded during the eighteenth century, Indian resistance grew throughout Guatemala and Chiapas (which was part of Guatemala at that time). The Tzeltal of Chiapas revolted in 1722. In 1768, there was a revolt in neighboring Vera Paz against the Indian alcalde, who worked closely with the Spaniards. The Ixil came close to open rebellion in 1799. The previous year, an epidemic had caused so many deaths that an outdoor cemetery was opened instead of the dead being buried inside the church as had been the custom. When the epidemic had passed, the Indian leaders requested that they be allowed again to bury their dead in the church. When the request was turned down, the Indians began to revolt ("llegaron a sublevarse"), and the priest acceded to it.[15] The parish records of the eighteenth century contain other references to the intransigence of the Indians in matters of religion, particularly in the matter of control over finances and activities of the religious brotherhoods.

Thirty years before the incipient Ixil revolt, Archbishop Cortes y Larraz visited Nebaj, and drew a picture of the region as being physically isolated and politically torn between several contending factions. The authority of both the central government and the clergy seemed seriously shaken. Cortes y Larraz complained that the road to Nebaj is the worst one can imagine. He started out on mule and foot, but was later transferred to a litter because the mud was so slippery and deep that, in places, the Indians sank to their knees and the mules to their saddle belts. The paths were not cleared of trees.

He arrived at Nebaj to find Friar Miguel de San Juán, who was new to the area and did not know Ixil, working alone. The priest in charge, Eusenio Puerra, who worked among the Ixil from 1749 to 1775 and knew Ixil well, was in the convent of Santa Cruz del Quiché. (Twice previously Puerra, the regular priest, had been withdrawn by his prelate, but he had been allowed to return. During his absences he was replaced by friars who did not have license to administer all sacraments.)

Cortes y Larraz goes on to comment that corn and beans are grown in great abundance in this country, but that

15 From documents Sig. A3.16 Leg. 242 ex. 4814 Guat. Natl. Arch. Apparently at some later time the priests were able to effect a permanent change to an outside cemetery, for this practice of burial within the church is no longer done.

transportation is so bad that nothing is exported from the area. To the north live Lacandon Indians, many of whom he believes to be fugitives from the Ixil towns. Ixil who do not attend mass are given eight or ten whip lashes by the fiscales (II, 48). There is no school in Nebaj.

In a rambling narration, the archbishop speaks with vehemence against the despotism of Juan Bacaro, alcalde mayor in Totonicapán. Through his puppet government in Nebaj, installed against the wishes of the people and contrary to the usual practice of choosing alcaldes locally through election, Bacaro has persecuted the principales of the cofradías and hermandades, arbitrarily arrested people, and seized their property down to the last chicken. Many Ixil had taken refuge in the mountains to escape arrest. The local priest complained that the fugitives were thus unable to receive the sacraments.

Previous to the archbishop's arrival, the audiencia had sent two or three investigating judges into the area. They were met with disrespect, and in the confrontation someone received a broken nose. The judges took several principales prisoners and condemned them to fifty lashes, but were afraid to carry out the punishment. The archbishop goes on to say that because of the strong-handed methods of those in power, the Indians were much given to prevarication, were afraid to complain, and changed their testimony for fear of punishment.

One infers that disorder and intimidation were prevalent, and that at least four different interest groups were involved in local political conflicts: the alcalde mayor, Magistrate of Totonicapán and his puppet government in Ixil territory; the principales, whose choices for Nebaj alcalde were ignored by the alcalde mayor; the priest, who seemed at odds with both the Ixil principales and the alcalde mayor; and the ostensibly impotent authorities from Guatemala represented by the investigating judges. The most powerful of these groups was clearly the alcalde mayor, who acted as an autonomous regional despot.

In the nineteenth century, the isolation and autonomy of the Ixil zone increased even further as a consequence of the withdrawal of Spanish power, the war of independence, and the political turmoil in the Central American Federation, and later the Republic of Guatemala. With this isolation went also greater resistance to orthodox Catholicism. In 1817 the Nebaj priest, Isidoro Luege, wrote:

The twenty ninth of August of 1817 Diego de Torres, married to Maria Medina, died without receiving any sacrament while I was in the town and in this one can see the faith of these wretches (*infelices*) and the good a priest can do among them. The first that I ask when I arrive at these towns is if there are sick people but they hide and never inform me, expressing fear. I know well enough that they burn copal in the mountains and if it were fear, more fear they would have of the whip lashes they received continually on my petition in the name of Justice as it applies to the sufferers of this place. He was buried in the Holy Church and I gave my signature.

Around the middle of the century another priest, Juan Raúl, thought it futile to take church inventory because what little the church owned was "in the power of the Indians from whom it would not be easy to retrieve." He went on to beg his successor not to condemn him for the abandonment, ignorance of doctrine, church poverty, and slovenliness in the things of God among the Ixil without first "spending some months experiencing the nature of these Indians." He himself had previously made this mistake of blaming his predecessors. Nevertheless he thought there was still some hope for the people of Nebaj and Cotzal because the Indians were, "if not of a docile character, at least timid, and with scolding and a few remonstrations one can make them do things." But the Chajul Indians, he says, are "indomitable and discourteous," and there is no hope for them without divine intervention. Another note from the Chajul death registry complains about Ixil burial practices conducted in defiance of priestly orders: "The Church of Chajul, 80 staves long and 14½ wide, serves as a cemetery; in each new burial they take out old bones and skulls which immediately are thrown in with the earth and left uncovered; it is a continual task of the priests to order the mortal remains covered in the church, to find out, threaten, punish and admonish them etc. In each visit they again sweep and clean [but] once the priest leaves they return to the same practice." (*Defunciones,* Chajul, 1846–1865).

Francisco Puente bemoans the power of the Indian sacristans. "The Indians are in control of items of the church and the priest would provoke a fight and quarrel to reclaim them" (1833, Book of Baptisms, Chajul, 1828–1846). Baltazar Balduini in the 1850's complains that Ixil parents expect him to marry their children without their knowing how to make the sign of the cross or pray the *credo,* insisting insolently that the customary engagement gift of money has already been made to the daughters, and then refusing to send the children to pray in the church. He mentions the Indians' disesteem for the mass and a high frequency of divorce and polygamy (Book of Marriages, Chajul, 1856–1867). In another book, he states that he refused to marry an Indian couple because of their disrespect and resistance.

Stoll, a late-nineteenth-century Swiss visitor to Nebaj, confirms that the town was regarded as an undesirable backwater, and that the resident priest enjoyed little trust and influence among the Ixil. The priest had been transferred to "this ultima Thule of Guatemala civilization" as punishment for political noncompliance, and his cousin "combatted his horrible boredom in his place of exile by playing the guitar" (Stoll, 1886: pp. 389, 395). Stoll also mentions that, although the priest referred to Indians as *inditos,* he had "a powerful fear of them," that the departmental authorities in El Quiché were not obeyed, and that the Indian fiscal was more intelligent and influential than the "unlucky priest who was the football of his municipality." Stoll himself was insulted by a drunk Ixil (pp. 391, 392, 393).

The historical evidence, then, scanty as it is, suggests that the Ixil zone was indeed isolated from ladino society until the late nineteenth century. From the eighteenth century on, the influence of the Spanish and later of the independent Guatemalan government was so minimal as to make even tax collecting precarious, and the role of the Catholic Church was nominal. The few resident priests seem to have been there on sufferance, and to have wielded limited power over the population. The number of ladinos in the area was relatively much smaller than today. The 1893 census lists 66 ladinos in Nebaj out of a total population of 5,945, 21 out of 2,825 in Cotzal, and 11 out of 3,329 in Chajul. When Doña Juana B. (Lincoln, 1945, does not give the full name of this early Ladino; see page 72 following) came to Nebaj in 1887 there were no ladinos in town except for the priest and a handful of mestizos who lived like Indians. A document of 1803 states that no ladinos at all lived in any of the three towns. However, a document of 1752 mentions one Calletano Balensuela, Spaniard, who was listed as a citizen of Nebaj. The same document mentions three Indian-mestizo marriages.[16]

It is clear that, until the 1890's, Ixil country remained almost completely isolated from the national life of Guatemala, though not from neighboring Indian groups. Some of the Ixil from Nebaj spoke the Quiché language easily because of their business contacts with the principal commercial areas to the south, but very few Indians spoke Spanish (Stoll, 1886: p. 235).

[16] Doc. A3.16 leg. 945, exp. 17657 Guat. Natl. Arch. Another census for the area for the year 1880 exists, but according to Stoll and others, the figures were mere estimates because the Ixil would not allow themselves to be counted.

On one occasion, however, the Ixil were almost fortuitously drawn into national politics. In 1868 Justo Rufino Barrios, after being wounded and failing in an attack against government soldiers in Huehuetenango, took refuge with some of his followers in the Ixil hamlet of Ȼ'alb'al, where they were received and cared for until their wounds healed.[17] After recovering his health, Rufino Barrios went to Mexico to organize another rebel expedition, returned to Guatemala in 1871, and became president of the Republic. Later, when Barrios redrew the political boundaries of Guatemala and divided Totonicapán into several departments including Quiché, Barrios gave full recognition to Ixil land rights. Diego de León was the leading *principal* under Barrios (Lincoln, 1945: p. 158), and Lincoln's statement that one or more of the Ixil leaders were exonerated from paying tribute suggests an unofficial expression of gratitude to the Ixil.

The independence and isolation of the Ixil allowed the survival of many cultural features of an earlier time which were lost in other Indian areas. One informant told Lincoln that, at the turn of the century, the Ixil were divided into four castes, or perhaps better, estates: warriors, priests, merchants, and workers (Lincoln, 1945: p. 61). The town itself was divided into cantons with a chief at the head of each. The workers, who wore blue jackets and skirts, were reported to have lived in a special area, the cantón of Salquilito.[18]

During the nineteenth century, Ixil religious activity was in full force, and religious art took the form of elaborate murals and other decorations. Aboriginal music of trum-

[17] The identification of the hamlet is from Ixil oral tradition.

[18] However, this has not yet been confirmed in our recent field work. Also, both in recent reports and in a written note by Baltazar Balduini shortly after the middle of the last century, the *cantón* of Salquilito was reported to be the site of the old town and that the second alcalde often was from that cantón. There is also a special tie between that cantón and the oldest, most prestigious *aldea* of Salquil Grande (Salč'il). People from that distant village have relatives and friends in the cantón of Salquilito.

pets, and log and turtle-shell drums accompanied religious ceremonies. Dances and dramas were elaborate affairs.[19] There was considerable praying at all the crosses and hills, particularly at the great cross in front of the church in Nebaj which was removed in 1935 (Lincoln, 1945: p. 61). The priests taught a few Indians Spanish to educate them for the office of fiscal or maestro de coro, but most of the Indians were illiterate and showed little inclination to learn Spanish.

According to Lincoln's informants, before the Ixil began to work in the coffee fincas, they were self-sufficient in food; there was a lively trade in pigs and cattle for export to Huehuetenango, Cobán, and Quiché. (Lincoln, 1945: p. 64). They drank *comiteco,* a rum made of pulque, which was imported from Mexico, and alcohol consumption was much more restricted than later when ladinos began to sell aguardiente on a large scale.

In the 1890's and later, Juan Brito and Diego de León, descendants of old warrior or top-caste families, were the two strongest principales. No taxes were paid to the central government until 1899. During this period, León and other chief principales extracted tribute from the lower castes of the area, most often in the form of corvée labor (Lincoln, 1945). This special privilege may have dated from the time of Rufino Barrios as suggested earlier.

Coffee cultivation destroyed the isolation of the Ixil zone, and led to its gradual impoverishment. In 1855, Guatemala exported only 5 tons of coffee; by 1870, the amount had climbed to 5,700 tons; by 1890, when the Ixil area was "opened up," coffee exports reached 25,000 tons. As coffee is a labor-intensive crop, the ever growing need for Indian workers led to the reestablishment of various

[19] This is extrapolating from our field observations of murals, dance drama, and music, all of which still exist but are fast disappearing. The dance drama is Hispanic in many respects, and the long trumpets are now made of brass. The murals are still visible in structures which are currently used. The last artist is said to have died some years ago.

forms of compulsory labor and debt peonage. Recruiters or contractors (known as *contratistas, enganchadores,* or *habilitadores*) scanned the countryside in an attempt to tap the labor reservoir at its source. They reached the Ixil area in the 1890's.

These economic transformations were accompanied in the political field by the series of liberal reforms beginning in 1871. Under Justo Rufino Barrios and Miguel Garcia Granados, the power of the Catholic church was curtailed, church land estates were confiscated, land was distributed both to municipalities and to medium-size private landowners, and the capitalist system of production was expanded.

Locally, Doña Juana B. arrived in Nebaj from Sacapulas in 1887 with the intention of opening a school, but did not settle in Nebaj until 1889 or 1890. Although the Indians tried to prevent her from building her house by burning the wood that she had assembled several times, she persisted and finally succeeded. Only later did she win the Ixil's confidence enough to start a small school. From about 1891 onward, Juana B. ran a boarding house. When ladinos came to the area, they all stayed at Doña Juana's house until they were settled. In the early 1890's, many ladinos came to look over the territory, but no new ladinos actually settled in Nebaj until 1894 (Lincoln, 1945).

Next to settle after Doña Juana was a Spaniard, Isaias P., who was sent by the central government to serve as municipal secretary, and thus became the first ladino of that period to be involved in local government. Later, Isaias P. turned to the more lucrative activity of labor recruiting, as did the score of other ladinos from Spain, Italy, France, Mexico, and Guatemala who came in quick succession during the last years of the century. Their labor-contracting activities expanded into money-lending which, combined with the sale of cane alcohol, and the spread of clandestine distilling, gradually reduced more and more Indians to a state of perpetual indebtedness (Lincoln, 1945).

A number of these early ladino settlers (whose children now constitute the older generation) acquired substantial land holdings by foreclosing on Indian debtors, by fraudulent contracts, or by other forms of trickery, although a few are reputed to have acquired land by honest means and without displacing Indians (Lincoln, 1945: p. 67). Some became owners of plantations of several hundred hectares, but the bulk of the land remained in Indian hands, as is still the case today. Other ladinos came as shopkeepers or liquor dealers, as schoolteachers, and as municipal employees, but many of them came when coffee prices were high, to leave again in periods of depression, and the ladino population remained unstable. The oldest ladinos in Nebaj can only trace their local roots to their own parents.

The economic life of Ixil country fluctuated with coffee prices and exports. In 1895, there were only two *estancos* (liquor stores) in Nebaj and not much drinking. By the good times of 1915–1929, there were a great many foreign-owned liquor stores and shops, and at one time there were nearly eighty canteens in town. These shops would frequently hire marimba bands to attract customers. This was a period of high coffee prices, when many Ixil were being advanced large amounts of money for their labor on the fincas. Most of this money was spent for drinking and ceremony, according to the ladinos. During the annual fiesta, there were as many as fifty or sixty marimba bands and private parties, compared to only two or three during the depression in 1940.

According to another of Lincoln's informants, during the early part of the century Nebaj exported as many as 6,000 laborers a year, whereas only about 600 were exported when Lincoln was there in 1940. The high point of prosperity was reached in 1909, when Guatemala exported more than 50,000 tons of coffee. In 1935, the number of men who went to the five important fincas in the coffee belt were 390 per week from Cotzal, 70 from Chajul, and 90 from Nebaj (McBryde, 1945: p. 34, map 12).

By 1921, the ladino population of Nebaj had grown to 421 (4.0 percent of the total), that of Cotzal to 280 (6.5 percent), and that of Chajul to 108 (2.2 percent). This demographic increase in the ladino population entailed economic and educational changes. Literacy and school attendance increased slowly. The region became increasingly incorporated in the Guatemalan money economy through a growing export of labor and coffee and import of textiles, metal tools, and other manufactured products. What had hitherto been a traditional Indian maize-and-beans subsistence agriculture became less and less self-sufficient because of population increase, soil erosion, partial loss of land to ladino-owned coffee plantations or cattle ranches, and the emigration of able-bodied men. As more maize had to be imported, the necessity for labor contracting increased, and subsistence agriculture degenerated further. At the same time, commerce expanded, particularly in Nebaj, which became the most important economic center in the region. A regular biweekly market became established in Nebaj around 1925, and in Cotzal around 1939 (Lincoln, 1945: p. 64).

On the local political scene, the ladinos gained increasing influence. Until 1917, the municipal government was solidly in the hands of the Indian alcalde and regidores (councillors), though these Indian officials were assisted by a literate ladino secretary. Juan B., who died (or possibly was assassinated) in 1904, was a powerful and autocratic Ixil *principal* who as *gobernador* of Nebaj ruled the town with an iron hand (Lincoln, 1945: p. 60). Three strong Ixil principales emerged in the next generation,

Diego B., Gaspar C., and Miguel B. The last one was the true head of the principales, held the title of *b'o·q'ol tenam,* and was thoroughly Indian in his cultural orientation. Diego B. and Gaspar C., on the other hand, were more ladinoized and were bitter rivals. Diego B. learned to read and write as a soldier in Guatemala and, on returning, dressed as a ladino, lived in ladino houses, married ladino women, and was socially accepted by the ladinos. Gaspar C. had a butcher shop and a small shop where the produce from his various fincas were sold. Don Gaspar owned two houses, one of them in the Indian style with no windows on the street (though the outside was painted in pastel color like ladino houses) and the other with windows and a large entrance on the street. His "ladino" house had three large rooms furnished with beds, mattresses, and armchairs. Diego B. had a ladino wife and ladino mistresses, while Gaspar C. had an Indian wife or mistress at each of his fincas. Don Gaspar wore Indian pants, but a ladino woolen coat and a Stetson hat; both wore shoes.

Don Diego and Don Gaspar both claimed ignorance of Indian customs, and in their actions generally acknowledged the superiority of ladino customs by denigrating their own. This attitude seems to indicate the growing influence and power of the ladinos, and the fact that some of the Indian principales deferred to ladino prejudices to maintain their own position. Both of these principales had served in the government of Nebaj and had accumulated land. According to Lincoln, Gaspar C. used his office to look up Indians whose lands were mortgaged, get them indebted to him, and foreclose on the properties (Lincoln, 1945: p. 88). Apparently the rest of the population considered these men to be honest but ruthless. They were often called "Don" by the ladinos. Expectedly, the two ladino-oriented principales of Nebaj were never fully accepted by the Ixil and their actual *b'o·q'ol tenam,* Miguel Brito de la

Paz, or Miguelón, as he was also referred to by the ladinos.

In 1922, two ladino advisers were added to the municipality, and in 1924 the ethnic dualism was fully reflected in the local government: there now was a ladino alcalde, an Indian alcalde, a ladino *síndico,* three ladino regidores, and three Indian regidores (Morales Urrutia, 1961: p. 471). Starting in 1932, during the dictatorship of President Jorge Ubico, the elected alcalde was replaced by an appointed *intendente* who was generally a ladino from outside the local community, and who typically only stayed in office for brief periods. In an eight-month period in 1939–1940, for example, there were six intendentes in Nebaj and four in Chajul (Lincoln, 1945: p. 73). Besides the civilian office of intendente, the central government also appointed a ladino in Nebaj as comandante in charge of a small military garrison of half-a-dozen ladino soldiers. These appointed ladino officials were under the authority of the *jefe político* in El Quiché.

As we shall see later, the Ubico dictatorship was a period of conflict between the Ixil and the ladinos. The most serious incident of violence in Nebaj's known history took place in 1936, as an indirect consequence of the labor reforms introduced by Ubico. In an attempt to abolish the system of debt peonage to which Indians had been reduced by the habilitadores, Ubico canceled the outstanding debts and limited liability for future debts to two dollars and a half. But, in order to retain control over the Indian labor force, two unpopular laws were passed, the *ley de vagancia* and the *ley de vialidad,* which obligated non-gainfully employed people (in effect, mostly Indians) to work on roads or for private employers for 150 days a year and at low wages (Monteforte Toledo, 1959: p. 101). Many Indians, however, now remember Ubico for having abolished debt peonage, and remember him with favor.

The revolution of 1944 had relatively little impact on

Ixil country, except for the reestablishment of elective alcaldes. Like the liberal reform movement of the late nineteenth century, the revolution of 1944–1954 was largely a middle-class movement in which the rural Indian masses played a very small role. The position of the local ladinos was not appreciably altered. Even when the Decreto 900 (the land reform law) was passed in 1952, the Ixil region was almost entirely unaffected. There were few large estates with unused land in the area, and hence there were few expropriations in Ixil country, although the Quiché department as a whole was more affected (Monteforte Toledo, 1959: pp. 435–436).[20]

Since the reestablishment of elective alcaldes in 1946, Nebaj has consistently had a ladino in that position, but Cotzal and Chajul now have Indian mayors. Until 1966, Nebaj retained its disproportional ethnic representation of three ladinos and three Indians on the town council, plus an elected síndico—a ladino until 1949 and an Indian since 1950. The election of a fourth Indian regidor in 1966 indicates that the local political ascendancy of ladinos is now being slowly reversed. Except for salaried civil servants, such as the treasurer and the secretary, who are ladinos, Cotzal and Chajul now have all-Indian municipal councils.

The "liberation" of 1954 and the counterrevolution which followed had some important local consequences. Reprisals were taken against some ladinos, mostly schoolteachers, who had been active in left-wing politics, and a few people were forced to leave the town. By far the most important effect of the counterrevolution, however, was the arrival of many militant foreign priests in Guatemala who launched an all-out effort to "reconvert" the Indians

20 Interestingly, the minister of agriculture in the Arbenz government was a co-owner of the largest finca and a close relative of the wealthiest ladino family in the Ixil region. Several ladino informants denied, however, that there was any relationship between these facts and the relative immunity of the Ixil zone to land reform.

through the indoctrination of *catequistas* (catechists). As we shall see later, this proselytism gave rise to an important new line of cleavage within the Ixil population.

In summary, social evolution in the Ixil area may be characterized in the following terms: After the Conquest, Spanish power was imposed through the Church, reaching its heyday in the seventeenth century. From the eighteenth century, Spanish control fell into decay; from the war of independence from Spain until the turn of the twentieth century, the region was only peripherally involved in the national society, and constituted a largely autonomous, monoethnic sub-society within it. Economically, the region was a largely self-sufficient economy with only minimal and periodic development of wage labor, market places, and commerce. There was a moderate amount of at least part-time artisanal specialization, and considerable stratification within the Ixil group. The towns of Nebaj, Cotzal, and Chajul were sizeable enough in the nineteenth century to be more than peasant villages.

Politically, local government in the nineteenth and early twentieth centuries was largely in the hands of the Ixil, with only occasional intrusions of the central government. Since the late nineteenth century, ladino influence increased through the arrival of ladino municipal secretaries who, as literate petty bureaucrats, acted as intermediaries between the Ixil and the larger society. A somewhat similar role was played earlier by the local priests, but, while Roman Catholicism importantly modified traditional beliefs and practices, it never came close to eradicating them. Instead, a syncretistic cult involving ancestor worship, the use of the Maya calendar, and a complex system of religious offices connected with the cofradías was evolved side by side with orthodox Catholicism. While the shock of the Conquest impoverished Ixil culture and decimated the population, the Ixil way of life has remained viable, resilient, and indeed locally dominant. Until the late nineteenth century, Ixil country had an almost entirely Indian population.

The development of coffee as a cash crop profoundly changed the Ixil area. The influx of substantial numbers of ladinos seeking to tap the Indian labor market undermined the subsistence economy and the political autonomy of the region, and introduced at the local level the cultural pluralism which already prevailed in other parts of Guatemala. The relative power and wealth of ladinos became increasingly disproportionate to their numbers until this trend began to be reversed in the last few years. At no time, however, did the ladinos entrench themselves to the extent of constituting a secure ruling aristocracy. The great increase in population also has profoundly changed the area, and land has become increasingly scarce. Where earlier Indians had to be forced against their will to work on the coastal plantations, now many landless Indians have no choice but to seek such seasonal employment on these fincas. Thus only during the last seventy-five years did Ixil country become significantly integrated into the complex plural society of modern Guatemala to which we shall now turn our attention.

III. SOCIAL CLEAVAGES: ETHNICITY, RELIGION, URBANISM, AND SOCIAL CLASS

To what extent does the Ixil area constitute a meaningful social unit? The Ixil area is certainly not a political unit. To be sure, the boundaries of the three *municipios,* Nebaj, Chajul, and Cotzal, coincide rather closely with ethnic lines (except for recent occupation of some Ixil land by Quiché speakers from neighboring districts), but Ixil country is divided into three semiautonomous and equal-status units, all of which are subordinate to the departmental authorities in El Quiché, outside Ixil country. The major sources of regional integration are cultural and economic. Culturally, the overwhelming majority of the population speak closely related dialects of the same Maya language, and although each municipio has its clearly identifiable dress, and its major cultural and dialectical idiosyncrasies, the Ixil regard themselves as an ethnic group distinct from the Quiché and other neighboring groups. Ixil from all three municipios regularly attend each others' markets and fiestas; they travel throughout the area to sell livestock, seek work on the coffee plantations, worship at rural shrines or at the town churches, visit friends and relatives, or take part in religious or secular feasts. Intermarriages of members of different municipios occur, though not frequently. In the practice of traditional religion, the Ixil do indeed constitute a community of worshippers recognizing common sacred shrines and places (such as the sacred mountain of Juil to which representatives from all parts of the Ixil area go to celebrate the first, twentieth, and two hundred and sixtieth days of the Maya New Year), very similar basic beliefs, and the spiritual paramountcy of Chajul and its titular saint.

In the economic sphere, the three municipios, though now far from constituting a self-sufficient unit, still maintain important ties with one another. There is not much specialization of production between them (except for extensive rope-making and agave fiber production in Cotzal), but the three towns alternate their market days (Cotzal on Wednesday and Saturday, Chajul on Tuesday and Friday, and Nebaj on Thursday and Sunday). Economically, the paramount position of Nebaj is evident. Nebaj has more permanent stores selling a wider range of goods than the other two towns, and its Sunday market is the biggest in the region. As the place of residence of almost all important labor contractors, Nebaj is virtually the only Ixil labor market. Nebaj is the terminus of the only two bus lines to link Ixil country with the outside towns of Huehuetenango and Santa Cruz del Quiché, and most of the fifteen-odd trucks and dozen private cars in Ixil country are located in Nebaj, which is thus the only significant center for motorized transport in the region. (Migrant workers, coffee, sugar, maize, and pigs are among the major items regularly carried into or out of the region by truck.)

The major occasions on which the economic and religious unity of the region becomes evident are when each of the three Ixil towns celebrates the feast of its patron saint. Whereas relatively few Ixil leave the region, except men (and a few women) on labor contracts, a great many Ixil men, women, and children attend each others' fiestas.

There are substantial differences between the three municipios. Culturally, dialectical variations between the three areas are noticeable, and women's dress and headgear immediately identify the wearer's origin. Of the three dialect areas, Chajul is the most distinct. Nebaj and Cotzal

Indians can understand each other more readily than either group can understand Ixil from Chajul. On the boundaries between the municipios, however, there is intermarriage and intermixture between the variants of Ixil culture.

Beyond these relatively minor variations in local Ixil culture, Ixil social relations in Chajul, Cotzal, and Nebaj differ in a number of important respects. Chajul with a total population of 13,497 in 1964 is in many ways the most traditionally Indian of the three Ixil municipios. The town of Chajul with its 4,172 inhabitants is smaller than Nebaj, and has proportionately only one fourth as many ladinos (234 compared to 1,040). Although the previous alcalde (mayor) was a ladino, the present local government, except for a paid ladino secretary and treasurer, is entirely in the hands of elected Ixil officials. There are only half-a-dozen small shops offering a narrow range of goods, and Chajul is the absolute end of the line as far as commercial activities are concerned. The dirt road goes no further, and all wheel traffic stops there. Chajul ladinos play a significant role in neither the commercial nor the political life of the town. Chajul Ixil are noticeably more provincial and more closed or even hostile to outsiders, both Indians and ladinos, than are the people of Nebaj and Cotzal.

The only field in which Chajul holds preeminence over Nebaj and Cotzal is religion. We have already noted how this was true of traditional Ixil religion; but this is also the case for orthodox Catholicism. The old church is nearly twice the size of those in Nebaj and Cotzal, and in 1966 and earlier there were two priests in residence compared to one in Nebaj and none in Cotzal. (Now one of the two Chajul priests has taken up residence in Cotzal.) In recent years, Catholic efforts at reconversion of the Ixil have met with more success in Chajul than in Nebaj or Cotzal. The priests claim the allegiance of about a thousand Ixil catechists in the municipio of Chajul compared to eight hundred in Cotzal and three hundred in Nebaj. Three of the Chajul catechists have even "infiltrated," with the encouragement of the priests, the stronghold of the traditional Ixil cult by holding office in the Indian *cofradías,* or religious fraternities.

Chajul, like Nebaj and Cotzal, has a primary school, but it only has three ladino teachers, and although the school consists theoretically of six grades, few pupils attend regularly. Total school enrollment was seventy-one in 1964.

The municipio of Cotzal (population: 12,150 in 1964) and the *cabecera*[1] by the same name (population: 3,609) are respectively the smallest in the Ixil zone. The town of Cotzal, however, is commercially more active than Chajul, though less so than Nebaj. Unlike Chajul, Cotzal has somewhat of a hinterland, since a dirt road goes on to the important coffee finca of San Francisco some eighteen kilometers away. The agave fiber industry also gives Cotzal a modicum of prosperity and gives it an advantage over Chajul. There are 272 ladinos in town—scarcely more than in Chajul—and local government is also entirely controlled by an elected Ixil alcalde and his Ixil regidores (councillors). The municipal secretary, treasurer, and two other petty officials are paid ladino employees. The primary school building is far inferior to Nebaj's but better attended than Chajul's. In 1964, the Cotzal school had 220 children on its rolls. The influence of the Catholic Church is not as great as in Chajul, but at the same time, Cotzal is much less traditional than Chajul. A number of upper-class Cotzal Indians are fluent in Spanish, dress as ladinos, and have ladino-style houses. Cotzal

1 The term *cabecera* refers to the main town which serves as the administrative center of each municipio. Its closest North American analog would be the county seat. Thereafter, in keeping with the Guatemalan census usage, we shall refer to the population of the cabeceras as "urban," and we shall call "rural" the people who live in the outlying villages and hamlets (*aldeas* and *caserios*) surrounding these towns.

Indians are regarded by the people of Nebaj and regard themselves as more progressive and *entendido* ("understanding," "in-the-know") than those of Chajul. In terms of economic development and openness to the outside world, Cotzal stands in an intermediate position between Chajul and Nebaj.

Nebaj is the most important center of contact between ladinos and Indians in the Ixil region. This was the chief reason Nebaj was chosen as the main locale of our field work.[2] Much of the subsequent analysis thus focuses on Nebaj. The municipio of Nebaj with a 1964 population of 23,374 is nearly twice as large as either Cotzal or Chajul. The town of Nebaj has 5,227 people, and is the largest commercial and labor recruiting center in the region. It is also the closest and most accessible Ixil town to El Quiché and Guatemala City, and it has the largest concentration of ladinos in the area. While, in 1964, ladinos constituted only 8.1 percent of the total population of the Ixil zone, they accounted for 19.9 percent of the population of the town of Nebaj where, in turn, 26.2 percent of the ladinos in the region are located.

As plural societies go, Nebaj represents an interesting intermediate case between a "colonial situation" where one group, whether immigrant or indigenous, is socially, economically, and politically dominant, and a "separate-but-equal" situation of the Swiss, Belgian, or Yugoslav type.[3] Indians hold a substantial, though not proportional, share of wealth and power in the municipio. The ladinos, though a superordinate group, hold only a partial

2 For a description of field methodology see the Preface.

3 For the concept of colonial situation see Balandier, 1963. The concept of internal colonialism has been used to describe situations in South Africa or Latin America where the dominant group has come to be regarded as indigenous and has created within a given body politic a sub-sector resembling a colonial empire (Gonzalez Casanova, 1963; Marquard, 1957; van den Berghe, 1965b). The equalitarian situation where several ethnic groups share power and wealth in a non-hierarchical and nearly proportional fashion is termed "consociation" by M. G. Smith.

and precarious political control over one of the three Ixil municipios, and play only insignificant roles in the other two. In terms of social class, there is considerable overlap between Indians and ladinos, though differences in status clearly favor the latter. Economically, the biggest shopowners and landowners are ladinos, but most of the retail stores, market stalls, and land are Indian owned and operated. In short, a situation approaching ethnic group parity in the distribution of social rewards and power prevails in spite of great numerical disparity.

Of course, one of the great advantages of local ladinos is that they belong to a much larger group which completely dominates the state and the economy at the national level. Local upper-class ladino families have extensive economic, social kinship, and political ties outside the Ixil area, which make them, in effect, local representatives of a national ruling class. The Ixil, on the other hand, are a strictly localized cultural minority, and one of the smaller ones in Guatemala at that.

The cleavage between ladinos and Indians is the deepest and most obvious one in Nebaj, as in the rest of Guatemala. At the local level it may be described as a caste or at least a quasi-caste system. The groups are hierarchized, nearly completely endogamous, and ascriptive, with membership by birth and for life. These groups are given semiofficial recognition insofar as ethnic affiliation is recorded in the census, and occasionally also in other official documents such as minutes of municipal council meetings, passport applications, and various legal documents. Questions concerning home language or literacy which are correlated with ethnicity are also routinely asked by the population and voters' registration offices.

Although Guatemala practices no systematic policy of racial or ethnic discrimination, there are at least two significant respects in which Indians are put *de facto* in a disadvantageous position as a consequence of government policy. First, Spanish is the sole official language of Guatemala, and Indians suffer therefore from a distinct handicap in having to transact government business or attend schools in a foreign tongue. Second, an electoral distinction is made between literate and illiterate electors. All adults may vote, but only literate people are obligated to do so under penalty of a fine. While this measure appears to discriminate against literate electors, it leads to the *de facto* disenfranchisement of many Indians. In 1964, only 15.4 percent of the Guatemalan Indian population over seven were literate compared to 54.5 percent of the ladinos. There results a much higher rate of voting for ladinos than for Indians in many parts of the Republic, and in Nebaj in particular. Thus, in the 1966 elections, when the eligible population of the municipio was around 10,000, only 1,306 ballots were cast. Obviously, the overwhelming majority of the Indians did not vote, partly because many lived in rural hamlets distant from polling places, partly because of political apathy or disinterest, partly because of fear of the consequences of political participation in a country which has not been notable for its stability or democracy. (In many parts of Guatemala, Indians have the reputation of being *"oficialistas,"* i.e., of voting for the party in power as the safest course.)

In Nebaj, as indeed in most Guatemalan towns, the social definition of an Indian is cultural rather than racial. Of a sample of 40 Nebaj ladinos [4] asked to name the

[4] The sample includes approximately 12 percent of the adult ladino population of Nebaj. Of 43 persons to whom an ethnic relations questionnaire was distributed, 40 returned it, a response rate of 93 percent. Because of high illiteracy rates among working-class ladinos, and among women, there is both a class and a sex bias in the sample. Of the respondents, 31 are men and 9 women; 10 have less than 6 years of school, and 11 have more than 10; the sample includes 14 professionals or semiprofessionals (10 of them primary school teachers), 9 merchants, rentiers, or landowners, 11 white-collar workers (mostly municipal employees), 4 manual workers, and 2 housewives. In age, the sample ranges from 19 to 65 with a mean of 37.9 years. The Guatemalan population census defines

differences between ladinos and Indians, 33 mentioned only cultural differences (clothing, language, and "customs" or "mode of life"); 6 mentioned both cultural and physical traits; and none listed physical traits only. (One person did not reply.) There are some phenotypical differences between ladinos and Indians. The ladino upper class is predominantly of recent European origin, and hence looks "white," but most working-class ladinos are physically undistinguishable from Indians. Conversely, illegitimate children of ladinos raised as Indians are accepted as Ixil even though, in some cases, they look more European than Indian. Physical differences are recognized by both ladinos and Indians, and both groups express an aesthetic preference for lighter skin and hair color, but phenotype is irrelevant to group membership. Ladinos and Indians constitute *ethnic* and not racial groups.[5]

Despite the largely cultural definition of group boundaries, the ethnic line is quite rigid. For a local person to "pass" from one group to another without going to live elsewhere is virtually impossible, and most informants

membership in an ethnic group in terms of "the social estimation in which a person is held in the place where the census is taken."

[5] The degree to which group distinctions in Mesoamerica are ethnic as distinct from racial is the object of some controversy. Some authors claim the existence of a Latin American brand of racism that is perhaps less blatant than in the United States, but nevertheless real (Monteforte Toledo, 1959: p. 116). Tumin (1952) cites consciousness of physical differences in San Luis Jilotepeque, and there is no question that both Indians and ladinos are conscious of phenotypical differences in most of Latin America. Aesthetic preference for certain physical types is also widespread. But the two core elements of "true" racism are generally absent in Spanish America, namely that genetically transmitted physical traits constitute basic criteria for membership in corporate groups, and that genetic characteristics be regarded as important determinants of human behavior and differential abilities. In Latin America, certain parts of Brazil exhibit mild forms of racism (van den Berghe, 1967); there is also some evidence of racism against African slaves in colonial Spanish America (Aguirre Beltrán, 1946, 1957), but in modern Mexico and Guatemala, racism has virtually vanished. Only one of our Nebaj ladino informants and respondents spontaneously made a remark which could be interpreted as racist, and it was directed against American Negroes, a group with which he had had practically no contact.

cannot give any cases. Twenty-three of the 40 respondents deny that an Indian can become a ladino, and 29 deny that a ladino can become an Indian. Of those, 16 mention "race," "blood," "ancestry," or "origins" as reasons which make passing impossible, but most of them also advance cultural reasons such as dietary and linguistic differences. On the basis of these findings, it may be argued that to a substantial number of ladinos, the ladino-Indian distinction is perceived at least partly as a racial one. At the subjective level, this is true to some extent, and in that sense traces of racism may be said to be present. But in terms of who is in fact classified as Indian or ladino, the criteria used are clearly cultural.

Nearly half of the ladino sample (17 out of 40) recognize that, given the cultural definition of the ethnic line, passing is at least a theoretical possibility. Those respondents tend to be more educated than those who think passing is impossible. (See Table 3.) The ladinos who regard passing as possible mention education, hispanization, change of clothing, and cultural "improvement" as means for Indians to become ladinos, but several qualify their statement by adding that this can only be done by leaving the community. Thirty-seven respondents perceive the Indians as changing in the direction of hispanization (learning Spanish, dressing as ladinos, becoming literate and more "civilized") , and most of them approve of the changes as indications of progress. Yet, most of them correctly perceive that gradual hispanization does not visibly affect the ethnic line locally. A bicultural Indian remains an Indian until such time as he loses all ties to Maya culture and language. In Cotzal and to a lesser extent in Nebaj, there are some persons who dress as ladinos and speak fluent Spanish, but regard themselves as Indians and are so regarded by others.

In a sample of 90 Ixil, 85 similarly recognized that Indians were becoming hispanicized.[6] But unlike the ladinos, most Indians were indifferent, noncommittal, or even hostile to hispanization. Of 85 subjects who expressed an opinion on the topic, only 6 approved of the change, 24 disapproved, 38 were noncommittal, and 17 explained why change was taking place. Cultural conservatism and ethnic identification on the part of the Ixil take the form of strong sanctions (such as gossip, ridicule, and ostracism) against those who take up ladino ways and adopt ladino clothing. Indian solidarity is unquestionably one of the important factors making the relative rigidity of the ethnic line at the local level.

Census figures corroborate ethnic stability in the department of Quiché. The Indian percentage of the Quiché population and of the three Ixil municipios has remained nearly constant between 1950 and 1964 (Table 2). If anything, it rose slightly from 84.1 to 84.7 percent for the whole department; from 91.7 to 92.3 percent for Nebaj; and from 92.5 to 93.6 percent for Cotzal. For Chajul it dropped from 91.0 to 89.6 percent. Such slight changes as

[6] As is true of the ladino sample, the 90 Ixil respondents were not randomly chosen. Included in the sample were some people who were selected because they held political office; most subjects were friends, acquaintances, and relatives of our literate Ixil informants. Respondents ranged in age from adolescence to their eighties. As indicated by the fact that 55 were literate, that 62 had held municipal office, and that 72 had held religious office, the sample is heavily biased toward high-status persons. There may also have been a bias toward religious traditionalism; the informants who administered the interview schedule and selected some of the respondents were themselves chosen by one of us because they belonged to traditionalist families. The 50-item schedule was administered in Ixil by young literate informants of both sexes who were trained for the task, and who pretested the instrument under our supervision. Somewhat less than one-third of the interviews were conducted in our field headquarters; the remainder were done in the subjects' homes. Approximately two-fifths of the questions were open-ended, and responses were written down verbatim in Ixil. The remaining questions required simple answers of quantity, choice, affirmation, or negation. Each question was standardized after extensive pretesting with three informants, and phrased in terms that seemed least ambiguous to the respondents.

did occur are attributable in part to differential net migration rates and rates of natural increase. When this local stability in ethnic composition is contrasted with the rapid relative increase of ladinos in the Guatemalan population as a whole (Table 1), it is clear that most of the "passing" takes place outside of the Quiché area, and indeed outside of the predominantly Indian areas.

As further tests of ethnic group definition, the ladino subjects were asked how they would call children of mixed parentage or Indian children brought up in a ladino home. Eighteen persons used the terms *mestizo* or *mezclado* to describe children of mixed parents. Sixteen subjects attributed them membership in either group, with a preference for the father's group because of the presumed tendency for the father to impose his culture on the household. The remaining respondents gave no definite answer, said there was no term for such people, or used universalistic terms like "Guatemalan" or "Christian." In the case of the Indian child brought up by ladinos, twenty said the child was still Indian, eight used the phrase "adoptive son" or "son of the house," and only eight said he would become ladino.

How can one resolve the apparent contradiction between the salience of cultural traits in the drawing of group distinctions, and the majority ladino opinion that passing is impossible for reasons that are at least partly "racial"? Passing is, *de facto,* at once locally rare and nationally fairly common. A local Indian cannot become accepted as a ladino in most Guatemala communities, but the rapidly declining proportion of Indians in the country's population (which cannot be accounted for in terms of either immigration or differential net reproduction rates) demonstrates that internal migration within Guatemala is, in fact, accompanied by ladinoization within a few years to a generation. Locally, the situation is quite different; even strongly ladinoized Indians are still regarded as

Indians, irrespective of their degree of wealth, power, and education. However, no local Indians in the Ixil zone are so completely ladinoized as to speak better Spanish than Ixil. It seems that only children of mixed unions can in time become accepted as ladinos, provided they speak Spanish without Ixil interferences and associate mostly with ladinos.

Given the existence of a strongly cohesive local Indian culture, passing only becomes possible by removing oneself from one's cultural milieu. At the local level, a system of ethnic castes prevails which some ladinos interpret in quasi-racial terms, but the virtual absence of completely acculturated Indians is fully consistent with a purely ethnic definition of the castes. Objectively speaking, cultural criteria are much better predictors of group membership than any combination of physical factors. Among cultural criteria, the stress has usually been put on the degree of hispanization by Indians, because this has been the main direction of culture change. However, this emphasis has somewhat confused the actual cultural differentiation between ladinos and Indians. The asymmetry in the process of culture change leads to a situation where nearly all ladinos are monocultural and monolingual, while most Indians exhibit various degrees of bilingualism and biculturalism. Thus, ignorance of Indian culture is a surer criterion of ladino status than knowledge of Spanish and of the dominant culture. Conversely, an Indian is a person who is either monoculturally "indigenous" or bicultural, except that if he is extensively hispanicized and leaves his place and group of origin he becomes a ladino.

Ethnic group membership can perhaps be even closely defined by stressing not so much *cultural* criteria as *social* ones. To be sure, if cultural differences between Indians and ladinos were to vanish, so would the ethnic line. But ladinos and Indians are not simply "carriers" of different cultures; they are also members of groups with a well-defined structure of patterned interaction and roles. Ethnic membership is defined just as much by a complex matrix of social ties and social roles as by the possession of certain cultural traits. When an Indian, for example, removes himself from his social network of kinsmen, friends, and neighbors, he retains his cultural characteristics and remains a "carrier" of his culture; but, to a considerable extent, he ceases to be an active interacting member of his ethnic group. A structural approach to ethnic relations in terms of networks of relationships and role structure helps explain better the link between "passing" and geographical mobility than an exclusively cultural view of the phenomenon in terms of dynamics of acculturation. The internal disparity between the locally rigid but nationally fairly fluid ethnic situation in Guatemala raises a number of interesting analytical problems which we shall take up again in Chapter VI.

The cultural and structural differences between Indians and ladinos in Nebaj, and the interaction between those two groups determine to a large extent the nature of the local plural society. Our present intention is not to describe either culture, but rather to analyze how the two groups interact, and how the institutional structures of each culture intermesh to form a single, culturally pluralistic sub-society. In spite of the fact that, with the exception of some children of mixed parentage, and of some ladinoized outsiders of partly Indian ancestry, every Nebaj person can readily be classified by every local adult as belonging to one of the two main ethnic groups, there are no simple, clear-cut criteria of ethnic membership. Some characteristics are closely associated with one group or the other, but none are both necessary and sufficient conditions of membership.

Mother tongue is perhaps the best distinguishing criterion, but a few ladinoized Indians have completely bilingual homes, and are almost equally fluent in Spanish and

Ixil. Most urban Ixil speak at least some Spanish, and a minority of the younger people speak it quite well. A number of ladinos speak some Ixil (thirteen out of forty in the sample), but very few are fluent in it. Generally, Indians speak more Spanish than ladinos speak Ixil, but few Indians speak a sufficiently fluent or unaccented Spanish to be accepted as ladinos even outside Nebaj.

In terms of dress, differences between Indians and ladinos are steadily diminishing, particularly among men. The vast majority of Ixil women and girls still wear their traditional costume in spite of the fact that its laboriously handwoven fabrics are about twice as expensive as cheap machine-made ladino clothes. Most Ixil men and boys dress in commercially produced clothes, but their preference for certain standarized items (white straw hats, black jacket) make them readily distinguishable as Indians. Increasingly, however, migrant laborers come back from coastal plantations in "ladino" clothes. Traditionally, Ixil women went barefoot, while men wore sandals or also went barefoot. The wearing of shoes is still regarded as an eminently ladino trait, but around fiesta time, many young men wear shoes, and two of our female Ixil informants began regularly to wear shoes after their return from a trip to the United States. In neighboring Sacapulas, a number of Indian women regularly wear cheap plastic sandals. While the assumption of footgear by local Indian women created a sensation among both ladinos and Ixil, the wearing of shoes by Ixil men is more and more accepted, and the symbolic character of footgear as a criterion of ethnicity will, no doubt, diminish in the future. Already, clothing is no longer a reliable basis of ethnic identification for Ixil men.

Literacy used to be almost a ladino monopoly, although many ladinos were illiterate; but today a small minority of Indians have gone to school and have become literate while some ladinos remain illiterate. Nationally, the ladino literacy rate is still three and one-half times that of Indians, and in Nebaj, the disproportion is probably greater. Of a sample of 180 persons who were listed in the Nebaj civil registry as having married between 1963 and 1966, 61.4 percent of the ladinos were literate, compared to 5.5 percent of the Indians.[7]

Religion was also, until recently, a reliable criterion of ethnic affiliation. The overwhelming majority of ladinos were orthodox Catholics, at least nominally so, although the actual degree of religious practice and fervor was low. The Ixil, on the other hand, nearly all practiced a syncretistic religion which the Catholic clergy and the ladinos regard as a form of "idolatry," "paganism," or "witchcraft." Traditional Indians call themselves "Catholics," and the polite term used by ladinos to distinguish them from orthodox Catholics is "old Catholics," but both Ixil and ladinos are aware that Ixil religion is clearly distinct and indeed antagonistic to orthodox Catholicism.

Ladinos are generally ignorant about Ixil religion. They know only that Indians go continually to the surrounding mountains and hills to perform ritual, or *costumbre*. For this and other reasons, they speak of the Indians as being "superstitious," although many rural and lower-class ladinos share some Indian beliefs and practices. Ladinos have been observed at the Indian shrine of Majobal in Chajul during the February pilgrimages. A ladino spiritualist was employed by well-dressed ladino women to bewitch a straying husband or boyfriend. The praying of the ladino spiritualist was in Spanish but with Indian phraseology and mixed Indian-ladino content. Divining shows at the market in Nebaj and at Chajul attract ladinos and Indians alike. An Ixil shaman has had ladino clients. Thus

[7] Possibly, bias on the part of ladino civil registry employees led them to assume that Indians were illiterate, unless they were known not to be so. But adult literacy among Indians almost certainly does not exceed 10 percent.

the distinction between Indians and ladinos in the religious sphere is not, as the ladinos would have it, one of superstition versus enlightenment, but one of specific content. Lower-class ladinos tend to share a pan-Guatemalan set of beliefs, partly Indian-derived and partly folk Spanish. The Ixil, on the other hand, have a set of religious beliefs and practices which, though of partly Spanish origin, are distinct in many ways from those of other Indian groups as well as from those of rural and lower class ladinos.

Generally speaking, therefore, ladinos and Indians live in different religious worlds, and Ixil life would seem to be dominated by religion to a much greater extent than is true of the ladinos, if one judges by time and money spent on religious activities. Pre-Conquest Ixil society was undoubtedly theocratic, and even today the political and the religious spheres are closely interwoven. Since orthodox Catholicism is widely known, we shall confine our comments to Ixil religion and we shall do so in summary form. (An extensive ethnographic description of Ixil religion will be the subject of a later monograph.)

Like Ixil society itself, and the municipio offices, some of the Ixil deities are stratified. In addition, most of the deities have more than one name, one of which is usually that of a Catholic saint. The many functions and attributes of the gods overlap in complex ways. A remote high god, Q'esla Kub'a·l, stands at the apex of the hierarchy. Under him is a matrimonial pair, Kub'a·l and Kuçuç, the sun and the moon, sometimes called Jesus and Mary. The sun has different manifestations, as does each of the twenty gods corresponding to the days of the calendar. The day gods are imagined as magnificent figures carried across the sky on litters by four lesser deities. The headdresses of the day gods are of such size as to require two additional deities to support them. The sun, a kind of third eye, shines forth from the gods' chests. With this enormous eye, the day god can peer into the smallest crack of a house and observe the behavior of its inhabitants. The female moon deity, on the other hand, was once such a gossipy individual that one of her eyes was closed so that she could not see so much to gossip about. She therefore shines with less brilliance.

Lower in status are various intermediate supernaturals such as the wind god, Kaqiq', the cloud god, Su·¢', and the storm god, Kaqsučkum'. Lower yet, intermediate gods called ˀanqel (from the Spanish) are vitally concerned with human affairs, for their existence depends upon the sustenance provided them by humans in the form of food, drink, incense, and candles consumed in the course of ritual. At the lowest stratum are the ancestral spirits living in one of three regions, the *klorya,* or sky, the *mundo,* or earth, and the underworld.

The great majority of the intermediate (and intermediary) supernaturals have been given the names of Spanish saints or angels, which reflects the success with which the early Spanish priests were able to effect at least a superficial semblance of Catholicism. The intermediary supernaturals inhabit specific regions. The saints occupy the *klorya* and the angels live in what is called "the world" consisting of caves, mountains, and rivers in the surrounding countryside. Each geographic location is the domain of a specific angel.

According to current oral tradition, there was a time when the high god, Q'esla Kub'a·l, was more directly connected with earthly events. He became angry with the inhabitants because they were too close to him and spied on him. He sought to destroy them with flood. By building boats and tall houses the people survived. He then made plans to destroy them with fire. Word got around that the fire would penetrate the earth by two staff-lengths. Many people accordingly buried themselves in large urns just below the two-staff line. Others hid in rivers, caves, and mountains. When the fire came it penetrated not two, but three, staff-lengths and killed all the people hiding in the urns. However, those who had taken refuge in the caves and rivers survived. Q'esla Kub'a·l then forgave these survivors and assigned them the job of watching over the next inhabitants of the earth, the humans. If the humans failed to provide these intermediary gods with ritual food or failed to serve them properly, the intermediaries would notify Q'esla Kub'a·l, who then would send sickness to the offenders.

The actions of the intermediaries thus depend entirely on the behavior of humans. If humans misbehave, the intermediaries become displeased and request that Q'esla Kub'a·l punish them with sickness. If humans are pious and carry out the necessary rituals, the intermediary gods can bring good luck, see that the crops and animals are abundant, and bring wealth and rain or dry weather as needed. The intermediary gods are thus both the indirect cause of illness and the source of good providence.

Another cause of illness arises from the displeasure of the ancestral spirits. To cite one example, a young man suffered from cramps because his mother had had an argument with his grandmother ten or more years previously. In the curing ceremony the curer invoked the name of the dead grandmother. Candles were burned at the house, cemetery, and calvary to placate the dead grandmother and ask forgiveness.

The twenty day-gods occupy the central place in Ixil religion. All ritual, whether for family, neighborhood groups, or the entire municipio, is done by the calendar. In Nebaj, there is an Ixil high priest, *b'o·q'ol b'a·lwa¢ti·š,* who keeps the day count and and determines the days on which government religious ceremonies and cofradía ceremonies are to be held (in addition to those ceremonies held on saints' days of the Gregorian calendar). There are also special prayer-sayers, called *b'a·lwa¢ti·š* in Nebaj, *mam* in Chajul, and *compadre* in Cotzal, who ask for good providence or cures in family and neighborhood ceremonies. Finally there are the diviners called *ʔa·q'i·* who know most about the calendar, and who use it with a divining bundle of *palo pito* seeds to count the days.

The twenty day-gods have differing attributes and domains of operation. Each god is said to reign when his day comes, and the attributes and special interests of the god are associated with the day. Thus the day god Ȼ'ikin is represented by the bird of that name, which is associated with the weaving of bird designs on the blouses of women. This is a day of praying for wealth. The day god Huna·pu represents the household deity at the shrine of every Ixil family. The day god Q'anil is in charge of corn growing; ʔA·ma represents the corn ear itself. B'a·¢' is the day for marriages and for praying for wealth. Ç'iʔ and Čo· are agents of witchcraft and counter-witchcraft.

Usually the ceremonies for a particular day-god begin the day previous to the god's appearance in the day count, and continue through the dawning of the day of the god to whom one is praying. Thus the day gods are sometimes thought of in pairs, and the special ceremonies span the change of days.

The day gods are divided in four groups of five gods in rank positions, showing that even the deities are brought into a system of government parallel to that of the municipios. Thus even after the Conquest and the cataclysmic changes wrought by the Spaniards, a theocratic tendency continued in the Ixil world view.

In addition to the series of twenty days are the numbers of the thirteen-day count which are also deities. These combine with the twenty day-gods to form the calendar. A complete cycle occurs in 260 days (13 times 20). The count then continues until 365 days are completed, and a new year begins. Thus, the Ixil have eighteen months of twenty days plus a special five-day period called *ʔo·q'i·* before the new year starts. Each year is given the name of the day which starts it, there being only four of the twenty which could appear as the first day of the new year. For example, the new year which started on March 5, 1967, was 7 ʔE· in the Ixil calendar. The year previous, the new year began on 6 Če· in 1968 it began on 8 Noʔq; and in 1969 it will begin on 9 ʔIq'. These four days will be repeated each time with a different number at the beginning of a new year until, after thirteen years the number thirteen is reached; at which time the next year begins with number one again. We are now in a thirteen-year period that began with 1 ʔIq' in 1961. In 1974 a new thirteen-year period will begin. For all four year-bearers to run through the thirteen numbers takes 52 years, a time interval which before the Conquest was a major marker throughout the Mesoamerican high cultures.

In various kinds of rituals and celebrations sometimes the twentieth or fortieth and especially the two hundred and sixtieth day following New Year's Day is celebrated with as much or more ritual than the actual New Year's Day. The two hundred and sixtieth day is especially important because it repeats the day on which the new year began (13 times 20). The two cycles, 13 times 20 and 18 times 20, are both in active use and well understood among Ixil calendar specialists today.

Because the Mayan calendar of 18 times 20 did not add a day every four years, it gradually moves out of phase vis à vis the Gregorian calendar. The Mayan New Year fell on the fourth of March in 1968 and will continue to fall on that date until the next leap year in 1972, when it will fall on the third of March. The Mayan New Year will not coincide with the Gregorian New Year until the year 2217. This calendar we shall call the ritual calendar.

In addition to the ritual calendar is another calendar of eighteen months associated with agricultural activities which has fallen into disuse, but it is still remembered in part by some of the older men. This eighteen-month agricultural calendar could not have been directly correlated with the 18 times 20 ritual calendar unless some sort of leap-year or quarter-day correction were added, because an agricultural calendar, to be in step with the seasons, must correlate closely with the solar year.

In addition to the full-time religious specialists for whom priesthood is a lifelong occupation, there are the non-specialists who take on one-year offices in religious brotherhoods or societies called *cofradías.* There are twelve cofradías in Nebaj, and ten each in Chajul and Cotzal. Each cofradía consists of ten ranked offices called *mertoma* in Ixil, *mayordomo* in Spanish. The highest office is called *b'a·l mertoma* or "father" mayordomo; the second office is *ka· mertoma* or second mayordomo, and the offices descend in rank and importance to that of *k'uˀč mertoma* or last mayordomo. This lowest office of a cofradía is so unimportant that it is usually filled by a young boy who performs menial tasks. The highest or *b'a·l mertoma,* however, is a very important office and, once discharged, qualifies the holder for the position of *principal* or community leader. In the past, *b'a·l mertomas* have been chosen only from men over forty who were in the upper stratum of Ixil society, according to Lincoln (1945) ; but the system seems to be opening now to admit members with lower-class origins if they have the necessary personal qualities and wealth to assume their role.

The purpose of the cofradía organization is to care for and honor the saint in its charge. This involves a series of ceremonies. The most important is for the day of the saint. Three of the twelve brotherhoods in Nebaj, though separate, are designated as companions to three others, each pair being a "man" and "woman." For example, the two cross brotherhoods are distinguished by the designation of *winaq* and *ˀiṣoq,* that is, man and woman. In the three "woman" brotherhoods, the wives of the officials (*mayordomas*) in charge of the statue participate to a greater extent than the wives of officials of men's brotherhoods, though mayordomas of all brotherhoods participate to some extent.

The list of Nebaj cofradías is as follows: Kuçuç Mariy, (also called Rosa·yo Winaq), Rosa·yo ʔIṣoq, Kru·s Winaq, Kru·s ʔIṣoq, Komsepsyon Winaq, Komsepsyon ʔIṣoq, San ʔAnto·nyo, Q'i· Santo, San Pedro, Lu·pa, San Sewástyan, Kayi·te. The first six are the ones in pairs. Paired saints are often celebrated on the same day although they occupy different houses. The statues are kept in the houses of the *b'a·l mertomas* of the respective cofradías. If a *b'a·l mertoma* comes from outside the town, as often happens, he may rent a house for the year. His wife is the *çuç* or mother mayordoma. In addition to the statue which is kept in the house of each mayordomo, there is a companion statue which is kept under wraps behind and to one side of the altar of the church. The companion statue is brought out during some of the ceremonies of the cofradía saints and, once a year, when the brotherhoods change personnel (and hence houses). During these times the brotherhood arranges for a marimba to play, and the statues are carried in procession. During important ceremonies such as Easter and the August 15 feast, all twelve brotherhood statues are carried in procession.

When the companion saint is visiting in the brotherhood house, it is usually placed together with the regular statue on the altar of the house. During crowded ceremonies, such as the feast of Kuçuç Mariy and San ʔAnto·nyo, one of the saints is kept on the covered porch of the house.

The father mayordomos have to attend mass in church and go there to "guard" the statue of the brotherhood. In the case of the three female brotherhoods, the father mayordomo is accompanied by his wife, the mother mayordoma. They go to church every Thursday and Sunday at 8:00 A.M.

In Chajul, the two highest ranking of the ten brotherhoods, Sacramento and Rosario, decide on who the father mayordomos will be for the following year, not only for their own brotherhoods but also for the others. They also are said to have a strong political influence. In Nebaj the three highest cofradías appoint the *b'a·l mertoma* for the others. Once the father mayordomo has been assigned, he chooses his own second mayordomo and together they decide on the remaining eight.

In addition to the aspects of Ixil religion we have just summarized, there exist a variety of curing rituals, many different kinds of neighborhood ceremonies, ceremonies at the sacred mountain of Juil where delegates are sent from all three Ixil municipios, and a number of municipio ceremonies in which government and religious officials both take part. Further, even among the traditional Ixils, there are several religious variants; the views of the head Nebaj priest differ from those of some of the calendar diviners, suggesting an early division analogous to the recent split between traditionalists and catechists to which we shall turn presently.

Two developments in the religious field have at once reduced categorical differences between Indians and ladinos and created new lines of cleavage. One is the establishment in Nebaj of two small Protestant denominations. Both of them are off-shoots of North American churches, but one of them is now locally run. Both Protestant groups have made a small number of ladino and Indian converts, referred to as "evangelists," who worship jointly, and constitute interethnic religious communities. The other development is more recent yet. In the last decade, the Catholic clergy and a lay organization, the Accíon Católica, have made a concerted effort to "reconvert" the Indians, and have succeeded in creating a small but highly militant group of "catechists" who are orthodox Catholics and deprecate traditional Ixil religion. These catechists, numbering some four to five percent of the total Ixil population, consist principally of adolescents and young adults who were often recruited in primary school, where the children are required to go to confession and attend other Catholic rites.

The position of the cathechists is interstitial between the rest of the Indians and the ladinos. Although they share the ladinos' religious beliefs, and tend to be more ladinoized and educated than the majority of Indians, they regard themselves and are regarded by others as Ixil. The Catholic clergy and the ladinos regard them as "better" and more "progressive" Indians, while the Ixil traditionalists generally resent their intolerance of customs, their militant proselytism, their discourtesy to their elders, and their organized attempts to disrupt or interfere with traditional forms of worship. The cleavage between traditionalists and catechists among the Ixil is secondary in importance only to that between ladinos and Indians, and if anything, it generates more open hostility. Although the catechists are only a small minority, they enjoy the support of influential ladinos with whom they tend to mix in politics, and being young and more educated, they feel that time is on their side.

Degree of urbanization (defined as residence in the town as distinguished from the rural *aldeas* of the municipio) differentiates ladinos and Indians, but not nearly as much as, for example, in neighboring parts of Mexico, such as highland Chiapas. As in other parts of Guatemala, there exists in Ixil country an established urban Indian culture, and urbanization, at least in its small-town form, does not entail rapid ladinoization. Conversely, a number of ladinos are dispersed in remote rural aldeas. Nevertheless, ladinos are more urbanized than Indians. In 1964, in Guatemala as a whole, Indians, who constituted 43.3 percent of the total population made up 22.0 percent of the urban population and 54.3 percent of the rural one. In the Ixil zone, 38.9 percent of the ladinos are urban, compared to only 25.4 percent of the Indians, and in the municipio of Nebaj the difference is even greater. Some 57.7 percent of Nebaj ladinos live in the town, compared to 19.4 percent of the Ixil. In recent years, the rural population of the Ixil zone increased *faster* than the urban one for both ladinos and Indians. Thus in 1950, 43.4 percent of the ladinos and 28.0 percent of the Indians were urban. The reverse was true for the country as a whole and for the department of El Quiché. The Quiché population was 9.4 percent urban in 1950 and 14.9 percent in 1964.

Within the Indian group, urban versus rural residence is not an important criterion of differentiation. The town of Nebaj offers certain facilities such as piped water and electricity which are not available in the rural aldeas. Hence town life tends to be somewhat more comfortable, and the standard of living somewhat higher. A greater proportion of the town houses have tile (as opposed to straw) roofs and adobe walls (as distinguished from wood and lattice covered by dried mud). Some Indian houses in town even have cement floors, and a few are large, multiroomed complexes with enclosed patios. The few well-to-do Indians are disproportionately concentrated in town, but some rich Indians also live in the countryside. For example, when a wealthy *principal* and landowner died a few years ago, several of his sons left town to live in the hamlets where they had inherited his land. The diet of townsmen offers perhaps slightly more variety because of easy access to the market, but the differences are minor. In style of clothing, there is no noticeable difference between urban and rural Ixil. The quality and length of schooling offered by the town is greater than in the outlying villages, and this is probably reflected in a somewhat higher urban literacy rate, but the vast majority of both urban and rural Ixil are illiterate.

Ixil townsmen do not look down on their country cousins. If anything, the reverse is true. Townsmen regard rural Ixil as more courteous and truthful than themselves, and country girls are considered to make more desirable and unspoiled wives. Urban and rural Ixil in each of the three municipios retain important kinship and *compadrazgo* ties with each other, and there is much weekly movement and visiting between the towns and their rural hinterland. Townsmen spend days with their rural relatives, and many aldea people come to the town market twice a week; farmers also come into town to attend to official business in the *juzgado,* such as paying taxes, registering a birth or death, or presenting a complaint against a neighbor to the alcalde.

Rural residence is no bar to holding political or religious office for the Ixil, though urban residence may be required during one's incumbency. Thus, the 1966 holder of the highest religious position in Nebaj (that of first mayordomo of the cofradía of Kuçuç Mariy, the patron saint of Nebaj) came from an outlying village, but he had to rent a house in town during his year in office. To the extent that political life centers in town and that religious processions and the cult of the cofradía saints take place in the town church and in the houses of the first mayordomos, Ixil principales have an advantage in living in town, though rural residence is certainly not disqualifying. Generally speaking, differences in life-style and culture between rural and urban Ixil are not nearly as pronounced as the differences in dress, dialect, and other culture traits between the three municipios of Nebaj, Cotzal, and Chajul.

Urbanism is not an important social cleavage among the Ixil, though it does differentiate between Ixil and ladinos.

Differential urbanization between ladinos and Indians is, of course, reflected in other structural characteristics. There are clear occupational differences between ethnic groups: proportionately more Indians than ladinos are farmers and agricultural day laborers. Conversely, more ladinos engage in commerce, white-collar jobs, artisanal production, and professional or semiprofessional work. With the exception of a few rural schoolteachers and a mestizo nurse from another town who is regarded as ethnically marginal, no local Indians engage in clerical or professional occupations. Indians and ladinos are both represented in certain skilled crafts, such as carpentry, bricklaying, and tailoring, but some trades, such as fireworks-making and flour-milling, are limited to ladinos. Proportionately, more ladinos than Indians are artisans. Of a sample of ninety men who married between 1963 and 1966, one-eighth of the ladinos were unskilled workers and one-half were craftsmen. Among Indians, 86 percent were unskilled, and 4 percent were artisans. Furthermore, virtually all Indians who are artisans supplement their income with part-time farming. The division of labor is not sufficiently advanced for more than a handful of people to devote themselves exclusively to a single specialized occupation, and most of those who do are ladinos. Many ladino artisans, however, engage in more than one trade, but unlike the Indians, they frequently do not cultivate any land.

The four largest shops in town are all ladino owned, and most of the smaller ones are Indian owned and operated, as are about 90 percent of the market stalls. Exactly two-thirds of the 72 Nebaj businesses registered with the municipality are owned by Indians, including 25 of the 26 butcher-shops. The smaller size of Indian businesses is compensated by the heavy preponderance of Indian merchants on market days, so that Indians probably control something close to an equal amount of trade in goods. The

Nebaj.

D. C. AND J. R. CLEMENT

Chajul.

Nebaj church and main street with ladino houses.

Chajul Market.

Nebaj market: ladino shopkeeper and Ixil customers.

D. C. AND J. R. CLEMENT

Typical two-room Ixil house in Nebaj.

D. C. AND J. R. CLEMENT

Planting with digging stick near Nebaj.

Cotzal market.

Ixil children in Nebaj.

Ixil mother and daughter from Chajul.

Climax of the August fiesta in Nebaj as the *cofradias* and their saints are about to enter church.

Cofradia procession in Nebaj with ladino onlookers in background.

D. C. AND J. R. CLEMENT

Cofradia procession in Nebaj. Catholic priest watches through window.

Nebaj fiesta: Ixil rocketeer lights skyrocket; behind him a drunken man has fallen unconscious.

Ixil municipal officials (*regidores*) in Nebaj holding their staffs of office.

Ladino clerk and Ixil citizen registering at the civil registry office.

D. C. AND J. R. CLEMENT

D. C. AND J. R. CLEMENT

Ixil voters and ladino electoral officials in Nebaj.

A minor dispute being settled in the council chamber of the Nebaj town hall. Official at table is ladino, others are Ixil.

D. C. AND J. R. CLEMENT

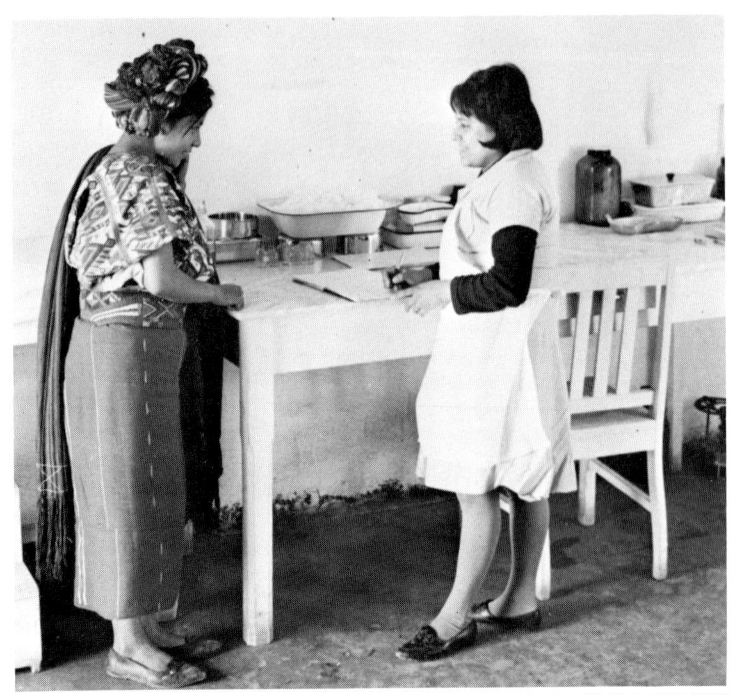

D. C. AND J. R. CLEMENT

Ixil woman and ladino nurse at government clinic.

Ladino marimba band playing in Nebaj.

ladinos do control, however, a lion's share of the Indian labor market and all of the local motor transportation. Among the six major and dozen-odd smaller labor contractors, there is only one Indian entrepreneur, who works with several of his sons.

The overwhelmingly agricultural basis of the Ixil region and of the whole department of Quiché is evident. According to the 1964 census, 82.2 percent of the 80,160 economically active people in the department were engaged in agriculture and related activities. An additional 8.2 percent were classified as craftsmen, and 5.5 percent as traders and merchants, but many of them are at least part-time farmers. This left only 4.1 percent of the economically active population for all other occupations (Anonymous, 1966: p. 116).

No accurate data about landownership exist, since many small peasants have no clear freehold title to land, and never registered their claim with the land registry office. (The land registry office lists 26,469 occupants of land estates for the department of Quiché. Of these, 19,177 were owners, mostly very small ones; 3,151 were tenants; 2,341 were *colonos;* 1,257 were unspecified "occupants," and 57 were administrators of large fincas. These figures do not include the vast majority of Indian peasants with no registered titles.) (Monteforte Toledo, 1959: p. 423.) Most of the land in the Ixil area is still in Indian hands, even though most of the larger holdings are owned by ladinos. There are few large estates in the region, the biggest one by far being the coffee plantation of San Francisco (approximately 5,000 hectares) in the municipio of Cotzal. In Nebaj, there are twenty-nine estates of over one *caballeria* (45 hectares), and of these, eight are owned by Indians. None exceeds 500 hectares, and all but three have less than 200 hectares. In addition, half a dozen Nebaj ladinos are absentee-landowners in other municipios. In summary, nearly three-fourths of the larger landowners are ladinos, and a majority of the Indians are either completely landless or have holdings that are too small for self-sufficiency. A few Indians, however, are relatively well-off, and have substantial land holdings. Virtually all Indians engage in some form of agricultural work, either as land-owners, tenants, or wage workers on fincas. Growing maize is a common denominator of Indian life.

The most clear-cut economic difference between Indians and ladinos concerns labor contracting. With the exception of one family mentioned earlier, all labor contractors are ladinos, and labor contracting has been the most important avenue of wealth accumulation and social mobility in the region for the last seventy-five years. Conversely, all agricultural laborers from the Ixil area who sign up to work on the coffee, sugar, or cotton plantations (for periods of four to eight weeks as a rule, at wages ranging from 70 cents to $1.05 a day) are Indians. Labor recruiting is one of the main factors making for the relatively unfavorable economic position of Indians vis à vis ladinos. Land scarcity, erosion, exhaustion, and unproductivity make the Ixil increasingly dependent on labor exports for survival. Once cash crops and wage labor were introduced, the subsistence economy entered a vicious circle of decline. A mayor of Nebaj aptly summarized the situation in 1957:

> . . . the major part of the indigenous people of this municipality must of necessity go to the coastal areas of the Republic in search of work in order to satisfy their most primary needs, because of the scarcity of articles of first necessity, and principally of maize. Their lands, for the time that they come to cultivate them do not satisfy their necessities; that is, in addition to being insufficient in quantity, their lands are not productive, and the increase in population has been rather steep. The result has been that many of the indigenous people neither have nor dispose of pieces of land for their cultivation, and, hence, the necessity in which they find themselves to emigrate

to the coasts of the country in search of more ample means of subsistence and often permanently.

Since that date, the situation has become even worse. Not only has the soil further deteriorated and the population increased, but able-bodied males have left the area in growing numbers, making for a local scarcity of labor for subsistence agriculture. Conversely, labor contractors have, as a result of their activities, accumulated capital with which to buy land from Indians. This land was diverted from subsistence to cash agriculture, and from intensive cultivation of maize to more extensive use for cattle ranches. These new cash-crop farms further stimulated the demand for agricultural wage labor, and its supply was further secured by the extension of credit to workers signing contracts, and by an increasing consumption of textiles, imported staple foods, alcohol, and manufactured products. As in most parts of the world where commercial agriculture was introduced in an economy hitherto based principally on subsistence farming, the latter gradually becomes *sub*-subsistence, and increasing numbers of peasants are drawn into an unorganized, mobile, easily exploited, low-paid, agricultural sub-proletariat.

Today, large numbers of Indians have to buy maize and beans for their own consumption, and consequently have to hire themselves out for at least a few months a year. Former subsistence peasants now have to spend much of their meager wages to buy relatively expensive maize produced in part by Indian labor on large ladino-owned fincas. Climatic and social conditions of work on the commercial plantations range from bad to abominable. The mortality and morbidity rates are high, and the Ixil regard plantation work as very undesirable. Yet, the majority of the Indian population derives few if any economic benefits from its labor exports, and the region grows increasingly dependent on the outside ladino world without much prospect of significant economic improvement within the existing system of production.

Nebaj is a clearly stratified society, and next to ethnicity and religion, class differences are probably the main lines of cleavage. Within both the ladino and the Ixil groups, there are substantial differences in prestige, wealth, and life-style. The ladinos are of too recent origin to have established a rigid class structure. Nevertheless, between the turn of the century and the partially abortive democratic revolution of 1944, two distinguishable social classes emerged among ladinos, the *sociales* (the "social ones") and the *obreros* ("workers"). The latter were mostly craftsmen, small shopkeepers, and petty white-collar employees, while the former were mostly schoolteachers, landowners, larger merchants, and successful labor contractors. From the 1920's until the mid-1940's, the sociales were politically as well as socially and economically dominant. Family heads among the sociales alternated as mayor of the town and controlled the town's affairs. During the ladino fiesta of September 15, obreros and sociales celebrated separately, each group having its own ball and marimba orchestra. Each group also had its football team, and during the fiesta, the obrero team played against the sociales.

An examination of old photographs reveals that the sociales were almost all European-looking, and were in fact mostly descendants of recent Spanish or Italian immigrants, while the obreros were predominantly Indian-looking. However, these phenotypical differences do not seem to have been socially significant. Now, at any rate, spontaneous mention of physical differences between ladinos is very seldom made. Of 32 subjects who listed differences between ladinos, 14 mentioned class or economic factors; 7, education; 25, cultural or life-style differences; 4, religion; 4, political beliefs; and only 1, physical appearance. (Figures add up to more than 32 because some persons listed more than one difference.)

Since the revolution of 1944, institutionalized class barriers between ladinos have largely disappeared, and today there are no two clearly distinguishable groups. The old upper class has lost much of its political power to working-class ladinos, from among whom the last mayors have been recruited. Economically, the old upper class has not been affected by the revolution, and there was no land expropriation in Nebaj. One of the factors weakening the upper class had been the steady attrition in its ranks brought about by their very success. Many of the upwardly mobile, well-to-do ladinos who "made good" in Nebaj left the town in search of better educational opportunities for their children, better political jobs, or a greater scope for their commercial activities. Today, only four families could be described as "upper class." They include the children of Guatemalan, Italian, and Spanish labor contractors who became large landowners and merchants. All have siblings or other close relatives holding important positions in the capital, such as cabinet minister, manager of a bank, or owner of a coffee export firm.

Wide differences in prestige and life-style persist among ladinos, however ill-defined class lines have become. The poorest ladinos live in Indian-type two-room houses made of whitewashed adobe walls and tiled roofs. They have no servants, own little furniture and household belongings, and live at much the same subsistence level as the majority of Indians, though in a different style. Their basis of subsistence is usually some combination of small-scale farming or market gardening, shopkeeping, and artisanal work.

A larger group of middle-class ladinos live in more spacious three- to five-room houses, which are better furnished and distinctly non-Indian in style—with windows, an inner courtyard, and the longest wall facing the street. Middle-class ladinos frequently own some land, horses, and other livestock, and employ an Indian servant. (Twenty-two of the forty ladinos in the questionnaire sample did have Indian servants.) While the typical Indian or ladino lower-class house measures about fifteen by five meters, middle-class ladinos live in houses of twenty to thirty by six to seven meters.

Upper-class ladino families occupy spacious one-story houses frequently taking up an entire town block of 50 by 50 meters with two enclosed patios. The absence of heating, indoor toilets, or running water makes even upper-class houses far from luxurious by North American standards, but the upper class eats and lives much better than the rest of the people. A few own private automobiles, the epitome of luxury in Nebaj, and all employ several servants and enjoy considerable leisure and freedom from manual labor. They own horses, cattle, land, well-stocked shops, and considerable furniture and household appliances.

Among the Ixil, social stratification has a long history. In pre-Conquest days there may have been a four-estate or four-caste system, which was reported to Lincoln as having survived until the nineteenth century (Lincoln, 1945). Today, this fairly rigid system has given way to an open class system. Differences in prestige, power, and wealth within the Indian group are as great as among ladinos, but there is considerable room for social mobility within the Indian group. In fact, several prominent Nebaj Ixil rose from the position of day laborer or small peasant to high political and religious office. The status of *principal* is achieved (and retained for life) after one has served as alcalde, fiscal, síndico, regidor, or as first mayordomo of a cofradía. Previously, that status was quasi-hereditary, but now political or religious office is within the reach of anyone who has accumulated the necessary wealth for the representation and entertainment costs which public office entails.

There is, therefore, a high correlation between economic and politico-religious status among Indians, so that most people of above-average wealth are present or past holders of municipal or cofradía offices. The present holder of the position of *b'o·q'ol tenam,* a kind of *primus inter pares* among the principales, is also the wealthiest Ixil in Nebaj. Indeed, many well-to-do persons have served several times, the terms being generally two years for political positions, and one year for religious ones. This relationship between wealth and political office is confirmed by our Ixil sample. The sixty-two respondents who have held municipal office tend to be more educated, to have more land, and to hire more Indians to work on their land than those who have not held political positions. These correlations do not hold for the seventy-two former incumbents of positions in the cofradías, even though people who have held office in one hierarchy also tend to have done so in the other. It must be remembered, however, that, in the sample itself, high-status persons are heavily overrepresented, and that the relationship between wealth and office-holding would probably be higher if the sample were more representative.[8]

In terms of standards of living, there is some overlap between Indians and ladinos, though this overlap area contains a much larger number of the latter. One Indian family, that of the one Ixil labor recruiter, lives in a large house fully comparable to those of upper-class ladinos. The same man owns one of the three television sets in town. One of his sons and perhaps a half-dozen other Indian families live at a material level comparable to that of middle-class or even upper-class ladinos; that is, they oc-

[8] This contrasts with parts of Guatemala and Mexico where a tradition of Indian political control is lacking and where status has been focused on the religious offices. Even where this has happened, however, as in Zinacantan, Chiapas, some anthropologists have overemphasized the cofradía or *cargo* system as a prestige-conferring mechanism, to the extent of making it a necessary and sufficient condition for ethnic identity.

cupy ladino-style houses with three or more rooms and more than the usual amount of furniture, some of which is upholstered. These upper-class Indians are geographically concentrated in the canton of Wi¢'al.

The vast majority of Ixil, however, are poorer than all but a minority of perhaps 20 percent of the ladinos. The "typical" Indian family lives in a two-room house composed of a kitchen and a living-and-sleeping room which also contains the family shrine. The typical Indian house has two doors leading to a covered porch and a fenced-in front yard with a granary. The walls are made of whitewashed adobe and the roof of round tiles, or grass for the poorer houses. Many houses have a patch of corn in the backyard and most people keep some poultry and a pig or two. Basic household furniture includes one or two beds, a bench, a couple of small chairs, and a table serving as house altar.

There are, however, sizeable differences among Indians in their material possessions and in the state of repair of the house. Some people keep their houses in spotless condition and repair, live in an enlarged version of the traditional house, adding a third room, or adopt ladino architectural features. Furniture, clothing, and other belongings are also important indices of status, distinguishing the modestly well-off from the poor and the very poor. A number of families are completely landless, and are forced to reside in a lean-to room in somebody else's house, in a flimsy grass shack on somebody's land, or in servants quarters in ladino households. Also, a number of young men who are mostly too poor to live at home spend practically the whole year on plantations, returning to Nebaj only for fiestas. A number of highland plantations in the Ixil area have colonos—landless Indian tenant-workers born and raised on the plantation. The largest finca in the Ixil zone is that of San Francisco; it has a large village of over 2,000 colonos.

Lincoln reports that the canton of Salquilito in Nebaj, which is located one kilometer from the town plaza in the center, was traditionally inhabited by the worker caste. Only two ladino families live there today. Though Salquilito contains no middle- or upper-class houses, it is not markedly poorer than other sections of Nebaj. Except for the fact that higher land values near the center debar poorer Indians from living there, there is no clear ecological pattern to social class among either Indians or ladinos.

Beyond quantitative differences in standard of living between ladinos and Indians, there are, of course, important qualitative differences in life-style, a description of which would take us beyond the scope of this book. Upward class mobility among Indians is almost invariably accompanied by the adoption of some aspects of ladino material culture, notably in men's clothing, in diet, and in furniture, but this does not represent a uniform trend toward ladinoization. In the religious field, for example, the most well-to-do Indian is also the leader of the conservative anti-catechist faction.

Ethnicity, religion, social class, and place of residence make for the main lines of cleavage and stratification in Ixil country. Of these, ethnic membership is the most basic, especially in Nebaj where the ladino population is largest. With the recent proselytism of the Acción Católica, there has been a reactivation of conflict and cleavage between orthodox and "old" Catholics. On the other hand, social class distinctions among both Indians and ladinos have declined in rigidity and importance during the last twenty-five years. Urban versus rural residence is not of great significance, perhaps because none of the Ixil towns fully qualify as an urban center. Nebaj, Chajul, and Cotzal are more like large peasant villages with the additional functions of marketplaces, low-level civil administration, and some artisanal production; more than anything, it is their ceremonial functions, in both orthodox Catholicism and Ixil religion, which give to the three towns whatever urban character they have. Among the Ixil, although the subcultural differences between the three municipios constitute important lines of cleavage, the Ixil dialects are all mutually (though not always easily) understandable.

IV. THE INSTITUTIONAL CONTEXT OF ETHNIC RELATIONS: POLITICS, ECONOMICS AND RELIGION

THERE ARE three main institutional areas in which Indians and ladinos interact in such a way as to constitute a single plural sub-society rather than two distinct and autonomous groups as do, for example, the Ixil vis à vis their Quiché or Kanjobal neighbors. The *political* area centers around the control of the municipio governments in each of the three towns and their outlying villages and hamlets; the *economic* sphere concerns the production, exchange, and distribution of goods and services; and the area of *religion* touches the interplay between traditional Ixil religion and orthodox Catholicism. In spite of significant conflict between traditionalists and orthodox Ixil, both groups use the church buildings and the services of the Catholic priests.

These are the three main institutional foci of integration between the two groups. In other areas, such as kinship (aside from ritual kinship), marriage (as distinguished from sexual relations and concubinage), mortuary practices, family religious ceremonies, and many other aspects of the daily lives of the Ixil and ladino, there is little interethnic contact.

Let us specify further the nature of the interaction in the political, economic, and religious areas. In the first two areas, the interaction takes place within the context of an institutional structure which is *common* to the two groups, in spite of internal role differentiation along ethnic lines *within* this unitary institutional structure. In the religious domain, the situation is different. Here we have two distinct sets of institutions which intermesh at some points and clash at others.

Two further considerations must be introduced. First, these three institutional areas are importantly related to each other in ways which have a direct bearing on interethnic relations. Second, all or nearly all interrelations between Indians and ladinos take place within the framework of standardized and ethnically ascribed roles and statuses. This mold of intergroup relations includes such things as a definite etiquette of group behavior, stereotyped attitudes about the out-group, and differential behavior based on ethnicity. These aspects of interaction constitute what is usually referred to as "ethnic relations" in the narrower sense, and will be discussed in Chapter V.

The political ascendancy of the ladinos from the turn of the century until recent years was a result in part of their numerical growth and of their economic position as labor recruiters, shopkeepers, and landowners. But cultural factors were also important. The ladinos spoke the official language of Guatemala as their mother tongue and had until quite recently a virtual monopoly of literacy. These cultural assets were of limited use so long as the Ixil zone was an isolated, autonomous, self-contained backwater. In fact, up until the last century, if an Ixil knew a second language it was more likely to be Quiché, which, before the Conquest, was the language of the most politically powerful group in Guatemala and subsequently remained the language of commerce in the more remote areas. But as isolation broke down, Spanish became the lingua franca. As the power of the central government percolated down to the grassroots, and as the area became economically integrated with the rest of the country, the ladinos increased their power by becoming an administrative group mediating with the outside world. The resentment of conservative ladinos at the spread of literacy among Indians is based at least partly on the realization that the power of knowledge has allowed a small minority to wield disproportionate influence.

In the town of Nebaj, Indians actively participate in the government primarily in matters relating to their fellow Indians. In administrative and secretarial work they are excluded, not by conscious design or discrimination, but simply because the great majority of Indians do not hold the necessary educational qualifications, and the few who do are likely to emigrate to places where they perceive the opportunities to be better, such as the capital. In Chajul and Cotzal the affairs of government are more directly under the control of the Ixil, though even in those towns the administrative and paper work is done by ladinos.

In the town hall, Indians behave toward both ladino and Indian officials in a respectful and submissive way which contrasts markedly with the behavior of the ladinos. The latter consider themselves to be more on an equal basis with the town officials and move about with more self-confidence. Indeed, in Nebaj they regard the municipio as theirs, and in fact, a large proportion of ladinos have served as alcaldes (mayor), regidores (town councillors), or municipal employees; if they themselves have not served, they have a close relative who has held such a position. Among the Ixil of Nebaj there is also a substantial number of people who have participated in government. Although there has not been an Ixil alcalde for half a century, perhaps one-tenth of the older Indian men have held the offices of regidor and síndico, and the great majority of Indian men living in Nebaj have participated in the more subordinate offices of *mayor* or *alguacil* and *policía*. However, excluding the four ranked mayores, these latter offices involve little else than running errands, patrolling the streets at night, and sweeping the marketplace. These menial posts are an Indian monopoly. They are not remunerated and are thus a form of labor exploitation of younger Indian men.

To most ladinos the ways of the bureaucracy are fairly familiar, though perhaps mildly irritating, and the municipio is not an impersonal and mysterious machine, but rather a small clique of friends, acquaintances, and relatives. To the Indians, on the other hand, the administrative details are less comprehensible for lack of education and experience. In Chajul and Cotzal, Indians are no more educated, but because the ladinos are less numerous and closer to the Indians in educational experience the discrepancy is much less. A ladino in an important post in one of these latter two towns impressed one of us as being barely literate. There is less administrative detail to handle in these latter towns primarily because of their smaller population and lesser importance as commercial centers.

Indians know that they have to go to the town hall on certain occasions: to obtain a permit, pay taxes, register land transfers, obtain citizenship papers, report births and deaths in the family, or be witnesses or plaintiffs in a legal case. When an Ixil goes to the administrative employees of the *juzgado* in Nebaj, he is typically treated in a way which is not openly discourteous, but which differs markedly from the paternalistic manner he often receives from other ladinos. Here municipio employees address him with studied boredom and impersonality, firing rapid questions at him, and showing either impatience or amusement if the Indian is too flustered to answer. For example, a man was asked how many children he and his wife had had. He answered "nine." Asked how many were alive, he replied "four." When he then said that three had died, the employees in the civil registry found his mistake very entertaining. (These same employees, one might add, are ignorant of the mathematical sophistication required by some of the Ixil calendar specialists in the use of the pre-Hispanic calendar with its permutations of thirteen, eighteen, and twenty elements. Nor do they understand the vigesimal system of counting which the Ixil language employs.)

Lower-class ladinos are also usually treated with the same impersonality at the town hall but are less likely to be made the butt of ridicule, and are not addressed in the familiar form of *tu* or *vos*.

Indians and ladinos are made to pay fees or taxes for practically everything. Many of these taxes are set by law and appear nominal to an outsider, but are in fact very substantial when measured by the standard of the local daily wage of 40 to 50 cents a day. The slightest petition or request has to be presented on a special "Spanish paper" costing at least 10 cents a sheet. The secretary is legally allowed to charge 40 cents per typewritten page of official document, and to keep the fee for himself. The unsalaried Indian síndico assisting him receives a $2.00 fee for arranging certain types of land documentation. There are innumerable direct taxes such as the $1.00 to $2.00 fee for a *boleto de ornato* (employment identification) which all men over eighteen years must pay. The effect of these charges is felt mostly by the poorest classes, that is, by the vast majority of Indians. In addition to the legal charges, some municipal employees have used their position to extort illegal fees. Thus, in 1960, a delegation of Indians demanded (and obtained) the resignation of a secretary who had extorted money for his services beyond the legally permissible fees.

Government positions in the three towns have a tradition going back to the sixteenth and seventeenth centuries when the Spanish system was imposed. According to a royal cédula of Philip III in 1618, all Indian municipios should have one *alcalde pedáneo* (petty mayor) if the town had less than forty houses, and two alcaldes and two regidores if the town had more than eighty houses. Above this, the upper limit was two alcaldes and four regidores.

In this early period, the tradition of having two alcaldes was unrelated to equal ethnic representation, since the same system existed in Spain. Some Guatemalan municipios preserve this dualistic structure and have both a ladino and an Indian alcalde, but this is not true of any of the Ixil municipios.

The alcalde of Nebaj, who receives a salary of $75 a month, is the only official directly elected at the municipio level. (His councilmen or regidores are decided upon after the elections and depend partly upon the showing of the various parties at the polls.) The powers of the alcalde are rigidly circumscribed, given the highly centralized nature of the Guatemalan government, but locally, the alcalde is by far the most powerful official. In addition to his prerogatives as mayor, he also serves as *juez de paz,* lowest-level magistrate. He has jurisdiction over minor criminal and civil cases, and is empowered to impose fines and short jail sentences. Since the alcalde is also ex officio chairman of the town council, he combines executive, judiciary, and legislative functions.

In addition to the alcalde post is that of síndico, concerned with litigation and documentation in matters of land ownership, seven regidores or councilmen who assist the alcalde in a wide variety of matters, four ranked mayores, and thirty unranked policías or alguaciles. The administrative personnel consists of some fifteen ladinos including a secretary, a treasurer, a scribe, a *registrador civil,* and various assistants. There is also a *comisionado militar* with assistants in some of the outlying villages, and two or three salaried, uniformed policemen commanded by a second lieutenant of the national police. In Nebaj, the alcalde, and the first, third, and fifth regidores are ladinos; the síndico and the second, fourth, sixth, and seventh councilmen are Ixil. All mayores, alguaciles, and policías are Indians.

The Ixil members of the Nebaj government have traditionally been selected by a group of older Ixil known as *principales,* who have held high government or religious office in the past. Principales are all those traditionally oriented Ixil who have passed the religious office of father mayordomo (*b'a·l mertoma*) or the office of alcalde (in earlier days when this post was filled by Ixil), síndico, regidor, *čusul,* and *piškal.* The leader of the principales is called *b'o·q'ol tenam,* and is a man of great prestige and considerable behind-the-scenes power.

The principales have a yearly meeting in October at which the four regidores, the síndico, the four *šaqal* or *šena·l* and *mayores,* the maestro de coro (*čusul*) and fiscal (*piškal*) are chosen. Thus religious as well as political offices are chosen at this meeting.

While the Indians fill the second, fourth, sixth, and seventh regidor positions, they refer to these positions as the first, second, third, and fourth. The first or *b'aṣa rišitol* is considered by both ladinos and Indians (in the absence of an Indian alcalde) as the official Indian leader. The Indians sometimes refer to him as the Indian alcalde because he must fill the position the alcalde used to fill in various traditional religious ceremonies in which the ladino alcalde is not culturally qualified to participate. However, the present ladino alcalde sometimes puts in an appearance at these ceremonies as a courtesy.

Principal meetings are also held in the sixteen outlying aldeas, where the leaders of the villages are chosen and later approved by the Nebaj town council. The aldea officials are alcalde auxiliar, regidor, and differing numbers of mayores.

With the new procedure of free elections, the Ixil principales in Nebaj chose a slate of officials for one of the political parties. Though their candidate for alcalde did not win, the other Indian positions, with one exception, were filled by people chosen at the meeting of principales. The exception was an Indian chosen by the winning party who, because of his conversion to modern orthodox Catholicism, does not recognize the principales as the true leaders of the Indian community.

The disproportionate influence of ladinos in Nebaj hinges largely on the continued control of the position of alcalde. In the 1966 elections, an Indian candidate (the son of the *b'o·q'ol tenam,* who is also the wealthiest Ixil in town, and himself a literate, ladinoized, and well-to-do man) nearly won the post of alcalde. These elections resulted at the national level in a transfer of government from a right-wing military junta, represented by the Partido Institucional Democrático (PID), to the mildly reformist, center-left Partido Revolucionario (PR) . Contrary to almost everybody's cynical expectations, the elections were honest and the opposition PR won, with behind-the-scenes diplomatic support from the United States. At the national level, there was no clear pattern of party affiliation following ethnicity, and none of the three main contesting groups emphasized the ethnic issue. Many Indian-controlled municipios voted for the conservative PID, following the trusted Guatemalan recipe that voting for the party in power was the better part of political wisdom.

It is interesting to examine the different effects the 1966 elections had on the social groupings and divisions in the three towns of Nebaj, Chajul, and Cotzal. In Nebaj, the elections activated the ethnic cleavages and brought the ladinos perilously close to a loss of their political power. Initially, a number of ladinos, tired of the military government, sympathized with the Partido Revolucionario. However, the PR worked through the existing *principal* structure, and the *b'o·q'ol tenam* assumed leadership of the PR in Nebaj, with the assistance of a former ladino alcalde of Nebaj who is a Protestant. The slate of officials decided on at the annual meeting of the principales in October thus ran on a PR ticket. The ladinos then decided to unite behind the PID; over 90 percent of the ladinos voted for the PID list, as did a number of Ixil *catequistas*. Party affiliation and national ideology were of little concern to either Indians or ladinos, except perhaps for the fact that PR party officials told the Ixil that they supported them in their wish to perform traditional ritual and ceremony. Thus, in Nebaj, the parties grafted themselves onto, and helped to crystallize preexisting cleavages.

To the ladino upper and middle class, an Indian-PR dominated town council evoked the spectre of land reform, agitation for higher agricultural wages, and similar "demagoguery" reminiscent of the period of the two progressive ladino alcaldes around 1950. In addition to economic considerations, ladinos of all classes saw in Indian control the threat of general stagnation for the town. Almost all ladinos define towns as being more or less progressive in terms of how predominantly ladino these towns are. By these standards, Nebaj is regarded as the most advanced of the Ixil towns, and Chajul the most backward. Ladinos were heard to say: "Would it not be a shame if such a nice town as Nebaj had an Indian mayor?" And in Chajul they speak of the all-Ixil government as being "dead," and not doing anything for the town's progress.[1]

For many Indians the main electoral issue was not economic reform or the wrenching of political control away from the ladinos, although these factors may also have played a role. More salient was the religious conflict between catechists and traditionalists. For the past several

[1] There is an important way in which material progress may be related to the ethnic group of the alcalde. Given scarce national resources and a highly centralized governmental structure, those municipios which are insistent and articulate in their demands for funds probably get a disproportionate share of subsidies. A ladino mayor will, on the average, have a better knowledge of Spanish, a greater understanding of the central government, and more influential relatives and friends in the capital. Hence, he is more likely to be successful in his requests for funds. During the summer of 1966, for example, the alcalde of Nebaj and one of the ladino regidores made several trips to the capital to request assistance, and during sessions of the municipal council, great concern was expressed toward securing central government support for local development.

years, the Ixil regidores on the town council had been catechists intent on stamping out traditional religion. As we shall see later, there is still an important interplay between political and religious institutions in Ixil culture, so that the composition of the municipality has a direct bearing on religious practices. Thus, an outwardly incongruous situation resulted in which a politically progressive party espoused the cause of religious revivalism and traditionalism.

Given the enormous numerical disproportion between the two ethnic groups, and barring electoral fraud, a ladino-PID victory was contingent on a very low voting turnout by Indians, and on the PID's ability to split the Indian vote. Both of these conditions prevailed and gave the PID a narrow victory margin of 606 votes to 516 for the PR. Most of the catechists and most of the Indian clients of prominent ladinos were brought into the PID organization and pressured into voting for the PID, and the overwhelming majority of the Indians (nearly 90 percent of the eligible population) did not vote at all. A sprinkling of progressive ladinos cast their ballot with the PR, but the election was overwhelmingly along ethnic and religious lines.

The high rate of abstentions is not unusual in Indian areas. Apathy, distance from polling places (a walk of several hours in each direction for many rural Indians), fear to commit oneself to a party which may lose, and the voluntary nature of voting for illiterates all reduce the Indian vote. (Literate electors *must* vote under penalty of a fine, though fines for not voting are seldom levied.) But additional chicanery and intimidation by the PID were also resorted to. Indians were told that voting against the then-ruling PID would result in sanctions; and the candidacy of the Indian to the mayorship was rumored to be illegal because of discrepancy in the spelling of his name in two different legal documents. (Behind-the-scenes moves can be even more complex in Chajul where, unlike Nebaj and Cotzal, the candidates pay their voters in a kind of institutionalized bribery.)

By electoral law, the representation of the two parties on the municipal council was made proportional to the votes cast, with the mayoralty going to the majority party. The PID thus holds the positions of alcalde and of four of the seven regidores. The PR has the post of síndico and three regidores. With the exception of the lowest-ranking PID regidor who is Indian, all PID members are ladinos and all PR members are Indians. To all intents and purposes, the two parties reflect the underlying ethnic cleavage complicated by the religious split.

The situation in Chajul and Cotzal is quite different. In Chajul the catechists are so numerous and well organized that they have had control of local government, except for administrative personnel, during the last three elective periods. Only on one occasion, the governor of the department of Quiché deposed the Ixil alcalde and replaced him with an appointed ladino alcalde. During the last elections the PR was the party of the ladinos, but their number was so small that they made a poor showing in the elections. In Cotzal, the PR also made a poor showing. The municipio has an all-Ixil, PID-dominated administration.

There is another dimension to the political expression of ethnic dualism in Nebaj. Ostensibly, the division is based on urban versus rural residence. On Sunday mornings, the Nebaj alcalde and his Indian regidores and síndico meet with the thirty-two auxiliary Indian alcaldes and regidores from the sixteen rural aldeas. (One of these is inhabited mostly by Quiché speakers. The other fifteen are Ixil.) This meeting is defined as one which concerns only Indians (even though there are a few hundred scattered rural ladinos), and is the one in which the highest-ranking Indian, the second regidor, takes the most prominent role. The auxiliary rural alcaldes and regidores are *de jure* appointed by the whole town council, but, *de facto,* the alcalde appoints them on the recommendation of the Indian regidores and principales. Thus, this group of auxiliary officials is chosen (on the recommendation of the aldea principales) and closely controlled by the second regidor, who dominates these Sunday meetings.

The proceedings of these meetings take place almost entirely in Ixil, which the alcalde imperfectly understands. The second regidor hears complaints or disputes, transmits orders on behalf of the municipio, and effectively runs the meeting in consultation with the síndico, the other Indian regidores, and the alcalde. The latter's ignorance of the Ixil language and customs make him almost completely reliant on the second regidor, to whom he refers as "my ears and my eyes." The second regidor is ostensibly in the position of interpreter of Ixil language and culture to the alcalde, but through his skillful screening and reinterpretation of information, he can manipulate to a considerable extent the outcome of decisions concerning such matters as road repairing, disputes, fiesta committees, and other affairs. In fact, he frequently suggests the solutions himself with the consensual approval of his Indian colleagues. The rural part of the municipio (which accounts for 77.6 percent of the population) is thus defined as an Indian sphere of interest, and here too the use of the esoteric potential of a cultural barrier for political purposes is manifest, this time to the benefit of the Indians.

The regular sessions of the municipality are generally held on Saturday, and are limited to the alcalde, the síndico, the seven regidores, and the secretary who takes the minutes. These meetings are mostly concerned with urban affairs in the town of Nebaj, and are formally defined as including both Indians and ladinos. In practice, however, these meetings are clearly dominated by the ladinos. The second regidor and his Indian colleagues play a distinctly subdued role, confining their participation to nodding approval of decisions, signing the minutes of the previous meeting, and answering questions from the alcalde concerning Indian customs or affairs. All of the debates take place in voluble rhetorical Spanish, which some of the Ixil can follow only imperfectly. The ladino regidores, the alcalde, and even the secretary, who is not a member of the council and whose official role is confined to taking and reading the minutes, nearly monopolize the conversation.

The alcalde and the other ladinos show great concern for and sensitivity to Indian opinion and are all aware of the precariousness of their political position. Verbally, the alcalde emphasizes the unity of "the people," and the irrelevance of ethnic distinctions, but ethnicity keeps intruding in the debates, as for example in discussions over the participation of the municipality in the Ixil fiesta of August 12–15, and the ladino fiesta of September 15. This year, the town allocated $50 to the former and $400 to the latter, the difference being justified on the ground that the latter was a national holiday (Independence Day) for the whole people, while the former was a religious fiesta for the Indians.[2] Indians are not deliberately excluded from the debates, but the ladinos implicitly assume that most of the technical matters (such as sanitation, education, road construction, and public utilities) around which most of the deliberations revolve exceed the competence of the Ixil councillors. The ladinos also assume that they retain a monopoly of *savoir faire* and wisdom in dealing with the higher echelons of government.

There are, of course, a number of politically influential ladinos and Ixil who do not currently belong to the council, though for the most part, they have held office at

[2] It should be noted, however, that the present alcalde has emphasized the rural areas more than his predecessors and in the face of opposition on the part of some ladinos in Nebaj who would rather see him improve the streets in town. The present alcalde, with the cooperation of the local villages, has built a road for vehicular traffic to ʔAk'ul as well as bridges and rural schools in the outlying areas.

one time. Since 1960, none of the members of the leading three or four ladino families have become alcaldes. This reflects in part their loss of influence since the 1944 revolution, in part their lack of incentive to assume the mayoralty. The salary of $75 a month is not attractive for an upper-class ladino; the appeal of power is mitigated by the prospect of incurring sanctions after the next change of government; the responsibilities of office are very time-consuming; and there is no better position in which to make enemies. However, several of the former alcaldes continue to exercise considerable influence. Two previous mayors who, some seventeen years ago, disregarded the wishes of what they called "the retrograde oligarchy" became the target of successful campaigns to unseat them before the completion of their terms. Today, the small upper class no longer constitutes an oligarchy; both the ladino working class and the Ixil are increasingly asserting their political independence.

The second institutional area of ladino-Indian interaction is the economic one. Some fifty or sixty years ago, the Ixil economy was based almost completely on self-sufficient subsistence production. There was, to be sure, some importation of manufactured goods and some sale of surplus food, textiles, pottery, and similar products on local markets. But the economy of the Ixil area was only marginally monetized; wage labor was just being introduced on a sizeable scale; local markets were much less developed than today; and reliance on goods and services produced elsewhere was much more limited. There was a substantial amount of artisanal specialization, and money and cacao beans were used as generalized exchange media, so the economy was more of the "peasant" than of the "primitive" type, but there was certainly no market economy in any but the most rudimentary sense.

Today, the area is still underdeveloped by modern industrial standards. In fact, it is still entirely nonindustrial if one excludes the small and rather antiquated cane and coffee processing plants in San Francisco. But now the economy is extensively monetized; wage labor has become at least as important as subsistence farming if not more so; the service or tertiary sector (commerce, motor transport) has greatly expanded; so have market places as centers for the sale of imported goods, including basic foodstuffs. Nor is the town market simply a place where local peasants sell their surplus to local townsmen. The town is now a place where peasants increasingly come to sell and export their labor and to buy their staple foods. While previously the town was more economically dependent on the countryside than vice versa, now the relationship has been reversed. At least, the town depends on its rural population more as consumers than as producers, and the peasants subsidize their consumption by exporting their labor.

To the extent that ladinos and Indians have developed differential relationships to the means of production, distribution, and consumption of goods and services, they are more narrowly dependent on each other than ever before. Probably the major nexus of interdependence is established through the region's major export, namely labor. Approximately 2,000 agricultural laborers, overwhelmingly younger men, leave and as many return to the Ixil area each month. They almost all do so through the Nebaj labor market, but the populations of Chajul and Cotzal are also tapped, though not as heavily as that of Nebaj. The latter municipio probably accounts for two-thirds of the region's labor supply. Putting the Ixil population at 45,000 and the working-age male population at no more than 10,000, this means that approximately one-fifth of the adult men leave each month. Since many people contract themselves for six, eight, or more weeks, and since some stay away permanently or return only for vacations during the fiestas. as much as 30 to 40 percent of the able-bodied men may be absent from the area at any given time. The number varies from year to year with economic conditions and world coffee prices, and from month to month with the harvest seasons.

The relationship between worker and labor recruiter takes place almost entirely across ethnic lines, since all workers are Indians, and the majority of recruiters are ladinos employed on a salary or commission basis by one or more ladino plantation owner. Each recruiter develops an Indian clientele for which he has to compete with other recruiters, using mostly advances on wages (of $6 to $8) as incentives for signing a labor contract. Labor contractors are thus the main source of short-term credit.

In terms of local purchasing power, most of the money which circulates in the Ixil zone comes from wages earned elsewhere. Migrant Ixil collectively earn at least $50,000 a month, and while some of it is spent in the region where they work, most of it probably enters the local market. In a town like Nebaj, where only fifteen to twenty families earn over $50 a month in cash, this is a very considerable sum, and one which together with the proceeds from the local coffee crop supports most of the commerce in town.

Another asymmetrical economic relationship across the ethnic line consists in local employer-employee ties. Almost every upper- and middle-class ladino hires Indians as domestic servants, as shop assistants, or as day laborers (*mozos*). Often these servants become lifelong dependents; occasionally the status of mozo with the same *patrón* is inherited from one generation to the next. The reverse situation of an Indian hiring a ladino other than casually (as in the case of a craftsman called to perform a specific task) is extremely rare.

Merchant-customer relations often cut across the ethnic line, but they do so both ways. Ladinos, especially women, go shopping in the market where practically all the merchants are Indians, and patronize other Indian-owned stores as well. Conversely, Indians constitute the bulk of the clientele in all ladino shops. At the market place, there is extensive bargaining on the part of both ladinos and Indians, and there is little evidence of ethnic discrimination. In both ladino and Indian shops, however, ladinos expect and usually receive preferential treatment in the form of more prompt attention and service, greater courtesy, and choice goods. This is especially true in butcher shops where the simple system of two official prices (for meat with or without bones) allows for a wide range of meat quality for the same price. Ladinos often demand the choicest pieces or complain if they do not get them.

In general, the permanent stores have a fixed-price policy. Some ladino shopkeepers show impatience or annoyance at attempts by Ixil to bargain, and adopt a take-it-or-leave-it attitude. Indian customers show a distinct preference for the shops in which they get more courteous treatment. All three of the maize mills (operated by small gasoline motors) are owned by ladinos and are used almost exclusively by Indian women, for whose patronage they compete.

Moneylending also establishes economic ties between ladinos and Indians. Although a few Indians do lend some money to other Indians, virtually all Nebaj moneylenders are ladinos, while most borrowers are Indians. The money lent by labor contractors is an interest-free advance on wages used as an incentive for recruitment. This money is disbursed, not by the recruiter, but by the employing plantation. Other forms of borrowing are done at very high interest rates, usually 5 or 10 percent a *month,* with land, houses, or livestock used as collateral. In 1935, in order to put an end to debt peonage, the central government abolished all outstanding debts and limited liability for further debts to $2.50 per person. This law is still in effect, but has not put an end to moneylending, although it has certainly curbed the use of moneylending as an indirect method of land acquisition. Moneylenders use Indian *caporales* to help them locate debtors and recover their loans, and occasionally resort to threats. Although debts are not legally recoverable beyond $2.50, to default is to jeopardize one's needed credit and even one's chance of employment as finca worker.

Much of the day-to-day interaction between ladinos and Indians involves a predominantly economic transaction, and both groups are aware of their mutual dependence in this field. The more monetized, based on wage labor, and integrated into the national economy the Ixil area becomes, the more this ethnic interdependence will grow.

The third main area of ethnic interaction is religious. Points of contact include common ladino-Indian worship by Protestants and by orthodox Catholics, the involvement of the Catholic priests in the cofradía cult and in Indian rites of passage, the participation of ladinos and Indians in certain processions and neighborhood rites, and the ties of ritual kinship or *compadrazgo* between Indians and ladinos.

A small but significant number of Indians worship in common with ladinos in the two Protestant churches and as orthodox Catholics. Protestant ministers and missionaries and the Catholic clergy stress the equality of men and the irrelevance of race and ethnicity in the eyes of the Creator. The services are integrated but held in Spanish (and Latin for the Catholic ones), and the cultural dominance of ladinos in orthodox Christianity is evident.

Orthodox Catholicism is relevant not only to "reconverted" catechists, but also to Ixil traditionalists, in that the Catholic clergy plays a ritual role which traditional Ixil regard as essential to the performance of their religion. The Catholic priest has to baptize all infants, and much of that is done during the August fiesta when the priest performs mass baptism in an assembly-line system. (He charges one dollar per infant for his services.) Ladino and Indian children are baptized at the same time without any distinction. Catholic baptism is regarded by Indians as an essential religious rite of passage, and hence may be said to have become incorporated into traditional Ixil religion. This is true, however, of none of the other Catholic sacraments. Generally, only catechists get married and buried in the Church, or go to communion or confession.

There is one other important ritual service which the Catholic priest performs. When a parish priest is in residence (which was not the case in the summer of 1966) he holds a daily mass for the cofradías and another one for the orthodox Catholics. On important occasions, like the August fiesta of Nebaj, this cofradía mass is usually a sung high mass, and is attended by the mayordomos and mayordomas, as well as by a sprinkling of ladinos and catechists. However, with the arrival of a new priest in Nebaj in 1967, the separation between cofradía activities and those of the Acción Católica has increased. During the Corpus Christi procession, for instance, the padre broke tradition by having his own procession led by flags of the Acción Católica and stopping at altars set up around the plaza instead of going with the cofradías to the street crosses as was done in the past. The degree to which a local priest compromises or clashes with Indian tradition obviously varies with his personality, religious outlook, and experience. Newcomers are frequently reported to go through a phase of militant purism which gradually gives way to a more tolerant and flexible approach to Indian practices.

Neighborhood crosses are also a focus of religious integration between Indians and ladinos. Common residence in a given section of town is more important here than ethnicity. On May third, ladinos as well as Indians leave flowers and contribute money offerings to the little cross shrines which are found in various parts of Nebaj and where rites are held.

Compadrazgo ties between Indians and ladinos are important because they extend their ramifications much beyond the religious area. Compadrazgo ties are not as extensive in Nebaj as in other parts of Latin America, for example, in neighboring Chiapas (van den Berghe and van den Berghe, 1966). Godparents are chosen for baptism, confirmation, and marriage, but as most Indians only get baptized in Church, interethnic compadrazgo is limited almost entirely to that occasion. As elsewhere in Latin America, the choice by the biological parents of godparents for their child establishes ties not only between godparent (*padrino, madrina*), and godchild (*ahijado*), but also between the two sets of parents who call each other *compadre* and *comadre*. These ties do not appear as strong as elsewhere in Mesoamerica, however, and we know of at least one case in which a comadre is suspected of witchcraft. The biological parents of the child, sometimes in consultation with other relatives, solicit a person who is almost always of equal or superior social status to become padrino or madrina of the child. To be asked to be a godparent is regarded as an honor which cannot be turned down without valid reasons. Godparenthood involves obligations, which can be onerous, such as gift-giving on the child's saint's day, acting *in loco parentis* in case the child is orphaned, and assisting both the godchild and his parents through money loans, help in negotiating official business, and seeking or providing employment.

Because of the political or economic advantages which a person can expect from compadres, powerful and well-to-do persons are in much demand as godparents, and the number of one's godchildren (well over a hundred in some cases) is a status symbol. Compadrazgo ties across the ethnic line are unidirectional (i.e., ladinos are frequently asked to become godparents of Indian children, but practically never request Indians to be godparents of their children). In a sample of forty middle and upper class ladinos, thirty-three said they had Indian godchildren, and two of those who did not, specified that they could not because they were Protestants. This indicates that almost all higher-status ladinos except a few who are Protestants, or who are known to turn down requests, have Indian godchildren. On the other hand, only two persons claimed to have Indian godparents, and internal evidence from their answers to other questions leads one to doubt their validity. The taboo against Indian godparents is about as strong as that against intermarriage.

In statistical terms, all or nearly all ladinos and most Indians select godparents from within their own ethnic group, yet a significant minority of Indians select ladinos. Of the 95 baptisms performed at Nebaj in November and December, 1965, 10 were of ladinos and 85 of Indians; all 10 of the ladino children had ladino godparents, and so did 9 of the 85 Indian children.

While compadres of the same ethnic group tend to treat each other as equals and have a symmetrical relationship, this is not true of interethnic compadrazgo. A ladino will typically treat his Indian compadre much as he would an ahijado. Interethnic compadrazgo thus becomes reinterpreted in terms of the patron-client relationship, and compadrazgo ties are one of the ways of reinforcing and extending the paternalistic clientage system between prominent ladinos and Indians. The interview data from our Ixil sample indicate that the 41 percent who claimed to have ladino godparents tend to be in an economically precarious position and to be low in traditional status. Indians with ladino godparents disproportionately report not having enough land for family subsistence, not to have ancestors of *principal* status, and not to be traditionalists. Interethnic compadrazgo thus seems to characterize those Ixil who are more dependent on ladinos and more insecure in their own group.

Religion also divides ladino and Indians, and creates a

cleavage within the Ixil between the traditionalists and the catechists. The Ixil have an ambivalent attitude toward the Catholic Church. They are ritually dependent on it; but to the extent that orthodox Catholics interfere with Ixil religion, they are resented. The Catholic priest is tolerated and even respected as long as he performs the rites requested of him without openly opposing the traditionalists. Nevertheless, he is regarded as an outsider living in the margin of local society. The local priests are in fact alien to both ladinos and Indians, for they are Spaniards who often spend only a few years in Ixil country. Furthermore, while the clergy has to compete among the Ixil against the religious fervor of the traditionalists, among ladinos it faces the religious indifference of most people. Very few ladino men and not many more women could be described as practicing Catholics, and the priests decry ladino irreligion even more than they do Indian "paganism."

When, some years ago, Catholic priests made a frontal attack against what they regarded as "paganism" and attempted to "reconvert" the Ixil by energetic methods, a number of clashes resulted, and in some cases the priest was pushed aside or even forced to leave the area. Today, the clergy are ostensibly more tolerant of Ixil practices and resort to subtler methods of converting young literate adults and infiltrating the cofradías with a few catechists. So far, their success has been limited to the conversion of some 4 to 5 percent of the Ixil population.

The church building in each of the three Ixil towns is an important center of both orthodox and traditional worship, and is thus a theater in which a continuous alternation of scenery takes place between the two religions. Sometimes, the church building becomes the scene of conflict between catechists and traditionalists when the catechists try to interfere with traditional worship. During the fiesta of the patron saint of the town, this ritual alternation is clearest; in the course of the same day, different groups "take over" the church three or four times. The priest gives a mass for the catechists in the early morning, followed by another one for the cofradías;[3] he will then baptize until noon, when the cofradías come in to take out the statues of the saints; the priest then assumes possession again to hear confessions, until the cofradías return for an evening service.

The ritual dualism of the church is also reflected in Nebaj in the fact that there is one young sacristan to represent orthodox Catholicism, and one older traditional sacristan and several assistants who represent the cofradías. In Chajul the priests have been strong enough to dismiss the cofradía sacristan. The clergy now tries to avoid any clashes and to temper the proselyting ardor of the more militant catechists, who blow out candles, use loudspeakers to make noise, and resort to similar tactics to disrupt traditional worship and the cofradía processions. (This behavior was reported, rather than directly observed.) The militancy of the catechists in recent years, and their capture of political offices in municipal councils has created a revivalist movement among traditionalists, which took a partly political expression in the organization of the Partido Revolucionario in Nebaj.

All three main areas of interaction (the political, the economic, and the religious) integrate ladinos and Indians by creating ties of interdependence, but they also constitute sources of conflict between the two groups and within the Indian group. The picture is further complicated by

[3] This practice of separate masses for the orthodox Catholics and for the "old Catholics" or traditionalists is a regular one throughout the year. During the summer of 1966, there was no Catholic priest in residence at Nebaj, for the previous incumbent had gone on leave to Spain. In 1967, a new Spanish curate was appointed to Nebaj.

the interplay between these three areas. Thus, as suggested before, there is a direct relationship between the cycle of Ixil religious life, labor contracting, and purchasing behavior. The August fiesta represents both a religious and an economic climax in the life of Nebaj. Many migrant laborers return home for the fiesta, and many more who have incurred debts during the fiesta have to sign labor contracts with the *contratistas*. Entire local handicraft industries such as candle- and fireworks-making are supported by the consumption of such items in Ixil religious ceremonies, and ladinos play an important role in the production of fireworks.

The connections between economic and political institutions are even more complex and numerous. There is a fairly close relationship between the distribution of wealth and of power among both Indians and ladinos. Only men of some means rise to political or religious office, and money is frequently converted into political influence. The most well-to-do Indian labor recruiter became the *b'o·q'ol tenam* and the local head of the PR; the largest ladino landowners, shopkeepers, and labor recruiters have been elected mayors. Similarly, a position of power can be used to acquire wealth, or at least to preserve and consolidate one's economic position. Municipal employees collect fees and gifts in exchange for favors. At another level, there is considerable regulation and taxation of economic life by the political authorities. The municipality collects rent for market stalls, it taxes business, it inspects weights and measures, and so on.

Perhaps most special to the Ixil region is the specific interplay between political and religious institutions. In both pre-Columbian civilizations and in the Spanish colonial system, church and state were closely associated. Since independence, the Guatemalan government has become increasingly secularized, and separation between church and state now exists in theory (though Catholic holidays are still observed nationally). At the local level, however, the theory breaks down to a considerable extent. First, as we have seen, religious cleavages and conflicts are expressed in the political arena. One might even say that, for most Indians, religion is the paramount political issue. Second, in the acquisition of prestige, a man's career frequently alternates between political office in the town council and religious office in the cofradías. The lifelong status of *principal* may be acquired through either political or religious positions.

Third, and most important, the government of the municipio itself plays a dual role vis à vis religion. In respect to the Catholic Church, the municipality is expected by the ladinos and the central government to play a neutral, secular role. For Indian traditionalists, on the other hand, the municipio and its elected Indian officials represent the Ixil community at large, and this community defines itself in religious terms. The municipio, for example, financed a large neon cross now adorning the Nebaj church. The separation between church and state is a concept alien to Ixil culture. On the contrary, the second regidor, as the highest representative of the Ixil, is expected to take an active part in the religious life of the community. He and his colleagues play a role in convincing reluctant persons to accept mayordomo positions in the cofradías; they take part in a religious ceremony in which the office staffs (*varas*) for the entire municipio are blessed by the head Ixil calendar priest. The whole town council, including its ladino members, have to participate actively in a ceremony which inaugurates the big annual fiesta of August. This important event takes place at the house of the first mayordomo of the cofradía of the Virgin of the Assumption on August 8, and involves drinking a maize gruel and alcohol; prayers and incense-burning on the altar of the Virgin by *b'a·lwa¢ti·š* (shamans or prayer-sayers); firing of firecrackers; dancing by the alcalde, the síndico, and all of the regidores; and ritual shattering of a large number (at least fifty or sixty) earthenware plates as each member of the town council dances past the altar. (Each person repeats that performance several times, breaking one plate at a time.)

In this inauguration ceremony, the "dual monism" of Nebaj is clearly expressed. The August fiesta is strictly an Ixil affair, but the participation of the whole municipal council, the composition of which is clearly dualistic, is essential. Similarly, the ladinos expect the municipality to play an active role in the September feast, though the latter is, of course, a secular national holiday.

The social structure of the plural society is held together by a set of intermeshing institutions which at crucial points create a complex network of ties of interdependence, but also of tensions between ladinos and Indians. The most important foci of integration are in the political and economic areas. The breakdown of geographical isolation has been accompanied by the extension of the power of the central government, the growth of cash crops and labor migration, and the general spread of the money economy. These trends have greatly increased the integration of the Ixil region to the rest of the country, as well as the mutual interdependence of ladinos and Indians within the Ixil zone.

Of course, these areas of integration are also potential sources of conflict between ladinos and Indians. Economically, the position of Indians has deteriorated considerably during this century, at least in terms of self-sufficiency if not in terms of absolute standards of living. Politically, Indians seem to be in the ascendancy in local government, and with better organization they could achieve further gains. However, at the national level, Guatemala is solidly controlled by a ladino ruling class, and the Indians as a declining group in the population can be expected to be faced increasingly with the alternative of impotent encapsulation in the western highlands, or assimilation to the dominant culture. Even the revolutionary movement of the last two decades has left the Indians largely to themselves.[4]

In the religious field, ethnic interdependence is much more tenuous because the points of contact are relatively few and the sources of conflict relatively numerous. In spite of certain religious ties, ladinos and Indians have fundamentally different conceptions of society. The ladinos are a largely secularized group with a large measure of indifference to the Catholic Church; the Ixil, like other indigenous Mesoamerican groups, are heirs to a deeply religious, indeed to a theocratic, society.

In all other aspects of life, especially in the areas of kinship, marriage, and most day-to-day affairs of a noneconomic or nonpolitical character, ladinos and Indians live side by side in two different cultural and social universes. Since we are primarily concerned here with group interaction, we are leaving these institutions outside the purview of this monograph.

[4] There is a third alternative which, though unlikely for the majority of Guatemala's Indians, should be considered. That is the local introduction of modern factories. Manning Nash (1958) studied the Quiché town of Cantel where a large textile mill had been introduced seventy years ago. After three generations, Indian factory workers still retain their dress, much of their religion, and many other aspects of their preindustrial life but have improved economically and changed slowly in other aspects. In the process, social integrity was maintained, and there was no special disruption such as has occurred with industrialization among peasant groups in other parts of the world.

V. THE FORM OF ETHNIC RELATIONS

FROM THE institutional structure of ethnic relations—that is, the network of normatively regulated ties which hold ladinos and Ixil together into a common plural society—we turn to what might be termed the morphology of ethnic relations, the specific forms which interactions take. It is immediately apparent that intergroup contact is not only highly patterned, but also that *inter*-ethnic behavior is strikingly different from *intra*-ethnic relations. Both ladinos and Indians engage in conscious role-playing when interacting. This is, of course, characteristic of nearly all, if not all, situations of race or ethnic relations.

Underlying the ladino treatment of Indians is the unquestioned assumption of the superiority of Spanish over Maya culture. We have not met a single ladino who rejected the stereotype of Ixil customs as backward, of Indian religion as a set of superstitions and idolatrous beliefs, and of the Ixil language as an inferior dialect. Few if any ladinos attribute any innate disabilities to Indians, and almost all agree that Indians are "improving themselves" and "becoming civilized," that they are in a process of ladinoization. Thirty-seven of the forty ladino questionnaire respondents said that Indians were changing and nearly all saw the major change as a process of ladinoization in dress, education, language, and customs.

Ladino feelings of cultural superiority are expressed in many different ways. For example, ladinos refer to the Spanish language by name (*español, castellano,* or erroneously, *castillo* or *castilla*) . Ixil on the other hand is spoken of *la lengua, el dialecto,* or *el idioma.* Similarly, ladinos regard Indians as practicing *costumbres* (customs), and being obstinately conservative in their "bad habits," but ladinos are not themselves consciously aware of also practicing "customs." The term *costumbre* is almost exclusively used in reference to Ixil customs. The most frequent and specific ladino criticisms of Indian culture are that the celebration of the fiestas entails a great economic waste, that the profuse drinking of alcohol which accompanies most religious rituals is detrimental to health, that lack of hygiene contributes to high disease and mortality rates, and that primitive agricultural practices make for low maize yields and soil erosion. Some of these criticisms are sound if one accepts certain premises and values regarding health and the accumulation of wealth, but ladinos generally condemn (and misinterpret) all of Indian culture simply because it is different from their own and because they regard Indians as a lower-status group.

Ladinos regard Indians as capable on the whole of becoming "civilized," but frequently unwilling to do so because of stubborn conservatism. Most ladinos approve of ladinoization by Indians. In the sample, eighteen persons said that Indians wearing ladino clothes were "improving themselves," "trying to make a better appearance," and so on, compared to ten who expressed neutral opinions, and six who disapproved or regretted the change. The few who disapproved did so because they regarded Indian dress as colorful and deplored its gradual disappearance. Indeed, clothing is practically the only aspect of Ixil culture which at least some ladinos regard positively, though with some condescension. Even though the tourist trade has not yet reached beyond Chichicastenango some hundred kilometers away, ladinos are aware that the colorful diversity of Indian dress in the Republic is a major tourist attraction, and their attitudes are beginning to be affected by this more cosmopolitan outlook toward Indian cultures. In some upper-class ladino families, women and young girls occasionally pose for photographs in Indian clothes as a kind of humorous or playful "disguise," but none ever customarily dresses so.

Ixil attitudes toward their own culture and that of ladinos are considerably more complex and ambivalent. Some material aspects of ladino culture are envied and admired, and within their limited economic means, Indians readily adopt imported goods. The practical value of learning Spanish, becoming literate, and attending primary school is also increasingly appreciated, particularly for boys. A small minority of catechists have also embraced with fervor orthodox Catholicism, and are vehement in their rejection of Ixil religion. But, beyond this selective adoption of, and adaptation to, the dominant culture, most Ixil value their way of life and reject the ladino definition of their culture as "pagan," "backward," and "inferior." Most Ixil are quite ambivalent toward ladino culture and orthodox Catholicism, though generally more tolerant toward ladino ways than the ladinos are toward Indian traditions. Indian women wearing shoes, and men imitating ladino ways are often regarded as ostentatious snobs, and traditional dress for women is highly valued for esthetic reasons as well as for purposes of group identity.

The Ixil have a strong consciousness of their past as shown in their ancestor worship and especially in their oral traditions where the historical and the mythical are intermixed. They are also aware of the past through ancient artifacts found accidentally or through clandestine excavation. Under some circumstances, archeological objects, when discovered, are placed on family shrines; but in other cases, such as deliberate excavation, they are thought to bring bad luck. There is a brisk traffic in these objects by ladinos and marginal Indians. Through archeological excavations, the commercial traffic in antiquities, and oral traditions, most Ixil have an awareness of the past, but they consider themselves different from their ancestors (*kuk'uykumam*) who produced the artifacts. The ancient Maya are viewed as superhumans, some of whom were destroyed and others deified by the omnipotent Kub'a·l.

Ladino ethnocentrism is probably the most important defining element of ethnic relations in Nebaj. As carriers of an allegedly inferior culture, Indians are regarded by ladinos as possessing certain properties which justify discriminatory treatment. The "positive" qualities most often attributed to Indians by ladinos are those which characterize their subordinate status: humility, docility, and willingness to do hard manual labor. Negative stereotypes, as previously mentioned, include tendency to idolatry, superstition, and alcoholism, lack of hygiene, mistrust, ignorance, and lack of desire to improve themselves.

The most common or at least the most overt treatment of Indians by ladinos is paternalistic. The Ixil are treated as backward and irresponsible grown-up children whom one has a duty to uplift and help within limits, provided, of course, that the Indians show the proper gratitude, dependence, and subservience. This treatment is especially characteristic of upper-class ladinos, all of whom have an Indian clientele of servants, compadres, debtors, tenant farmers, and other dependents.

This paternalistic model of ethnic relations is reflected in the etiquette prevailing between ladinos and Indians. The diminutive *indito* is constantly used in reference to adult Indians, and Indians are referred to as *muchacho* ("boy," "youth") or *chico* ("little one") by ladinos irrespective of either absolute age or relative age of the ladino speaker and the person to whom he refers. With few exceptions, ladinos call Indians by their first name without any title such as Don or Señor, and use either the familiar *tu* form (which is also used among ladinos when adults address children) or the equally familiar *vos* form, which has become archaic in most parts of the Spanish-speaking world but is still widely used in Central America. The *vos* form when used between relatives marks great familiarity, but in the interethnic context it symbolizes condescension and social distance. The only breaches of this etiquette which we have witnessed involved the mayor and some of the municipal employees when they spoke to prominent Indians in their official capacity, such as during a session of the municipal council. Then, they used the formal *usted* form.

This familiar and condescending treatment of Indians by ladino upper-class people is in marked contrast with the refined and elaborate courtesy which ladinos use among themselves. Social intercourse between ladinos who are not close relatives or friends is punctuated by the profuse use of titles (Don, Doña) and of courtesy phrases ("I am very pleased to greet you," "How did you wake up?" "I am always awaiting your orders," and the like).

In the ladino working class, condescending paternalism gives way to a more egalitarian or a more competitive attitude. The latter sometimes erupts in open rudeness and conflict. Gossiping, the exchange of ethnic insults between schoolchildren, trespassing by ladinos on Indian property, discriminatory treatment in shops (such as the common practice of serving ladino customers first), and the use of verbal threats in the collection of debts are so many sources of irritation and conflict in ladino-Indian relations. Paternalism is, however, the most common form of treatment of Indians by ladinos, both as an ideology and in practice. Of twenty-four ladino subjects who gave a classifiable answer to the question: "What is the best way of treating Indians?" fourteen gave paternalistic responses ("with affection," "try to uplift them," "introduce them to civilization"), eight responded in equalitarian terms ("just as you would a ladino," "the same as anybody," "without discrimination"), and two gave competitive answers ("with mistrust," "firmly and energetically"). The fifteen unclassifiable answers were generally positive or neutral ("decently," "in a friendly way," "tactfully," "carefully").

Most ladinos expect Indians to behave toward them with a certain deference, using the courtesy title of Don, Señor or, less commonly, *patrón,* and the polite *usted.* Some Indians conform to these expectations, particularly toward upper-class ladinos with whom they have patron-client ties. They express a certain subservience or at least meek reserve in conversation with ladinos, leaving the initiative to the latter, waiting patiently, hat in hand, for the ladino to pay attention to them, asking permission to leave, and using the courtesy titles. All of these practices are not reciprocated by ladinos. Many ladinos feel quite free to upbraid Indians in public for failure to repay a debt, laziness, forgetfulness, or some other alleged fault, and Indians are expected to appear contrite and accept the criticism without "talking back."

Many Indians do not use the *usted* in speaking to ladinos; instead, they reciprocate the familiar *tu* or *vos* with which they are addressed, but with the use of courtesy titles. This is tolerated by ladinos, and is not regarded as disrespectful because ladinos often rightly ascribe this form of address to inadequate knowledge of Spanish by the Ixil. (The use of *tu* or *vos* together with titles such as Don and Señor is not idiomatic in standard Spanish, and Indians who are more fluent in that language do address ladinos as *usted.*)

In fact, ladinos are frequently amused when Indians use unidiomatic Spanish or exhibit other evidence of lack of familiarity with ladino culture, because this reinforces their stereotype of the Indian as a childish, ignorant, inept person. Often, shows of "ignorance" or illiteracy, solecisms in Spanish, *faux pas* in etiquette, lengthy hesitation in the purchase of small items of current consumption such as cigarettes or soap, or other forms of "un-ladino" behavior on the part of Indians elicits smiles and winks between ladinos. In short, any evidence of the Indian's unfamiliarity with the ladino world is interpreted as ignorance and simplemindedness, and enjoyed as a kind of social comedy which enhances the ladino's opinion of himself and his culture. In line with this outlook is the resort by many ladinos to a simplified variety of Spanish when talking to Indians. Of course, most Indians who have never attended school and have had no other exposure to Spanish also use this limited dialect, and the ethnographer himself, after extensive contact with Indians, sometimes lapses unconsciously into it to the point of starting to use simplified Spanish with ladinos.

Some ladinos also speak Ixil and use a pidgin version of that language in interaction with Indians. However, of the thirteen ladinos out of forty who said they knew an Indian language, only one claimed to be fluent in it. Generally, ladinos speak much less Ixil than the Ixil speak Spanish, and Spanish is much the more common language of intergroup relations. Whether Spanish or Ixil is used, however, limited knowledge on the part of one of the parties makes for frequent misunderstandings, and this is a common cause of conflict.

A number of Ixil, particularly younger ones, do not conform to the subservient model which many ladinos expect of them. In crowded places, such as the market, Indians will push ladinos, and vice versa, to make room. Indians also frequently interrupt ladinos when they are speaking and are commonly rebuked by ladinos for doing so. These practices are common among the Ixil, and in arguments or debates one sometimes hears two Ixil talking simultaneously at each other. Sometimes, Indians insult ladinos or address them very curtly. On one occasion a woman shouted angrily at one of the authors for several minutes because he had unwittingly trespassed on her maize field. Another time, the Indian second regidor curtly rebuked working-class ladinos for interrupting a session of the municipal council. In 1883, Stoll reports an incident when a drunken Indian called him "son of a whore" (Stoll, 1886: p. 392).

Generally speaking, however, the Ixil exhibit courtesy toward ladinos, give preferential treatment to ladino guests in their houses (offering them the best chair, and giving them choice food and drink), and show a much greater tolerance of ladinos than ladinos do of Indians. Nevertheless, outside of the patron-client context, there is no generalized subservience of Indians toward ladinos. Many ladinos feel very insecure in their minority status, and tolerate what they regard as misbehavior on the part of Indians rather than risk arousing their hostility. Indians, on the other hand, are conscious of their majority status, and tend to regard ladinos as interlopers in a land that legitimately belongs to them.

Ethnic attitudes of ladinos toward Indians vary considerably, though there is agreement that the Ixil are culturally inferior to the ladinos. Basically, ladino attitudes can be reduced to three broad types which tend to go together with social class and educational status. There are those who regard the Ixil as inferior and irresponsible people who must be uplifted and helped in a paternalistic way. This outlook is generally accompanied by an acceptance of ladinoization, although some of the more conservative ladinos fear and resent the spread of primary-school education among Indians on the theory that a little education is a dangerous thing. Characteristic of this paternalistic and assimilationist outlook are the following statements: "The Indians must be well-educated so that they can be incorporated in society as good people in every sense," or "I think it is urgent to incorporate the indigenous race of Guatemala who constitutes 90 percent of the population so that they would no longer be the obstacle that they now are for the country in their present conditions of backwardness." These sentiments are most frequently expressed among middle- and upper-class people.

A second and much less common outlook is the egalitarian one. A few of the younger or middle-aged ladinos who are well-educated and are politically more radical advocate a non-discriminatory treatment of Indians as fellow citizens. Even they, however, regard Maya culture as backward and primitive and hence view themselves as "uplifters," so that, in practice, their attitudes are not markedly different from those of the more conservative paternalists. They do, however, regard the Indian as an adult rather than as a dependent child, and favor a more rapid pace of social, economic, and educational change which would improve the relative position of Indians vis à vis ladinos. This more progressive attitude has been advocated by two of the younger ladino mayors of Nebaj in the late 1940's and early 1950's. Both of them encountered considerable opposition from the conservative upper class and were prevented from completing their term in office. The following quotation typifies this more egalitarian outlook: "For many obvious reasons, the philosophical principles and aims of Guatemalan education have not yet been implemented, but, when they are, we shall be able to speak of social improvement, partly in economic terms, but fundamentally by educating our rural communities. . . . I think that every necessary opportunity must be given to the Indian so that his civilization shall be more distinguished in the future, but we must not interfere in any situation where the Indian can develop all by himself."

A third ladino attitude toward Indians consists in distrust, hostility, and fear. Such sentiments are more common among the ladino working class, though not entirely absent in the upper and middle classes. In practice, these negative sentiments are frequently tempered by a realization that ladinos are dependent on Indians for their livelihood. These people tend to regard Indians not only as ignorant, superstitious, and backward, but as untrustworthy, dishonest, lazy, and addicted to alcohol. One quoted a saying: "A dog shows more gratefulness than an Indian in need." Another said, "In my long experience, I have observed that the Indian never forgets his race; whether he believes himself superior or inferior to the ladinos, he is always resentful of them."

Different types of contact with Indians elicit widely different responses from ladinos. The responses of our forty subjects to the question whether they would accept Indians in given situations fall in three clear clusters, depending on the degree of equality and intimacy implicit in the type of contact. All or nearly all ladinos accept Indians as servants, as neighbors, as godchildren, or as companions in casual social activities such as taking a walk, visiting, or playing sports. (See Table 4.) Only two-thirds of the respondents accepted more intimate and egalitarian contacts with Indians—for example, as close friend, dance partner, or guest at one's table. Finally, only one-fourth of the sample would consider marrying an Indian or choosing one as godparent for his child.

Acceptance of contact with Indians is closely related to actual contact in given situations. Those forms of interaction which are in fact common are widely accepted, while those that are extremely rare are generally disapproved. The incidence of hypothetical acceptance of unusual situations such as ethnic intermarriage is, however, considerably higher than the actual occurrence of such events. The relationship in the ladino sample between actual contact with Indians and acceptance of such contact in hypothetical situations is shown in Table 5.[1]

The ladinos sample was broken down along the vari-

[1] Scores for actual and hypothetical contact were obtained by simple addition of positive responses to individual questions. There were eight items testing actual contact and eleven items dealing with hypothetical contact.

ables of sex, age, and education. The small size of the sample and its nonrandom character only allow tentative conclusions here. There was a clear tendency, however, for ladino women to have less contact than men with Indians, to be less favorable toward such contact, and to disapprove more of ethnic intermarriage. Respondents over thirty-five years of age were slightly (but not significantly) more tolerant of intermarriage and of interethnic contact, than people of thirty-five or less.

The relationship between education and ethnic attitudes was much closer. All six people approving of intermarriage belonged to the *less* educated half of the sample. The least educated fourth of the sample (those with less than six years of school) had most contact with Indians and was more willing to accept such contact. It seems probable that a higher rate of contact with Indians on the part of working-class ladinos results in more tolerant attitudes, although as we have noted, there is also considerable friction and competitiveness between Indians and working-class ladinos.

Ladino-Indian relations cover a wide gamut from paternalistic master-servant relations, to neutral, impersonal ones, to hostile, competitive ones. The traditional Ixil attitude toward outsiders, if we are to trust written and verbal accounts by ladinos, has been mistrust and hostility. Considering the experiences the Ixil have had with ladinos since the Conquest, these sentiments are easily understandable. Most local ladinos report that this hostility has abated in recent years. As far back as 1940, Lincoln encountered much friendliness and hospitality among the Ixil, and so have more recent visitors, ourselves included. There seems to be, however, a higher level of xenophobia in Chajul than in either Nebaj or Cotzal. Of course, foreign social scientists are readily recognized as being different from local ladinos, and attitudes toward them are probably not typical.

There have been several open and violent clashes between Indians and ladinos in recent decades in the Ixil zone. Some were provoked by a Catholic priest's brutal interference with traditional Ixil religion (such as destroying sanctuaries or trying to prevent processions from taking place). In 1925, an Indian insurrection against ladino landowners took place in Ilom (an aldea in the municipio of Chajul) as a consequence of a land dispute (Lincoln, 1945: p. 69). The most serious incident happened in Nebaj in 1936. A group of Indians, disturbed at recent legal changes in the status of debts and in the system of compulsory labor, were insulted and tactlessly handled by the ladino military commandant. The latter was assaulted, and his garrison of seven ladino soldiers was disarmed. The Ixil then dispersed and hid in the neighboring hills, while the ladinos telegraphed for troops from El Quiché. A general and a detachment of fifty soldiers arrived during the night, several Indians were arrested, and the following day seven Ixil men were shot. For several weeks, many Indians stayed away in the mountains, afraid of further punitive action. This episode was the last major outbreak of violence in Nebaj and in the Ixil area. But some latent hostility persists. The Ixil have many reasons to distrust and dislike ladinos, a fact which some ladinos readily concede. In particular, the Ixil resent the overbearing and superior attitude of many ladinos. Treated with respect, the Ixil generally respond with kindness and hospitality.

The sample of ninety Ixil yields additional data on the ethnic attitudes of Indians toward ladinos. As is true of ladinos, Ixil who report a high incidence of contact with out-group members also tend to have favorable attitudes toward the out-group. Indians who have ladino neighbors tend to like them and to visit them frequently. Beyond these none-too-surprising results, several more complex patterns of Indian-ladino interaction emerge. The Ixil who report more actual contact with ladino friends and neighbors and express more favorable attitudes toward such contact tend to have higher status and to be better educated. (As we just saw, the reverse is true of ladinos.) They also tend to perceive Indians as becoming ladinoized and to disapprove of this change. This indicates that, while high-status Ixil may enjoy contact with ladinos and like them as individuals, they are not necessarily attracted to ladino culture and do not seek to become assimilated into the ladino group. Favorable attitudes toward ladinos as persons are frequently associated with conservatism and a rejection of many aspects of ladino culture.

The favorable qualities most frequently attributed to ladinos by the Ixil respondents are their readiness to give advice to and teach Indians (mentioned by 37 persons), their willingness to speak to Indians (14), and their usefulness as sources of gifts (14) and employment (8). Most resented are the ways in which ladinos allegedly mistreat Indians (30), their refusal to speak to or give advice to Indians (20), and their proneness to ridicule or insult Indians (11). Unlike ladinos who ascribe to Indians a wide gamut of qualities and defects thought to be intrinsic to Indian culture or character, the Ixil evaluate ladinos almost exclusively in terms of interethnic relations. Good ladinos are those who are friendly or helpful to Indians; bad ones are those who refuse to help or are contemptuous of Indians.

Ostensibly, then, the Ixil refrain from evaluating ladino culture and individuals in terms of their own characteristics. In one respect, however, the pattern of responses reveals an indirect acknowledgment of ladino superiority. Ladinos are regarded as a source of information and advice, and are criticized when they do not fulfill these functions. While this acknowledged superiority may be limited to the technological field, these responses do nevertheless indicate some measure of acceptance of the paternalistic model of ethnic relations fostered by the ladino upper class.

Other interview responses confirm this finding. Those Ixil who have had contact with ladinos through political office or parish jobs and through longer school attendance tend to prefer the paternalistic model of interethnic relations over the egalitarian or the competitive alternatives.[2] Thus, those Ixil who, because of greater literacy, education, and knowledge of Spanish understand ladino culture best, and because of their position in the municipality or the parish have had important and extensive dealings with ladinos, seem to have learned to "play along" with the patron-client model of interethnic relations preferred by most upper-class ladinos.

Expediency and material gain seem to be the principal motivations of much interaction across the ethnic line. This is probably as true of ladinos as of Indians, and reciprocal mistrust reinforces the expectation of exploitative motives in much ladino-Indian interaction. Relations across ethnic boundaries are highly segmental, functionally specific and instrumental, and are circumscribed by well-defined roles. In a society with a past history of intergroup treachery, exploitation, and conflict, and a present stress in both ladino and Indian cultures on money and material possessions, ladino-Indian relations are to a large extent a contest for wealth and for power. This contest includes a widespread and reciprocal use of deception.[3]

2 Respondents were asked which of the following three ways was the best form of interaction with ladinos: It is good that ladinos look at us as a father, as a keeper of us, that likes us. It is better that they don't order us, just as we cannot order them because we are equals. It is better that we fight for our living to become richer, that we become smarter than the ladinos.

These three statements are literal translations from the Ixil. They are meant to elicit respectively the paternalistic, egalitarian, and competitive attitudes toward ethnic relations.

3 Both authors have frequently been told untruths, and open accusations of lying are common among both Ixil and ladinos. *"Son mentiras"* is a recurrent phrase and in Chajul protestations of truth are frequently pref-

There is little if any residential segregation which could be attributed to ethnicity in Nebaj. Ladinos and Indians live side by side in most parts of town, although one barrio (Salquilito) has only two ladino families. Thirty-three ladinos, out of 40 in the sample, report having Indian neighbors. So do 78 out of the 90 Ixil respondents.[4] Generally, there is a greater concentration of upper- and middle-class houses along the main street (Calle Real) and within two blocks of the central square, but the relationship between either class status and ethnicity, and distance from the center is not very close. Poor houses are interspersed between more substantial ones. The few middle-class Indian families tend to congregate in one barrio, but a number of ladinos also live there.

Indians are not debarred by either law or custom from any public place such as government buildings, churches, marketplaces, and the like. There is however, considerable ethnic separation in schools, in that most of the small minority of Ixil children who attend school go to lower-primary rural schools which are *de facto* all Indian, or to the Escuela de Castellanización. The latter was especially established to teach Ixil children Spanish and basic literacy in order to prepare them for the four urban primary schools in Nebaj, Cotzal, and Chajul. The two urban schools of Nebaj are entirely ladino in terms of teaching staff, and predominantly so in terms of pupils. Both Nebaj schools have a sprinkling of Indian pupils (some 12 to 15 percent of the total enrollment), but ladinos are vastly

aced with "Why should I lie to you?" Also, in spite of the fact that we were generally well received and had no difficulty in establishing rapport, our presence in town was accompanied by gossip, some of it malicious, and several people tried to take advantage of us for monetary gain.

4 These findings may be contaminated by the fact that the Ixil term *b'esi·no* is derived from the Spanish "vecino," which in local usage can also mean "fellow townsman" or "citizen." However, in the context of the questionnaire most respondents probably interpreted the word in a narrower sense. In any case, the questionnaire responses confirm observation and interview data.

overrepresented in them. While virtually all ladino children now attend at least the first three or four grades of primary school, only a small minority of Ixil children do so. Indian children constitute a higher proportion of the school population in Cotzal and Chajul, since the ladino population of these towns is considerably smaller. In the entire Quiché department, 19.0 percent of the ladino population over seven years old were enrolled in schools in 1950, compared to only 1.8 percent of the Indians. The ladino-Indian differential probably declined somewhat since 1950, but it certainly remains very great.

In the field of entertainment, the free Sunday evening motion pictures shown in the *juzgado* of Nebaj and just recently, the nightly television showings also in the juzgado, are attended by both ladinos and Indians without any pattern of ethnic seating or other form of segregation or discrimination. Nebaj sport clubs, however, are organized along ethnic lines. Basketball is played only by ladinos; in soccer, there are two ladino teams and, for a while, one Indian one now disbanded. Occasionally, all-ladino teams played against all-Indian teams. (One Ixil informant reported a fight once after the Ixil team had won a game.) Both Protestant and Catholic religious services are attended by ladinos and Indians, but traditional Ixil rites and practices are generally restricted to Indians. Each group has its religious brotherhoods or cofradías (twelve for the Indians, two for the ladinos). The two ladino cofradías do not take part in the processions and other religious rites associated with the Indian cofradías. In fact, they are of very peripheral importance to the ladinos, unlike the central role of cofradías in Ixil social and religious life.

Once a year, the ladino school children elect a ladino queen and king, and the Indian schoolchildren elect their own "royalty." Nebaj barbers practice ethnic discrimination, more by custom than by design. There are no barbershops in Nebaj, but the couple of ladinos who give haircuts as a part-time job charge twenty cents and serve only ladinos. Indians are accustomed to get their hair cut by the five or six Indian barbers who set up shop on the marketplace on Sunday, or receive customers on the verandas of their houses, and charge ten cents.

Both Indians and ladinos are buried in each of Nebaj's two cemeteries, but in each location there is a covered sanctuary where only Indians come to pray and burn incense for their ancestors. (The cult for the dead plays a much greater role in Indian culture than in ladino culture, and mortuary practices are quite different.) Indians and ladinos visit each other when they need to transact business (such as signing a labor contract, borrowing money, or collecting debts), but purely casual visits are rare. Commensality and more intimate and equalitarian forms of intercourse between Indians and ladinos are even more exceptional. On several occasions when the authors were traveling with Indians and were invited to eat in a ladino house, the Indians were served in the kitchen even though they were not servants. Indian visitors in ladino houses are seldom invited to come into a room and sit down; they are generally received on the veranda or in the patio and left standing.

Two more intimate forms of interethnic relations are fairly common. One involves ladinos serving as godparents for Indian children. These ties of ritual kinship are important, as we have seen in Chapter IV. The second involves sexual relations in and out of marriage. Miscegenation is an old theme in Ixil country, and has entered local folklore. At various fiestas, for example, the Ixil perform a dance drama called *Čawela Hu·* in which a young Indian woman ridicules her old Indian husband and has promiscuous relations with seven dancers impersonating Spaniards. The dance, which involves much slapstick, is a favorite among the Ixil. Actual ethnic intermarriage is extremely uncommon. Out of ninety cases of civil marriage registered in Nebaj between 1963 and 1966, only one involved persons of different ethnic groups. The one exception consisted of a ladino man and a non-Ixil Indian woman who was an outsider from Huehuetenango. Both partners were Protestants, and their marriage was religiously endogamous in a society which only has a small minority of Protestants.

Interethnic concubinage is relatively common. About two-thirds of the cases involve ladino men and Indian women. In the ladino sample, 28 respondents out of 40 said that they knew of unions between ladino men and Indian women, and 22 reported cases of ladino women living with Indian men. The subjects mentioned an average of 3.4 cases of the former type, and 2.5 of the latter. Concubinage is by no means limited to interethnic unions. The majority of both Indians and ladinos do not get married either in church or at the civil registry, and hence are legally considered to be living in *matrimonio de hecho* (common law marriage). Most Indians go through a set of agreements, exchanges of gifts, and rites which constitute a real traditional marriage, but many ladinos simply live together without any traditional or other marriage.[5]

There is considerable disapproval of interethnic concubinage, mostly among women of both groups. Ixil women regard it as a form of exploitation of Indian women by ladino men, but generally condone the practice if the man takes good care of the woman and her children. Ladino women tend to view Indian women as unfair competition, and regard affairs between ladino men and Indian women as distasteful. But among ladino men, who

[5] Thus, the legal term *matrimonio de hecho* has a different significance for ladinos and Indians. For ladinos it represents a real case of concubinage, while for most Indians, matrimonio de hecho constitutes a true marriage according to cultural traditions which are denied legal recognition in the Republic of Guatemala. The use of a single legal category obscures a fundamental structural difference brought about by cultural pluralism.

stress the value of *machismo* (masculinity) and adhere to a dual standard of sexual morality, affairs with Indian women are regarded with amused tolerance. Several men are famous in the region for the number of their illegitimate progeny by Indian mistresses. Some ladinos keep several households in the same town, or in town and elsewhere, and reside alternatively with their wife and mistresses according to a system somewhat analogus to "hut polygyny" in African societies.

In fact, these extramarital unions form an interesting nexus of ties between some Indian and ladino families in town. Two Indian and two ladino families seem to have paired off in a complex and enduring sexual partnership in which the Indian family furnishes daughters as mistresses of ladinos, get their sons married to daughters of similar ladino-Indian unions, or marry former Indian mistresses of ladinos. These various sexual ties are also accompanied by economic, political, and patron-client relations between these families.

Interethnic concubinage seems to be declining if one compares the present situation with Lincoln's account of offers of sexual hospitality of Indians to him, of the eagerness of Indian women to have children by ladinos, and of the cavalier way in which ladinos had intercourse with married Ixil women in their husbands' absence (Lincoln, 1945: pp. 78–79). (Neither author was ever offered sexual hospitality, but we were rumored to have had such relations with Ixil informants.) Lincoln also reports that Indian principales had ladino mistresses, that a number of Indian women engaged in prostitution, and that ladinos encouraged promiscuity among Indian women. We have only heard of one Indian woman who sells the sexual services of her daughter for twenty-five cents. A number of Indian children look phenotypically more European than Indian. Some of these are rumored to be children of Catholic priests, brought up by their mothers since they could not be acknowledged by their fathers. (More significant than the veracity of the rumor, which in this age is unlikely, is the fact that priests are not exempt from this kind of gossip.) To be genetically mestizo does not necessarily imply acceptance as a ladino, and a good many of those children are brought up as Indians and are regarded as such.

Nebaj's ethnic dualism is perhaps most clearly symbolized by the fact that each of the two groups has its own great annual fiesta. The Ixil fiesta coincides with the Catholic holiday of the Assumption of the Virgin Mary, the patron saint of the town. Its cult is celebrated by the highest-ranking Ixil cofradía, that of Kuçuç Mariy. Preparations begin early in August, and the festivities begin on the eighth, go crescendo until the climax on the fourteenth, and finish on the fifteenth. This is primarily a religious occasion which attracts thousands of Ixil from Chajul and Cotzal as well as Nebaj. There are also numerous Indian visitors from Sacapulas, Cunén, Huehuetenango, Totonicapán, El Quiché, and other neighboring towns. The main religious rites consist of lengthy processions organized by the cofradías; during these, the statues of the twelve cofradía saints are taken out of the church, and each statue is left in the house of the *b'a·l mertoma* of the corresponding cofradía; later the statues are collected again one by one and led back to the church in procession.

All this is accompanied by much marimba playing, dancing, shooting of fireworks (*cohetes* and *bombas*), and drinking of alcohol. Some 1,300 liters of aguardiente worth $3,100, and some 3,500 pieces of fireworks worth some $525 were consumed during the 1966 fiesta, in addition to unknown but large quantities of illegally distilled alcohol. Some 20 to 30 percent of the adult Ixil are intoxicated at any given time during the fiesta. Large sums of money are also spent on the marimba orchestras, several of which come from other towns. The largest nine-man band from Totonicapán charged $350 for four days of playing. There were fifteen other orchestras in town, charging from $150 to $250 for the fiesta period.

While the Ixil fiesta is first and foremost one of these great religious events reaffirming the social solidarity of all Ixil (to use Durkheimian terminology), it is accompanied by a great deal of commercial activity. A continuous market is held, beginning around August 8, and coming into full activity around August 12. Many ladinos and non-Ixil Indians come to sell a variety of unusual goods and services. Some articles are sold, such as toys, shoes, decorated pottery, wooden chests, packaged sweets, and similar "luxury" items, which seldom appear on regular markets. Similarly, photographers, shoe-shiners, keepers of gambling tables and lotteries, and diviners offer a range of services which are not normally available. Pickpockets making the circuit of local fiestas come from as far as El Salvador.

Ladino participation in the August fiesta is only marginal. When processions go by, ladinos often step outside to look. Occasionally, a few ladinos are seen drinking in the bars and dance-halls set up for the occasion. The ladino members of the municipality take part by custom in an inauguration ritual to be described later. Ladino shopkeepers, truck owners, and labor recruiters make the most of the fiesta economically. A number of the marimba players hired by the Indian cofradías are ladinos who earn a living by making the fiesta circuit throughout Guatemala. But the ladinos regard the whole fiesta as an Indian affair. Their attitudes range from amused detachment to strong disapproval. A few ladinos enjoy the colorful pageantry of the events; many more are amused at what they regard as the childish or backward behavior of the Indians; most dismiss the fiesta as a noisy, wasteful, drunken orgy which impoverishes the Indians and contributes to their alleged degeneracy.

Nebaj ladinos celebrate their annual fiesta from September 12 to September 15, the latter date being the anniversary of the National Independence of Guatemala.[6] In principle, this is a national holiday for the whole population, but in practice, Indians express about as much interest and participate in it about to the extent that the ladinos do in the August festivities. Representatives from important ladino families are called together by the alcalde, and they elect an all-ladino fiesta committee to organize the activities. In contrast to the Ixil feast, the ladino feast is entirely secular. It consists mostly of amateur theatrical performances by ladino children, of basketball and soccer games between ladino teams from Nebaj and neighboring towns, of a parade, and of Western-style dancing to marimba bands. Indians participate on the sidelines as spectators to the sport events. The entire municipal council elects an Ixil queen and maids of honor. These Indian women, dressed in traditional clothes, take part in the parade to the sports grounds.

The "origin myth" of the September fiesta accounts for the ethnic dualism of public festivities in Nebaj. Around the turn of the century, the leading ladinos, most of whom were Spanish labor recruiters, decided to hold their fiesta in September because, during the August events, they were too busy recruiting Indians to celebrate. Thus, it came to pass that Spaniards chose as their fiesta the anniversary of the independence of Guatemala from their own country. (The narrator, himself a Guatemalan of several generations' standing, told the story with great relish.)

In Chajul, where there are fewer ladinos in town and where the discrepancy in economic well-being between the two groups is much smaller, there is a single large fiesta which takes place preceding and during the second Friday of Lent in February. While busloads of pilgrims come to Chajul sporadically throughout the year, large numbers

6 Information on the September fiesta was gathered from Indian and ladino informants. Neither author was able to attend the event.

come only during this Lenten period. The high point occurs Friday night, when the church is brightly lit with thousands of burning candles. Thousands of pilgrims, both Indians and ladinos, come from all over Guatemala to visit the statue of Christ of Golgotha, a bent figure carrying a cross, situated in a glassed-in area behind the altar. During the high point of the fiesta a line of several hundred people waits to see the statue of Christ. From six to twelve priests come from other towns in the department of Quiché to assist the local priest. The Chajul fiesta thus has much less of an ethnic character than the fiesta of Nebaj. Nor is it as closely linked with the Indian cofradía rites as the main fiestas of Nebaj and Cotzal.

The long line of pilgrims slowly moves forward. Each person carries a spray of camomile and other flowers, candles, and religious pictures. In addition to the line of pilgrims waiting to see the statue of Christ, the church is full of people who come to pray and burn candles. Candles are lit in front of altars, in the aisles, and behind the last row of seats before the entrance of the church. The large quantity of wax which accumulates is scraped up by Chajul women who presumably will use it for making new candles. Overhead are weird figures of people, animals, monstrances, and other objects painted on the ceiling of the church by earlier generations of Chajul Ixil. Local Chajul people as well as the pilgrims come and go in the church, some making numerous visits in a single day. A lesser number of both Indians and ladinos visit the pagan shrines in and around Chajul, and some of the Indians go as far as the sacred shrine of Juil, a Chajul god connected with the origin of corn and the ritual calendar.

In the market, people buy hats adorned with ground pine and trinkets around the rim. Religious pictures, statues, and other objects are sold. A line of a dozen photographers with their backdrops of city streets and other scenes is at the entrance of town. The market area which normally occupies one end of the large grassy common extends in all directions and up into the central plaza and fountain area in front of the church and juzgado. A mass of white tarpaulins over the market stands, milling crowds, and the din of people talking, loud-speakers blaring, and horns of buses trying to move through the crowded street all add to the effect which is in marked contrast to the normal quiet of the town.

As many as three dozen buses, trucks, and other vehicles are parked at the end of the common opposite the market. Located there also is usually a carousel, or a whirling-chairs device run by a loud gasoline motor, which always attracts a large group.

During the major Ixil fiestas of the three municipios there is an interesting institution shared by the three Ixil dialect groups, known as *weȼ k'aol,* in which families exchange hospitality. People from Cotzal and Nebaj go to specific houses in Chajul, where they are given bed and meals for as long as they stay. On departing they are often given gifts of food to take with them. In exchange, those from Chajul visit their *weȼ k'aol* families in Nebaj during the fiesta in August and in Cotzal during the San Juan fiesta in June. Interestingly, although Nebaj and Cotzal Indians say they understand each other much better and consider each other to be generally more friendly than the Chajul people, there is much less *weȼ k'aol* exchange between Nebaj and Cotzal than either has with Chajul. This may be due to the greater religious importance of Chajul.

In addition to the *weȼ k'aol* privilege, Chajul people allow non-Ixil Indians to build fires in their front yards and sleep there. This contrasts with the usual inhospitality which Indians of the other two municipios attribute to the people of Chajul.

As during the August fiesta of Nebaj, the market includes a wide variety of agricultural produce and manufactured products. There are also dining places. Fortune tellers with various gimmicks, vendors of patent medicines, and tables where games of chance are played are also in evidence. Several loudspeakers of people hawking their wares or their fortune-telling services compete cacophonously with each other.

In contrast to the August fiesta of Nebaj there is considerably less public drunkenness. This is due to the fact that the major religious activities in Nebaj at the August fiesta are concerned with the cofradías, where drinking is an institutionalized part of the religious ceremony.

The fiesta of San Juan Cotzal in June, like the Nebaj fiesta two months later, is primarily a cofradía fiesta. However, in the number of marimba bands, the duration of the fiesta, and various other criteria of the importance and intensity of a fiesta, the San Juan Cotzal festivities are on a smaller scale.

Having described both the institutional context and the morphology of ethnic relations in Ixil country, and especially in Nebaj, we shall now discuss ethnic relations at once from a more dynamic perspective and from a broader one. What social and cultural changes are taking place in Guatemala as a whole as a consequence of interaction between ladinos and Indians?

VI. THE SOCIOCULTURAL DYNAMICS OF THE PLURAL SOCIETY

THOUGH OUR STUDY has focused on a relatively small region of Guatemala, we have tried to stress the dependence of Ixil country on the national society of which it is a part. In dealing with the central problem of social and cultural change, the national perspective is essential.

The Guatemalan ethnic situation is characterized by two sets of seemingly paradoxical facts. The first paradox is that, in many communities, the ethnic line at the local level is so rigid as to constitute almost a caste barrier (Tumin, 1952); but if one takes the country as a whole, there is considerable hispanization; thus the national situation could be described as ethnically fluid.

Ethnic fluidity is indicated by the steady decline in the Indian percentage of the Guatemalan population. In 1921, 64.8 percent were Indians; in 1950, 53.5 percent; and in 1964, 43.3 percent.[1] (See Table 1.) Some of the decrease in the Indian population may be attributable to the lower Indian net reproduction rate as a consequence of a higher death rate (Monteforte Toledo, 1959: p. 86). But demographic differentials are not sufficient to account for the change in the ethnic composition of Guatemalan population. There is no clear relationship between the ethnic composition of departments and their relative rates of population increase, especially if one excludes the five departments with a high rate of in-migration. Thus,

[1] In the last censuses, "ethnic group" has been consistently defined in terms of "social estimation in which a person is held in the place where the census is taken."

changes in the proportion of ethnic groups is a result principally of ladinoization rather than ethnic differentials in net reproduction rates.

Assuming that changes in ethnic ratios reflect mostly cultural assimilation, an examination of statistics by department reveals wide regional differences in rates of assimilation. (See Table 7.) Two main factors seem to affect the situation. The first one is relative size of Indian population. In all of the departments that were heavily Indian (75 to 95 percent in 1964)—Totonicapán, Sololá, Alta Verapaz, Chimaltenango, and Quiché—the ethnic ratio remained quite stable. In all five departments, there was a large absolute increase in the Indian population, and in Quiché there was even a slight relative increase of 0.6 percent between 1950 and 1964. The other four departments showed a relative decline of only 1.1 to 1.5 percent. With the exception of Chimaltenango, these departments were also remarkably stable between 1940 and 1950. In short, there has been little change in ethnic composition of the heavily Indian western and central highlands for the last quarter century.

On the other hand, in four of the seven departments where Indians numbered only 10 to 20 percent of the population in 1950, the decline has been rapid. In Jutiapa, the percentage of Indians declined from 19.6 to 0.4, and absolute numbers went from 27,249 to 840; in Progreso, from 9.4 to 0.4 and from 4,482 to 240; in Santa Rosa, from 9.4 to 0.9 and from 10,294 to 1,460. Escuintla experienced an absolute decrease from 19,660 to 17,880 and a relative one from 15.9 to 7.1 percent. Of the seven departments with Indian populations of less than 20 percent in 1950, only Izabal, Zacapa, and Guatemala retained Indian minorities in excess of 10 percent. Where Indians are in the minority, especially in the eastern part of the country, they are becoming rapidly absorbed into the ladino group. Ethnic ratios by department account for approximately 30 percent of the variance in rate of assimilation. (The Spearman rank correlation between Indian percentage in 1964 and relative decline of Indian population between 1950 and 1964 is –.54.)

There are, however, five departments which had Indian majorities of 52 to 73 percent in 1950, and which nevertheless experienced large declines of between 18 and 12 percent between 1950 and 1964. With the exception of Chiquimula, these departments are located in the southwestern zone of large-scale coffee, sugarcane, and cotton plantations. San Marcos, Quetzaltenango, Retalhuleu, and Suchitepéquez are all rapidly growing because of the steady influx of agricultural laborers. It might be thought that the Indian population declines relatively (despite a slow rate of absolute growth) because of ladino in-migration. Such is not the case, however. We know that much of that in-migration consists of Indians coming from the adjacent western highlands. If it were not for assimilation, the Indian proportion should rise rather than decline as a consequence of in-migration into that zone. The region of large-scale commercial agriculture is probably, with the capital city, the one where "passing" takes place most rapidly and on the largest scale. The fifth department with a relatively large but rapidly declining Indian population, Chiquimula, does not resemble the other four. Its rate of population growth is the lowest in the Republic, indicating considerable out-migration. Its location in eastern Guatemala is probably the main factor accounting for the rapid Indian decline. Chiquimula is surrounded by predominantly ladino departments and is also relatively accessible to the capital city. A number of Indians probably emigrate to neighboring ladino areas and become assimilated.

The seeming paradox between local rigidity and national fluidity is resolved by the fact that where the population is heavily Indian and where little in-migration takes place, the ethnic line acquires the quasi-caste characteristics reported in the anthropological literature. Conversely, in large cities or in zones of commercial agriculture where the Indian population is locally polyethnic as a result of in-migration, hispanization is more rapid, and ethnic boundaries become ill-defined. Adams has spoken of "modified Indian labor populations" and "ladinoized Indian communities" which are probably of this type (1956).

Some of the "passing" is undoubtedly temporary. When Indians from the highlands come to work in the coastal fincas, they frequently dress as ladinos and use Spanish as a lingua franca. They may even "pass" for ladinos in the work situation, but when they return home they regard themselves and are regarded by others as Indians.

Another factor which probably contributes to ladinoization is the ambiguity in the ethnic status of the Indian who does not belong to the local majority group. Local Indians will regard him as a stranger, and, of course, unless he speaks the local Indian language, he will be forced to use Spanish as a lingua franca. Ladinoization and "passing" of Indian "strangers" are probably more the consequence of marginality than of any conscious desire to become assimilated to the ladinos. Rejection by local Indians makes ladinoization almost inevitable. In the municipio of Chajul, for example, Quiché-speaking immigrants who settled on vacant land among the Ixil are referred to by the Ixil as "Chiquimulas," regardless of whether they originated from the Quiché town of that name. The word has come to be a generic term for "Indian stranger." Yet, discrepancies between the 1964 census and statements by Ixil informants suggest that many of these non-Ixil Indians were sufficiently ladinoized to be classified as ladinos by the census enumerators.

A second seeming paradox concerning assimilation and ethnic boundaries is that, in local communities, the ethnic line between ladinos and Indians often remains quite rigid in spite of considerable hispanization. That is, lines of social cleavage persist despite a gradual acquisition of Spanish culture by Indians. This situation is, of course, common where "race" rather than culture is the criterion of group membership. However, this criterion is not used in Guatemala. If ethnic group membership is determined by cultural differences, why should hispanization leave the ethnic line largely unaffected at the local level? The actual degree of westernization which the Indian population has undergone, and the resultant degree of *objective* cultural difference between the indigenous and ladino groups are only two of the many factors making for the relative flexibility or rigidity of the ethnic line. Indeed, they are not as important as the *subjective perception* of cultural differences; the way in which each of the two groups defines its boundaries; the attitudes of members of both groups toward assimilation, their own culture, and that of the outgroup; the self-sufficiency or "social viability" of each group; and the relative economic, social, and political positions of the ethnic groups.

Both apparent paradoxes in the Guatemalan situation are best explained by shifting the analysis from the cultural to the sociological aspects of ethnic relations. In their insistence that ladino-Indian distinctions were not "racial" or phenotypical, most anthropologists have stressed cultural distinctions, including differences in value systems, between the two groups as the relevant criteria. Ethnic relations were interpreted primarily in terms of dynamics of acculturation between "carriers" of different traditions engaged in a complicated exchange, selection, reinterpretation, and syncretism of culture traits or complexes.

To be sure, objective cultural differences are important defining criteria of ethnicity in Guatemala, the rest of Spanish America, and numerous other countries; and culture change through interethnic contact is a legitimate and important topic of study. But the predominantly cultural approach gives an incomplete view of ongoing systems of ethnic relations. Indians and ladinos are also members of groups structured by well-defined networks of ties of kinship, friendship, neighborliness, economic exchange, and power relations. This interaction takes place within the matrix of structured roles and statuses both within and between ethnic groups.

Viewed from this perspective, it is clear why partial hispanization does not typically lead to passing so long as the distinct social structure of the local Indian group remains. Only complete cultural homogeneity would presumably lead to a monistic structure, unless, of course, "racial" criteria of membership were introduced to preserve the pluralistic structure, as happened in South Africa and the United States. Migration is thus a chief factor in "passing" because, by moving outside the area occupied by his own ethnic group, the Indian has largely removed himself (if only temporarily) from his group, and finds himself among strangers. It is almost a foregone conclusion that, under those conditions, he uses Spanish as a lingua franca, dresses as a ladino, and gradually or at least temporarily assimilates to the dominant ladino group rather than to the alien Indian group.

Let us now turn to a basic property of stratification systems: What makes for relative fluidity or rigidity of ethnic membership? An answer to this kind of problem is best sought through the use of comparative evidence. The available literature suggests that in Mexico, even in the neighboring state of Chiapas, which has close similarities and historical links with Guatemala, the ethnic line between Indians and ladinos or mestizos is more fluid than in Guatemala, even at the local level. Thus, in the town of San Cristóbal de las Casas located in the Chiapas highlands in the middle of the Tzeltal-Tzotzil zone, Indians who come to live in the urban area (e.g., domestic servants) become assimilated to the ladino group in a few years (de la Fuente, 1965).[2] We found that such is not the case in Quetzaltenango and other urban areas of Guatemala (Colby and van den Berghe, 1961). We then suggested two possible explanations for the greater rigidity of the ethnic line in Guatemala compared to Mexico. The first had to do with the longer and more successful revolutionary tradition of Mexico, with the strong assimilationist ideology and practice of its government. Secondly, we argued that the much higher proportion of Indians in Guatemala gave much greater salience and omnipresence to the ethnic cleavage than in Mexico where the indigenous population constitutes a residual tenth of the nation (1961, pp. 786-789).

Other crucial differences in the structural position of Indians in the two countries also seem related to the rigidity of the ethnic line. Briefly stated, the Indians of Guatemala, protected from massive contact with the Spaniards by greater isolation and the relative absence of mines and other natural resources, preserved a more complete, internally differentiated and autonomous version of their pre-Columbian culture than was the case in most of Mexico. In the latter country, the Indian groups are scattered remnants in what Mexican anthropologists have called "refuge areas" (Aguirre Beltrán, 1957). The Indians of Mexico represent "decapitated" peasant cultures. The "great tradition" of the stratified, urbanized, and highly differentiated societies of pre-Columbian Mexico was effectively

[2] The highlands of Chiapas are probably the part of Mexico where the Indian-ladino distinction is most pronounced. (In fact, the word "ladino" is not generally used elsewhere in Mexico in the sense of "non-Indian." In most of Mexico, the term "mestizo" means a monolingual Spanish-speaking person as distinguished from monolingual or bilingual speakers of indigenous languages. Thus, in modern Mexico, the word "mestizo" has lost the racial meaning it had in colonial times to refer to a person of mixed European-Indian ancestry.) In most other parts of Mexico, the remaining Indian pockets are for the most part strongly hispanicized, and the distinction between Indians (most of whom also speak Spanish) and mestizos is a very fluid one. See, for example, Foster, 1967, and Foster and Ospina, 1948, on Tzintzuntzan, Michoacán, in the Tarascan area.

smashed by the Conquest, as were the ruling classes who transmitted that tradition. Indian cultures survived only in their "de-differentiated" peasant variety, which is rural, relatively unstratified, and usually with only minimal artisanal division of labor. Also, the implantation of Catholicism and the ritual dependence of the Indians on the clergy seems much greater among groups in Chiapas than in much of Guatemala.

In the western Guatemala highlands, on the other hand, the various Indian groups managed to remain, until the late nineteenth century, virtually autonomous cultures and complete, self-sufficient, ongoing societies. They retained their stratified, partly urbanized, and highly differentiated character; they preserved nearly complete religious independence from the Catholic Church, continuing in some cases to use the Maya calendar in the cycle of ritual activities. In Guatemala, many Indian groups were until recently tribute-paying, but otherwise largely autonomous societies, living on the fringe of the area of Spanish control. In most of Mexico, the Indians were survivors of broken societies reduced to a direct symbiotic serfdom involving a sixteenth-century Spanish ethos of disdain for manual labor (Colby, 1966). Such symbiosis led to their hispanization or forced them to live as fugitive peasants in the refuge areas. In Mexico, to remain Indian means staying permanently on the margin of political, economic, and social life, at both the national and the local levels. In Guatemala, the various Indian groups are in a subordinate position nationally, but not locally in areas where they are in overwhelming majorities.

The Ixil area illustrates the two basic cultural facts of the Guatemalan situation mentioned earlier. The use of Spanish as a lingua franca is quite widespread even among Ixil women and children. In the urban Ixil areas bilingualism, at least in its elementary form, is considerably more common than, for example, among the Tzeltal-

Tzotzil groups of Chiapas. Also, the Ixil have more knowledge of the ladino world; they are more familiar with the material culture (e.g. houses, furniture, implements), the monetary economy, and with the organs of government; this is particularly true of the urban population and the migrant workers. Yet, "passing" is less frequent than in Chiapas. This is not due to resistance to assimilation on the part of the ladinos. In both areas, the local ladinos tend to be favorable to assimilation, even though very few do anything actively to foster it.

It is true that the Guatemalan government has not undertaken nearly as much to hispanicize and integrate the Indians as has the Mexican government through the Instituto Nacional Indigenista (INI). Nebaj's Escuela de Castellanización and some rudimentary lower primary schools in the rural areas represented until quite recently the only significant achievements of the government affecting Indians in the Ixil zone.[3] The Mexican INI, on the other hand, conducted many extensive projects in the fields of rural education, hygiene, road construction, water supply, soil conservation, reforestation, and agriculture. INI has undoubtedly been a major source of planned social change in Chiapas. Much of the answer to the problem of the rigidity of the ethnic line in Ixil country is found, however, in the characteristics of the Indian group itself.

Since Ixil culture is itself partly urban and differentiated in terms of occupations and social status, none of the phenomena which, in Mexico, are first steps in a nearly inescapable process of ladinoization have the same consequences in Guatemala. Urbanization, literacy, knowledge of Spanish, and the adoption of an urban occupation such as shopkeeping are all compatible with retention of mem-

3 Now the Guatemalan Department of Education has begun to emulate the Mexican INI by training Indian *promotores* who, after finishing the sixth grade, are given a year's training in Chichicastenango and return to teach in Indian villages. Some of them have begun to work in the Ixil zone.

bership in a group which already incorporates these elements.

At the level of individual motivation, there is little incentive to "pass." Those aspects of ladino culture which are most desired, primarily material objects and technical skills, can be acquired through a process of social mobility within the Indian group. Other facets of ladino culture, such as religion, are perceived as alien and undesirable. Ixil culture is differentiated enough to make selective adaptation from a similarly differentiated culture quite possible while preserving one's cultural identity. Also, the advantages in "passing" are not all that obvious. Local ladinos are in a position vis à vis Indians that is too precarious and not sufficiently superior to make membership in their group very desirable. The security of membership in the Ixil community must seem to most people preferable to the uncertain prospect of acceptance into the ladino group.

In addition to all of these factors, the Ixil community itself exhibits considerable group solidarity. This is clearly illustrated in the recent revival of traditional religion, resentment of the catechists, and recapture of political offices by the traditionalists. Those few individuals who emulate ladino manners and dress are regarded with a mixture of hostility and ridicule, and are the subject of adverse gossip. Conversely, most Ixil show great pride in their dress and traditions, and in Nebaj and Cotzal welcome the stranger who expresses respect for and interest in their culture.

Ixil ethnic solidarity is reinforced by a stress on harmonious social order in Ixil culture. Fear of social discord places considerable restraint on types of self-assertion that would be disruptive. Among the Tzeltal-Tzotzil groups of Chiapas, on the other hand, there seems to be more emphasis on the protection of individual integrity than on social harmony (Colby, 1967). In Chiapas, cases of homicide against suspected witches, for example, are relatively common, a fact which has no counterpart in Ixil country. (Though the Ixil believe in witchcraft, suspects are not murdered.) These regional differences in values probably affect collective reactions to passing. To a Chiapas Indian, "passing" is more a personal matter affecting his personal identity; to an Ixil, passing is potentially a breach of ethnic solidarity, and tends to be looked upon with disfavor, as we have seen earlier.

As soon as the Guatemalan Indian moves out of the area inhabited by his own language group, however, the situation changes entirely. He finds himself in the position of a stranger to both ladino culture and the local Indian group. Lacking any strong incentives to assimilate into the latter, and encountering little resistance from the former, the advantages of membership in the dominant group are sufficient to explain gradual ladinoization. This is all the more likely if, as is frequently the case, the migrant already had more knowledge of Spanish than of the local Maya language when he first arrived, and if he moved as an individual or as a nuclear family and had to sever most kin ties. Thus the apparent paradox—of relative fluidity of ethnic distinctions at the national level and local rigidity of the same—is readily understandable. Horizontal mobility is *the* way of crossing the ethnic line.

In fact, it is somewhat misleading to characterize Guatemala as a bicultural country. To be sure, the various Maya language groups are fairly closely related, but from the point of view of the subjective perception of group differences, cleavages and solidarity, there are two "models" of Guatemalan society which are equally valid. Most ladinos tend to view their country in dualistic terms; of course, they perceive differences between Indian groups, but to them the all-important cleavage is that which separates ladinos from all Indian groups put together. Generally, the Indians tend to have a more fragmented view of their country. Although they readily perceive linguistic similarities between their own group and other Maya groups, they have relatively little feeling of solidarity qua Indians. Rather, they tend to regard their own local municipio group, or perhaps their linguistic group, as one community among many. The ladinos are simply one such group, albeit an important one.

Terms of reference used by ladinos and Indians are a good indication of the subjective perception of group differences. When referring to the out-group, the ladinos almost invariably use the terms *indígenas, naturales, indios,* or *inditos,* all of which refer generically to all Indians. They only specify the language or local group when that specific item of information is relevant. Indians also use the above terms, especially *naturales* when speaking Spanish, but they will also frequently speak of themselves as "kumo·l" or "Ixil," and will refer to Indians from other areas as "people from Sacapulas," for example; ladinos, on the other hand, are called by the generic term *muˀs* irrespective of place of residence. (Indians now begin to use the word *gringo* in reference to North Americans, and more generally to foreigners.)

Thus, by putting different degrees of salience on different criteria or at different levels of group segmentation, ladinos and Indians have widely different views of their society. The former tend to think in dualistic terms, the latter in terms of multiple groups. This differential subjective perception of pluralism within the same society is one of the least studied and yet one of the most important aspects of plural societies.

The whole problem of culture change as it relates to ethnic membership calls for more complex models than have often been used. The first coherent approach, that of acculturation theory, was concerned mostly with changes in cultural forms. When users of different cultures come into contact, they "borrow" or exchange culture traits.

The main direction of change is from the more differentiated and technologically developed culture to the "simpler" one. Material culture, especially those items which increase productive capacity, safety, comfort, or various forms of gratification (e.g., tools, weapons, clothes, liquor) tend to be adopted first. The main questions then become:

What factors, beyond the obvious technological and utilitarian ones, determine the selectivity of culture change? Why are certain groups highly receptive to change and others less so; why are there individual differences in receptivity to change within groups; and why are certain foreign items "accepted" in a given culture while others are rejected?

Given the functional view of the society-culture, what kinds of adaptive changes are unleashed within the "recipient" culture in response to exogenous changes? Why do certain cultures seem to be highly adaptive while others are shattered by contact?

At least in North America, whence the bulk of culture-change studies have come, answers were sought mainly at two levels. At the individual level, psychologically or psychoanalytically inclined anthropologists have searched for those factors in the personality or life experience of individuals which account for differential responses within a given culture. At the sociocultural level, the explanation was sought in terms of congruence or compatibility of basic values and institutions. "Superficial" items—that is, those that are value-neutral and do not appreciably affect the institutional structure—are easily adopted, and so are those items which are generally congruent with the recipient cultures. Forced culture change from the outside, on the other hand, frequently results in "social disorganization" because of basic incompatibilities in institutions or values.

Much previous work attempted to understand processes of change in the "cultural inventory" of groups defined in terms of observable cultural uniformities. Legitimate as this approach is, it underemphasizes at least two important elements of the problem. First, an ethnic group is not only defined objectively by cultural uniformities of language, values, child-rearing practices, and so on. (In fact, the individual range of behavior within a group is often quite wide, but we are not concerned with this aspect of the problem here.) More important, for our purposes, is the fact that ethnicity is also a matter of *subjective* identification by members of the group. This subjective identification is itself the product of a context of social relationships both within the group and between ethnic groups. In other words, the subjective definition of ethnicity is determined partly by ties of social solidarity within the group and partly by relations of cooperation, conflict, domination, rejection, and so on with members of other groups. Ethnic cleavages, or indeed cleavages within ethnic groups, result from both centripetal and centrifugal forces. Since there can be no sense of "we" without a corresponding sense of "they" (however shifting the reference groups may be), a pluralistic approach is imperative. When distinct groups are present, their perceptions of each other reciprocally affect their view of themselves and even their overt behavior.

In Guatemala, the ability to speak Spanish does not make one a ladino. This linguistic skill is a necessary but not a sufficient condition for being regarded as a ladino. In last analysis, the test of ethnic membership is the complex interplay of subjective definitions by the individual, his group, *and* the other groups. As we have seen, these subjectively defined affiliations are in good part a function of spatial mobility and the resulting patterns of physical propinquity.

This leads us to our second and related point, namely that cultural change must also be studied within the total social structure within which it takes place. For example, changes in the modalities of bridewealth payment must be understood within the context of the marriage and kinship structure, and changes in dress style in a stratified society must be related to the class structure. This point—that the social and the cultural are but two sides of the same reality—is, of course, widely accepted. However less obvious is its corollary—that, in plural societies, the study of culture change through contact must incorporate the social structure of the entire society and, more specifically, those aspects of it which define the relationships between constituent ethnic groups. Social stratification, political power, and relationships to the means of production, to mention only three crucial aspects of interethnic relations, are essential to an understanding of cultural dynamics. Sheer amount of contact allows one to say little about acculturation; more significant is whether contact came about through military conquest, trade, voluntary immigration, or chattel slavery; whether the economy is monetized or not, agrarian or industrial; whether the settlement pattern is dispersed or concentrated, nomadic or sedentary; whether the political system is representative or colonial; and so on. For example, one cannot study the acculturation of Afro-Americans without understanding the institutional complex of plantation slavery.

In summary, we have attempted to show in this monograph how the relations between two distinct yet interdependent ethnic groups constitute the source of both integration and conflict in a small, plural sub-society in Guatemala. Each group has its own clearly defined sphere of autonomy with its separate sets of institutions. Yet, the two groups share, albeit differentially, political, economic, and religious institutions. On the one hand, these common institutions are the very bases of integration of the plural society; on the other hand, the asymmetry in many of the interethnic relations generates conflicts. The area of institutional overlap which determines both the form and content of ethnic relations constitutes the very core of the plural society.

Beyond simply applying a new label to the study of ethnic relations, we try to show that in plural societies, the area of ethnic relations occupies a key analytical vantage point. To the extent that the constituent groups have lost their independent viability, they cannot be understood purely in terms of themselves. An understanding of each culture and, even more so, of change processes within it presupposes a historical and sociostructural study of the place occupied by each ethnic group in the larger plural society. Conversely, and whatever its intrinsic merits might be, the most competent monograph using the "culture group" as its unit of analysis will tell us less and less about contemporary societies and the significant social processes taking place within them.

APPENDIX A: NOTE ON SPELLING OF TERMS AND IXIL PHONOLOGY

The names of well-known towns, languages, and objects will be kept in their usual Guatemalan spelling even though Indian words are often inaccurately and inconsistently rendered. Thus Nebaj, Chajul, and Cotzal, representing Spanish approximations to the Ixil, are incorrect, ignoring as they do vowel length and glottal stops. We have retained these spellings, however, as they have long been the accepted way in Guatemalan writing. For smaller villages, hamlets, and other types of referents where the incorrectly spelled word-forms are less well known or have not appeared in print, we have used a more accurate spelling according to the rules of Ixil phonology in those cases where the terms were elicited.

Most of the phonemic values used in the transcription of Nebaj Ixil words have been suggested by R. Elliott (1960) in his phonemic analysis of Nebaj Ixil. For the purposes of our own work the following modifications have been made:

(1) *Length* has been added to the phonemic inventory, signalled by a raised dot.

(2) Standard linguistic symbols have been used instead of a practical alphabet.

The linguistic forms cited in the text have been rendered in terms of phonemic symbols whose sound values can be inferred from their respective position in a linguistic grid which specifies points of articulation horizontally and manner of articulation vertically:

MANNER	POINTS OF ARTICULATION							
	labial	*apico-dental*	*alveolar*	*apico-palatal*	*apico-palatal, retroflex*	*dorso-palatal*	*dorso-velar*	*glottal*
plain stops & affricates	p	t	¢	č	ç	k	q	
glottalized stops & affricates	b'	t'	¢'	č'	ç'	k'	q'	?
fricatives			s	š	ş			h
nasals	m	n						
flap		r						
lateral		l						
semivowels and loan phonemes	w	(d)		y		(g)		

The five vowel phonemes /a,e,i,o,u/ contrast with /a,e,i,o,u + length/, indicated by a /vowel + raised dot/ sequence.

Comparison of phonological and lexical properties is the base for placing Ixil together with Mam and Aguacatec in a Mayan language group called Mamean*. (*Terrence Kaufman, Review of: Languages of Guatemala, ed. by Marvin K. Mayers. In: IJAL 34, no. 3, 1968.)

APPENDIX B: GLOSSARY OF SPANISH AND IXIL WORDS

ˀA·q'i·, a calendar specialist and diviner; one of the types of Ixil priests who specialize in divination and knowledge of the Maya calendar. *ˀA·q'i·* is used when the day-keeping function is stressed, *'A·me·ša* when the divination function is signified.

Acción Católica, a militant lay Catholic organization engaged, among other things, in the "reconversion" of Guatemalan Indians.

Aguardiente, a form of cane alcohol over which the state claims a monopoly.

Ahijado, a godchild; *ahijada* in the feminine.

Alcalde, the mayor or highest municipal official.

Alcalde auxiliar, an official recommended by the principals of an *aldea* and approved by the municipal council to head an aldea. Can be removed from office by the *alcalde.*

Aldea, a subdivision of a *municipio,* consisting of a small village and surrounding hamlets called *caseríos.*

Alguacil (*şe·mpo·b'al*), a low-status municipal official in charge of menial chores, sometimes called *mayor,* but not to be confused with the four *mayores* of a higher-level office.

B'a·l mertoma, the "father" or highest ranking religious official in an Ixil *cofradía.*

Ba·lwa¢ti·s, a prayer-sayer; one of the types of traditional Ixil priests.

B'aşa rišitol, the highest Indian municipal official in Nebaj who holds the position of second *regidor.* (In Ixil *b'aṣa* means first.) In Chajul and Cotzal, where all the officials are Indians, this term is used for the first regidor.

B'o·q'ol b'a·lwa¢tis, the Ixil high priest in Nebaj who keeps the day count and decides on the dates of ceremonies.

B'o·q'ol tenam, the Ixil leader of the *principales* in Nebaj; a kind of *primus inter pares* among "elder statesmen."

Caballería, a land area equal to approximately 45 hectares.

Cabecera, the town which serves as the administrative center of the *municipio.*

Cantón, a section of a town, a neighborhood.

Caporal, a foreman; on a plantation, the lowest-level supervisor, often an Indian.

Caserío, a hamlet pertaining to an *aldea;* with the town *cantones,* the smallest subdivision of the *municipio.*

Catequista, an Indian who has been recently "reconverted" to orthodox Catholicism, usually a member of *Acción Católica.*

Čusul (*maestro de coro* in Spanish), an Indian church official who officiates at important *cofradía* ceremonies, burials, and other religious activities traditionally associated with the church.

Cofradía, a religious brotherhood linked with the cult of a saint; the most important type of religious association in Ixil society. The distinction between *cofradías* and *hermandades* of earlier centuries no longer exists in the three Ixil towns.

Colono, a settler or permanent worker on a *finca.*

Compadrazgo, literally "co-fatherhood"; the ties and customs connected with ritual kinship in the Catholic Church; the ties linking godchildren, godparents, and biological parents.

Compadre, literally "co-father"; a reciprocal term of address and reference used between a person's godparent and his biological parents; its feminine form is *comadre,* or "co-mother."

Contratista, a labor recruiter, often a ladino; also known as *enganchador* or *habilitador.* The term *contratista,* emphasizing the contractual aspect in which indebtedness is limited, is preferred.

Costumbre, literally "custom"; the term generally used by both Ixil and ladinos to refer to Indian religious ritual.

Cuerda, a measure of area equal to 625 square *varas,* or slightly over 500 m^2.

Departamento, any of the 22 largest administrative and geographical units into which Guatemala is divided; a province; *departamentos* are subdivided into *municipios.*

Encomendero, the holder of an *encomienda.*

Encomienda, a land grant made by the Spanish Crown to settlers in the New World.

Finca, a land estate or plantation.

Finquero, owner of a *finca.*

Fiscal, in colonial times, a religious official who was the right hand of the parish priest. Current functions are similar to that of the *čusul* and involve *cofradía* ceremonies, funerals, and other activities associated with the church.

Gobernador, the chief official of a *departamento.*

Habilitador, a labor contractor; also called *contratista* or *enganchador.*

Indígena, one of the terms used to refer to Indians; the most common official term; other terms include *indio* and *natural.*

Instituto Nacional Indigenista, the Mexican Indian Service; its Guatemalan counterpart is called the *Instituto Indigenista Nacional.*

Intendente, an appointed municipal official who, during the presidency of Jorge Ubico, performed the functions of alcalde.

Jefe político, the chief appointed official of a *departamento* who, during the presidency of Jorge Ubico, performed the functions of *gobernador.*

Juez de paz, the lowest judge in the Guatemalan court hierarchy; this function is often combined with that of alcalde.

Juzgado, tribunal or courthouse; the term used in Nebaj to designate the town hall, which is formally known as *Alcaldía Municipal.*

Kub'a·l, the supreme god in the Ixil pantheon; literally "our father."

Kuçduç Mariy, the highest ranking *cofradía* in Nebaj, that of the Virgin Mary of the Assumption, the patron saint of Nebaj.

Madrina, a godmother.

Maestro de coro (*čusul* in Ixil), an Indian church official who officiates at important *cofradía* ceremonies, burials, and other religious activities traditionally associated with the church.

Mam, one of the largest Maya language groups in Guatemala; also an Ixil prayer-sayer in Chajul.

Manzana, a measure of area equal to 16 *cuerdas,* or 10,000 square *varas.*

Matrimonio de hecho, a common-law marriage; stable concubinage.

Mayor, one of four ranked municipal officials below the status of *regidor,* but above that of *alguacil* and *policía.*

Mayordomo (*mertoma* in Ixil), one of ten ranked office-holders in an Indian *cofradía.*

Mertoma (*mayordomo* in Spanish), one of ten ranked office-holders in an Indian *cofradía.*

Minifundia, a small land estate.

Mozo, an unskilled wage laborer.

Municipio, a subdivision of a *departamento;* a district or county including a town and its rural hinterland; *municipios* are themselves divided into *aldeas.*

Muʔs, the Ixil term for ladino.

Natural, an "aborigine"; one of the terms used in reference to Indians.

Obreros, the lower social stratum of Nebaj ladinos; literally "workers."

Oidor, a member of the *Audiencia,* which was a kind of supervisory commission overlooking the Spanish colonial administration.

Padrino, a godfather.

Partido Institucional Democrático (PID), the conservative party, which lost power in 1966.

Partido Revolucionario (PR), the liberal-reformist party, which won the presidency of Guatemala in 1966.

Piškal (*fiscal* in Spanish), in colonial times, a religious official who was the right hand of the parish priest. Current functions are similar to that of the *čusul* and involve *cofradía* ceremonies, funerals, and other activities associated with the church.

Policía, the police; in Nebaj, the unpaid Indian youths whose main duty is to patrol the streets at night.

Principal, an Indian "elder statesman" who has occupied high political or religious office.

Q'esla Kub'a·l, the supreme god in the Ixil pantheon; "great father."

Regidor, a municipal councillor ranked from one through six or seven according to the number of council members.

Sacristán, a parish official who combines custodial, care-taking, and ritual functions.

Šaqal, one of four assistants of the *maestro de coro* and *fiscal.* Duties include ringing the church bells during processions.

Síndico, an official of the municipal council whose functions include registering land transactions.

Sociales, the upper social stratum among the ladinos of Nebaj.

Trago, cane alcohol of legal or illegal manufacture.

Tributario, a tribute-paying Indian in colonial times.

Vara, measure of length equal to 836 mm; a ceremonial staff of approximately that length carried by officers of municipal councils. Also used to refer to the sacred divining bundle of the *ʔa·me·ša.*

APPENDIX C: STATISTICAL TABLES

TABLE 1

ETHNIC COMPOSITION OF GUATEMALA [a]
(1778–1964)

Year	Percent Indian	Percent ladino	Total population in thousands
1778	78.4	21.6	396
1880	64.7	35.3	1,225
1921	64.8	35.2	2,005
1940	55.7	44.3	2,400
1950	53.6	46.4	2,791
1964	43.3	56.7	4,284

[a] The census divides the population into "indigenous" and "non-indigenous" according to the criterion of "social estimation in which the person is held in the place where the census is taken."

TABLE 2

POPULATION OF THE THREE IXIL MUNICIPIOS

	Total population	*Area in km²*	*Inhabitants per km²*	*Percent urban* [a]	*Percent Indian*	*Percent illiterate*
			1950			
Nebaj	13,253	608	21.8	26.3	91.7	92.7
Cotzal	9,244	182	50.8	28.5	92.5	92.6
Chajul	8,258	1,524	5.4	34.8	91.0	95.1
Department of Quiché	174,911	8,379	20.8	9.4	84.1	91.7
			1964			
Nebaj	23,374	608	38.4	22.4	92.3	92.0
Cotzal	12,150	182	66.7	29.7	93.6	88.8
Chajul	13,497	1,524	8.9	30.9	89.6	93.6
Department of Quiché	255,260	8,378	30.5	14.9	84.7	— [b]

[a] "Urban" refers to the population which lives in the town which serves as administrative seat of the municipio. Each municipio has a town as its center and a rural hinterland.

[b] Information not available.

TABLE 3

EDUCATION AND PERCEPTION OF PASSING, LADINO SAMPLE

	Education		
	8 years or less	*More than 8 years*	
	frequencies		
Passing possible	5	12	17
Passing impossible	16	7	23
Totals	21	19	40

$\chi^2 = 4.8$, $p < .05$

TABLE 4

LADINO ACCEPTANCE OF CONTACT WITH INDIANS

Question	*Yes*	*No*	*No reply*
Would you accept an Indian as servant?	40	0	0
Would you visit an Indian in his house?	40	0	0
Would you accept an Indian as neighbor?	38	1	1
Would you accept an Indian as godchild?	38	1	1
Would you go for a walk with an Indian?	34	5	1
Would you play sports with an Indian?	32	5	3
Would you accept an Indian as a close friend?	26	13	1
Would you dance with an Indian?	25	12	3
Would you invite an Indian to a meal in your house?	25	14	1
Would you choose an Indian as godparent of your child?	10	29	1
Would you choose an Indian as a spouse?	9	26	5

TABLE 5

RELATIONSHIP BETWEEN ACTUAL INTERETHNIC CONTACT AND ACCEPTANCE OF HYPOTHETICAL CONTACT, LADINO SAMPLE

	Actual Contact with Indians		
	High	*Low*	
	frequencies		
Acceptance of hypothetical contact with	15	4	19
Indians	4	17	21
Totals	19	21	40

$\chi^2 = 12.1,\ p < .001$

TABLE 6

AGE OF DEATH, PARISH OF NEBAJ [a]
(Jan. 1965–July 1966)

Age in years	*Frequency*
Less than 1	43
1–5	174
6–10	38
11–20	64
21–30	43
31–40	38
41–50	27
51–60	23
61–70	27
71–80	18
81–90	7
91–100	3
Total	505

[a] This is a fairly complete registry of all deaths in Nebaj and vicinity, for practically everybody gets buried in the Nebaj cemeteries according to Catholic rites. (It excludes only the small Protestant minority.)

TABLE 7

CHANGES IN ETHNIC COMPOSITION BY DEPARTMENT
(1940–1964)

Department	*Percent Indian*			*Change in percent Indian*		*Rank order of change in Indian population*	
	1940	*1950*	*1964*	*1940–50*	*1950–64*	*1940–50*	*1950–64*
Alta Verapaz	93.9	93.4	91.9	− 0.5	− 1.5	18	18.5
Baja Verapaz	60.4	58.5	52.3	− 1.9	− 6.2	12	13
Chimaltenango	86.6	77.6	76.1	− 9.0	− 1.5	2	18.5
Chiquimula	61.0	61.9	49.6	+ 0.9	−12.3	21	5
Escuintla	18.9	15.9	7.1	− 3.0	− 8.8	8	8
Guatemala	19.5	18.1	10.3	− 1.4	− 7.8	14	11.5
Huehuetenango	76.5	73.3	67.5	− 3.2	− 5.8	6.5	15
Izabal	19.0	17.2	11.5	− 1.8	− 5.7	13	16
Jalapa	49.5	50.5	42.6	+ 1.0	− 7.9	22	10
Jutiapa	22.2	19.6	0.4	− 2.6	−19.2	9	1
Petén	32.3	27.9	24.9	− 4.4	− 3.0	4.5	17
Progreso	16.1	9.4	0.4	− 6.7	− 9.0	3	7
Quetzaltenango	69.8	67.6	54.0	− 2.2	−13.6	10.5	4
Quiché	84.8	84.1	84.7	− 0.7	+ 0.6	17	22
Retalhuleu	56.3	51.9	33.9	− 4.4	−18.0	4.5	2
Sacatepéquez	54.8	51.6	45.6	− 3.2	− 6.0	6.5	14
San Marcos	73.8	72.5	60.5	− 1.3	−12.0	15	6
Santa Rosa	10.5	9.4	0.9	− 1.1	− 8.5	16	9
Sololá	93.3	93.8	92.7	+ 0.5	− 1.1	19	21
Suchitepéquez	66.9	67.7	54.0	− 2.2	−13.7	10.5	3
Totonicapán	96.1	96.8	95.4	+ 0.7	− 1.4	20	20
Zacapa	30.9	19.2	11.4	−11.7	− 7.8	1	11.5

BIBLIOGRAPHY

Adams, Richard E. W.
1966 The ceramic chronology of the southern Maya. Dittoed manuscript.

Adams, Richard N.
1956a Encuesta sobre la cultura de los ladinos en Guatemala. Guatemala, Seminario de Integración Social Guatemalteca.
1956b Cultural components of Central America. American Anthropologist, 58:881–907.

—— (editor)
1957 Political change in Guatemalan Indian communities. Middle American Research Institute Publication 24, New Orleans, Tulane University.

Aguirre Beltrán, Gonzalo
1946 La población negra de México, 1519–1810. México, Universidad Nacional Autónoma de México.
1957 El proceso de aculturación. México, Universidad Nacional Autónoma de México.

Anonymous
1965 Guatemala: Tenencia de la tierra y desarrollo socioeconómico del sector agrícola. Unión Panamericana, Comité Interamericano de Ciencias Agrícolas.
1966 Censo de población 1964. Guatemala. Departamento de Censos y Encuestas.

Arriola, Jorge Luis (editor)
1958 Economía de Guatemala. Guatemala, Seminario de Integración Social Guatemalteca.

Balandier, Georges
1963 Sociologie actuelle de l'Afrique noire. Paris, Presses Universitaires de France.

Bancroft, Hubert Howe

1883 History of Central America. San Francisco, A. L. Bancroft and Co.

Barth, Fredrik

1966 Models of social organization. Royal Anthropological Institute Occasional Paper No. 23.

Becquelin, Pierre

1966 Excavations at Acul, Guatemala, a preliminary report. Typed manuscript.

Benedict, Burton

1961 Indians in a plural society. London, Colonial Research Studies.

1962 Stratification in plural societies. American Anthropologist, 64:1235–1246.

Boeke, J. H.

1953 Economics and economic policy of dual societies. New York, Institute of Pacific Relations.

Brasseur de Bourbourg, Charles Etienne

1857 Histoire des nations civilisées du Mexique et de l'Amérique centrale. Paris, Arthur Bertrand.

1961 Der Mann von Rabinal, oder der Tod des Gefangenen. Frankfurt, Suhrkamp.

Bunzel, Ruth

1952 Chichicastenango, a Guatemalan village. Locust Valley, N.Y., Augustin.

Burkitt, Robert

1930 Explorations in the highlands of western Guatemala. The Museum Journal, 21.1:41–72, illus. University Museum, University of Pennsylvania.

Carranza, Jesus E.

1956 El general Justo Rufino Barrios. Guatemala: Editorial del Ministerio de Educación Pública. 3rd ed. (pp. 14–15).

Coe, Michael D.

1966 The Maya. New York, Frederick A. Praeger.

Colby, Benjamin N.

1966a Ethnic relations in the Chiapas highlands of Mexico. Santa Fe, Museum of New Mexico Press.

1966b The Ixil Maya, a culture variation study in Guatemala. El Palacio, 73.4:26–38.

1967 Mesoamerican Psychological Orientations. In: Handbook of Middle American Indians, Vol. 9. Manning Nash (ed.).

Colby, Benjamin N., and Pierre L. van den Berghe

1961 Ethnic relations in southeastern Mexico. American Anthropologist, 63.4:772–792.

Colby, Lore M.

1966 Maal Ts'uch: Portrait of a young Ixil girl. El Palacio, 73.3:26–30.

Cook, S. F., and Woodrow Borah

1960 The Indian population of central Mexico 1531–1610. Ibero-Americana 44.

Cortes y Larraz, Pedro

1958 Descripción Geográfico-Moral de la Diocesis de Goathemala. Tomo II, pp. 45–50. Biblioteca "Goathemala" de la Sociedad de Geografía e Historia de Guatemala, Vol. XX.

de la Fuente, Julio

1965 Relaciones interétnicas. México, Instituto Nacional Indigenista.

Despres, Leo A.

1967 Cultural pluralism and nationalist politics in British Guiana. Chicago, Rand McNally.

1968 Anthropological theory, cultural pluralism, and the study of complex societies. Current Anthropology, 9.1:3–26.

Dessaint, Allain X.

1963 Effects of the hacienda and plantation systems on Guatemala's Indians. Practical Anthropology, 10, no. 4.

Elliott, Ray

1960 Ixil clause structure. In Mayan studies. I. B. Olson (ed.), Norman, Summer Institute of Linguistics.

Evans-Pritchard, E. E.

1940 The Nuer. London, Oxford University Press.

Ewald, Robert

1954 San Antonio Sacatepequez. Ann Arbor, University of Michigan, Ph.D. thesis.

Ferdon, E. H.

1959 Agricultural potential and the development of cultures. Southwestern Journal of Anthropology, 15:1–19.

Fortes, Meyer

1949 The web of kinship among the Tallensi. London, Oxford University Press.

Foster, George M.

1965 Peasant society and the image of the limited good. American Anthropologist, 67:293–315.

1967 Tzintzuntzan, Mexican peasants in a changing world. Boston, Little, Brown and Company.

Foster, George M., assisted by Gabriel Ospina

1948 Empire's children: the people of Tzintzuntzan. Mexico, Smithsonian Institution, Institute of Social Anthropology, Publication no. 6.

Fuentes y Guzmán, Francisco Antonio de

1933 Recordación Flórida. Guatemala, Biblioteca Goathemala, 8.

Furnivall, J. S.

1948 Colonial policy and practice. Cambridge, Cambridge University Press.

Gage, Thomas

1958 Thomas Gage's travels in the New World. J. Eric S. Thompson (ed.). Norman, University of Oklahoma Press.

Garcia Pelaez

1951 Memorias para la Historia del Antiguo Reyno de Guatemala. Guatemala.

Geertz, Clifford

1965 The social history of an Indonesian town. Cambridge, MIT Press.

Genet, Jean

1927 Histoire des peuples mayas-quichés. Paris, Genet.

Gillin, John

1948 Race relations without conflict, a Guatemalan town. American Journal of Sociology, 53:337–343.

1951 The culture of security in San Carlos. New Orleans, Tulane University.

1952 Ethos and cultural aspects of personality. In:

Heritage of conquest, S. Tax (ed.). Glencoe, Free Press.

1958 San Luis Jilotepeque. Seminario de Integración Social Guatemalteca, no. 7. Guatemala, Ministerio de Educación Pública.

Gluckman, Max

1958 Analysis of a social situation in modern Zululand. Manchester, Manchester University Press.

Gonzalez Casanova, Pablo

1962 Sociedad plural y desarrollo: el caso de México. América Latina, 5, no. 4:31–61.

1963 Sociedad plural, colonialismo interno y desarrollo. América Latina, 6, no. 3:15–32.

1964 Société Plurale, Colonialisme Interne et Développement. Tiers Monde, 5:291–312.

1965 La democracia en México. México, Ediciones Era.

Goodenough, Ward H.

1963 Cooperation and change. New York, Russell Sage Foundation.

Haug, Marie R.

1967 Social and cultural pluralism as a concept in social system analysis. The American Journal of Sociology, 73:294–304.

Hoyt, Elizabeth

1955 The Indian laborer on Guatemala coffee fincas. Inter-American Economic Affairs.

Hunter, Monica

1936 Reaction to conquest. London. Oxford University Press.

Juarros, Domingo

1936 Compendio de la historia de la ciudad de Guatemala. Vol. II, Guatemala. Tipografía Nacional.

Kaufman, Terrence

1968 Review of: Languages of Guatemala, Marvin K. Mayers (editor). In: International Journal of American Linguistics, 34:224–231.

King, A. R.

1952 Changing cultural goals and patterns in Guatemala. American Anthropologist, 54:139–143.

Kuper, Hilda
1947 The uniform of colour. Johannesburg, Witwatersrand University Press.

Kuper, Leo
1965 An African bourgeoisie. New Haven, Yale University Press.

LaFarge, Oliver
1956 Etnología maya: secuencia de las culturas. In: Cultura indígena de Guatemala. Guatemala, Seminario de Integración Social Guatemalteca.
1947 Santa Eulalia: the religion of a Cuchumatan Indian town. Chicago, University of Chicago Press.

Las Casas, Bartholomé de
1909 Apologética historica de las Indias. Madrid, Bailly Bailliers e hijos.

Lewis, Oscar
1951 Life in a Mexican village: Tepoztlán restudied. Urbana, University of Illinois Press.

Lincoln, Jackson Steward
1945 An ethnological study of the Ixil Indians of the Guatemala highlands. Chicago, University of Chicago Microfilm Collection.

Malinowski, B., and J. de la Fuente
1957 La economía de un sistema de mercados en México. Un ensayo de etnografía contemporánea y cambio social en un valle mexicano. México, Acta Antropológica.

Marquard, Leo
1957 South Africa's colonial policy. Johannesburg, South African Institute of Race Relations.

Mayer, Adrian C.
1961 Peasants in the Pacific, a study of Fiji Indian rural society. London, Routledge and Kegan Paul.

Mayer, Philip
1961 Townsmen or tribesmen. Cape Town, Oxford University Press.

Mayers, Marvin K. (editor)
1966 Languages of Guatemala. The Hague, Mouton.

McBryde, Felix Webster

1934 Sololá: A Guatemalan town and Cakchiquel market center. New Orleans, Tulane University.

1945 Cultural and historical geography of Southwest Guatemala. Washington, D.C., Smithsonian Institution.

Milla, José

1882 Historia de la América Central, Vol. II. Guatemala, El Progreso.

Mitchell, J. Clyde

1960 Tribalism and the plural society. London, Oxford University Press.

Monteforte Toledo, Mario

1959 Guatemala, monografía sociológica. México, Universidad Nacional Autónoma de México.

Morales Urrutia, Mateo

1961 La división política y administrativa de la república de Guatemala. Guatemala, Iberia-Gutenberg. Vol. I.

Morley, Sylvanus Griswold

1946 The ancient Maya. Stanford, Stanford University Press.

Mosk, Sanford A.

1958 Economía cafetalera de Guatemala durante el periodo 1850–1918. In Jorge Luis Arriola (ed.), Economía de Guatemala. Guatemala, Seminario de Integración Social Guatemalteca.

Nash, Manning

1955 Cantel, the industrialization of a Guatemalan Indian community. Chicago, University of Chicago, Ph.D. thesis.

1958a Machine age Maya. American Anthropological Association, Memoir no. 87.

1958b Political relations in Guatemala. Social and Economic Studies, 7:65–75.

1966 Primitive and peasant economic systems. San Francisco, Chandler.

Olaverreta, Joseph de

1935 (Description of three Ixil towns, written in 1740). Boletín del Archivo General del Gobierno de Guatemala. Vol. I, no. 1. Octubre, pp. 22, 23.

Parsons, Talcott

1951 The social system. Glencoe, The Free Press.

Recinos, Adrian

1947 Popol Vuh, las historias antiguas del Quiché. México.

Redfield, Robert

1939 Primitive merchants of Guatemala. Quarterly Journal of Inter-American Relations, 1:42–56.

1941 The folk culture of Yucatan. Chicago, University of Chicago Press.

1956a The relations between Indians and ladinos in Agua Escondida, Guatemala. América Indígena, 16:253–276.

1956b Peasant society and culture. Chicago, University of Chicago Press.

Reina, Ruben E.

1959 Continuidad de la cultura indígena en una comunidad Guatemalteca. Seminario de Integración Social Guatemalteca, no. 4. Guatemala, Ministerio de Educación Pública.

1960 Chinautla, a Guatemalan Indian community. New Orleans, Tulane University.

1966 The law of the saints. Indianapolis: Bobbs-Merrill.

Remesal, Antonio de

1919 Historia de la provincia de San Vincente de Chiapa y Guatemala. Madrid.

1932 Historia general de las Indias occidentales, y particular de gobernación de Chiapa y Guatemala. Guatemala, Biblioteca Goathemala.

Roberts, Robert E. E.

1948 A comparison of ethnic relations in two Guatemala communities. Acta Americana, 6:135–151.

Rodriguez, Mario

1965 Central America, Englewood Cliffs, Prentice-Hall.

Schmidt, Lester

1966 Migrant labor on the Pacific Coast of Guatemala. University of Wisconsin, Ph.D. thesis.

Siegel, Morris

1941 Religion in western Guatemala: a product of acculturation. American Anthropologist, 43:62–76.

1942 Effects of culture contact on the form of the family in a Guatemalan village. Journal of the Royal Anthropological Institute, 72:55–68.

1954 Culture change in San Miguel Acatán, Guatemala. Phylon, 15:165–176.

Silvert, K. H.

1954 A study in government: Guatemala. New Orleans, Tulane University.

Smith, A. L., and Alfred V. Kidder

1951 Excavations at Nebaj. Washington, D.C., Carnegie Institution Publication, no. 594.

Smith, M. G.

1965a The plural society in the British West Indies. Berkeley and Los Angeles, University of California Press.

1965b Social and cultural pluralism. In Pierre L. van den Berghe, (ed.), Africa, social problems of change and conflict. San Francisco, Chandler.

Stevens, Rayfred L.

1964 The soils of Middle America and their relation to Indian peoples and cultures. In Robert C. West (ed.), Handbook of Middle American Indians, Vol. I. Austin, University of Texas Press.

Steward, Julian H., and others

1956 The people of Puerto Rico; a study in social anthropology. Urbana, University of Illinois Press.

Stoll, Otto

1884 Zur Ethnographie der Republic Guatemala. Zürich.

1886 Guatemala, Reisen und Schilderungen aus den Jahren 1878–1883. Leipzig, Brockhaus.

1958 Etnografía de Guatemala. Guatemala. Seminario de Integración Social Guatemalteca.

Tamayo, Jorge L., and Robert C. West

1964 The hydrography of Middle America. In Robert C. West (ed.), Handbook of Middle American Indians, Vol. I. Austin, University of Texas Press.

Tax, Sol

1937 Municipios of the midwest highlands of Guatemala. American Anthropologist, 39:423–444.

1942 Ethnic relations in Guatemala. América Indígena 2, no. 4:43–48.

1952 Heritage of conquest. Chicago, The Free Press.

1953 Penny capitalism. Washington, D.C., Smithsonian Institution.

1956 La visión del mundo y las relaciones sociales en Guatemala, in Cultura indígena de Guatemala. Guatemala, Seminario de Integración Social Guatemalteca.

Termer, Franz

1957 Etnología y etnografía de Guatemala. Guatemala, Ministerio de Educación Pública.

Thomas, Olive B.

1954 The labor and social policies of coffee fiqueros in Guatemala. Iowa State College, Ph.D. dissertation.

Thompson, J. Eric S. (editor)

1958 Thomas Gage's travels in the New World. Norman, University of Oklahoma Press.

Tumin, Melvin

1949 Reciprocity and stability of caste in Guatemala. American Sociological Review. 14:17–25.

1950 The dynamics of cultural discontinuity in a peasant society. Social Forces, 29:135–141.

1952 Caste in a peasant society. Princeton, Princeton University Press.

van den Berghe, Gwendoline and van den Berghe, Pierre L.

1966 Compadrazgo and class in southeastern Mexico. American Anthropologist 68:1237–1244.

van den Berghe, Pierre L.

1963 Dialectic and functionalisms, toward a theoretical synthesis. American Sociological Review, 28:695–705.

1964 Toward a sociology of Africa. Social Forces, 43:11–18.

1965a Africa: social problems of change and conflict. San Francisco, Chandler.

1965b South Africa: a study in conflict. Middletown, Wesleyan University Press.

1967 Race and racism. New York, John Wiley.

1968 Ethnic membership and culture change in Guatemala. Social Forces.

van den Berghe, Pierre L., and Benjamin N. Colby

1961 Ladino-Indian relations in the highlands of Chiapas, Mexico. Social Forces, 40, no. 1:63–71.

Vasquez, Francisco

1937–38 Crónica de la provincia del santisimo nombre de Jesús de Guatemala. Tipografía Nacional.

Villacorta Calderon, José Antonio

1938 Prehistoria e historia antigua de Guatemala. Guatemala, Tipografía Nacional.

1942a Historia de la capitanía general de Guatemala. Guatemala, Tipografía Nacional.

1942b Rabinal Achí. Adaptación al castellano e interpretación nueva. Anales de la Sociedad de Geografía e Historia de Guatemala, 17, no. 5:353–375.

Vivo Escoto, Jorge A.

1964 Weather and climate of Mexico and Central America. In Robert C. West (ed.), Handbook of Middle American Indians. Vol. I. Austin, University of Texas Press.

Vogt, Evon Z.

1967 Tendencia de cambio en las tierras altas de Chiapas. América Indígena, 27:199–222.

Wagner, Philip L.

1964 Natural vegetation of Middle America. In Robert C. West (ed.), Handbook of Middle American Indians, Vol. I. Austin, University of Texas Press.

Wagley, Charles

1941 Economics of a Guatemalan village. American Anthropological Association, Memoir no. 58.

1949 The social and religious life of a Guatemalan village. American Anthropological Association, Memoir no. 71.

1953 Amazon town, a study of man in the tropics. New York, Macmillan.

1957 Santiago Chimaltenango. Seminario de Integración Social Guatemalteca, no. 4.

Wallace, Anthony F. C.

1961 Culture and personality. New York, Random House.

West, Robert C. (editor)

1964 Handbook of Middle American Indians, Vol. I. Austin, University of Texas Press.

Whetten, Nathan L.

1961 Guatemala, the land and the people. New Haven, Yale University Press.

Wisdom, Charles

1940 The Chorti Indians of Guatemala. Chicago, University of Chicago Press.

Wolf, Eric R.

1959 Sons of the shaking earth. Chicago, University of Chicago Press.

1966 Peasants. Englewood Cliffs, Prentice-Hall.

Woodward, R. L.

1966 Class privilege and economic development. The Consulado de Comercio of Guatemala 1793–1871. Chapel Hill, University of North Carolina Press.

Ximenez, Francisco

1926 Las Historias del origen de los indios de esta provincia de Guatemala. San Salvador, Biblioteca Nacional.

1929–30 Historia de la provincia de San Vicente de Chiapa y Guatemala. Guatemala, Biblioteca Goathemala.

Young, John Parke

1958 Moneda y finanzas centroamericanas. In Jorgé Luis Ariola (ed.), Economía de Guatemala. Guatemala, Seminario de Integración Social Guatemalteca.

Zarate, Alvan O.

1967 Principales patrones de migración interna en Guatemala, 1964. Estudios Centroamericanos no. 3, Guatemala.

INDEX

ʔA·q'i· (diviner), 98
Acción Católica, 78, 82-83, 102-103; mentioned, 115; separate rituals, 135
Acculturation: theory, 2, 24, 180; dynamics, 92
Address forms, 147-149
Agave fiber industry, 83
Age differences in ethnic attitudes, 154. *See also* Ethnic Relations
Agrarian Reform Law (Decreto 900), 35
Agriculture: 29-30, 32-33, 145; subsistence, 33-34, 109; cash, xi, 12, 33-34; calendar, 99-100; labor, 107, 131-132; commerce, 172. *See also* Contracting, Wage labor
Aguirre Beltran, Gonzalo, ix
ʔAk'ul, road to, 129*n*
Alcalde: Mayor, 47, 66, 77; Pedaneo, 121; functions, 122; nomination of, 123; salary (Nebaj), 130
Alcohol consumption, 71, 73, 163-164, 168
Aldeas, colonial, 43, 60
Alvarado, Pedro de, 41
Ancestral spirits, 96-97
Arbenz: overthrown by United States, 35
Architecture: Spanish influence, 52;
Ixil, 58, 114; ladino, 111-112
Area of Ixil region. *See* Ixil region
Arias, Gaspar, 41
Art, 70, 71*n*. *See also* Dance
Artifacts, Ixil, 39
Assimilation rates: regional differences, 170, 175, 177
Audiencia de los Confines, 50
Autonomy of Ixil zone. *See* Ixil

Bacaro, Juan, 66
Balduini, Baltazar, 40, 47, 52, 52*n*, 53*n*, 60, 62, 68
Balensuela, Calletano, 69
B'a·lwa¢ti·š, 97, 141
Baptism, 134-135, 137
Barrier, ethnic. *See* Ethnic relations
Barrios, Justo Rufino, 70, 72
B'a·¢, 98. *See* Day gods
B'aṣa Rišitol, 123
Behavioral sanctions: religious, 97
Benedict, Ruth, 9
Biculturalism, 88; and ethnic membership, 91; in Guatemala, 179
Bilingualism: related to ethnic membership, 91, 92-93, 176
Black legend, 48-49
Blacks and social pluralism, 9; in U.S. status hierarchy, 18
Boleto de ornato, 121
B'o·q'ol b'a·lwa¢ti·š, 59, 97
B'o·q'ol tenam, 75, 113, 123, 124, 140
Brito, Juan, 71
Burial customs, 65, 68

Cabecera: defined, 83*n*
Caciques, 43 51
Calendar: described by Las Casas, 54; deities, 95-96, 98; 260-day ritual, 98-99; cycle, 98-99; agricultural, 99-100; correlation, 99, 120-121
Caletohil, 42
Cantons, 43, 115
Caste: in status hierarchies, 18; Ixil, 70; mentioned, 85, 91; workers, 115; barrier, 169-183. *See also* Ethnic affairs, class

Castellanización, Escuela de, 177
Castellanos, Francisco de, 42
Catechists, 788, 82-83, 102-103, 146; contact with traditionalists, 117; voting, 125; militancy, 135, 139
Catholic Action. *See* Acción Católica
Catholicism: resistance to, 67-69, 138, 176; orthodoxy, 82-83, 94, 146; influence on traditional religion, 96, 134
Čawela Hu·, 160. *See also* Dance
Census: definition of ethnic group, 87*n*
Ceremonies, 54; dawn, 98; music, 101; Government inauguration, 142; Čawela Hu·, 160
Chajul: interethnic commuting, 21; altitude, 27; prehispanic period, 40; reduction of, 52; hostility, 67, 81; religious importance, 81; school, 83; cofradías, 102; party affiliation, 127; fiesta, 165-168
Chama Mountains, 26
Change: religious, 82-83; in ladino stratification, 111
Chiapas, 103, 113, 136, 174, 178; ethnic fluidity in, 174, 177
Chols, 60
Chichicastenango, 38, 145
Christ of Golgatha, 166
Church: early locations, 53; colonial organization, 55-56; colonial income and wealth, 56-57; colonial power, 59; records, 62; wealth and influence in 18th century, 64-65; size, 82; Cotzal, 83; attendance, 101-102; confession, 103, 135; worship, 134; function, 138; Chajul, 139; dualism, 139; relations with the state, 140-141. *See also* Religion
Citizenship: in plural societies, 12*n*
Class. *See* Social Class
Clothing: Ixil, 93
Cloud god, 96
Čo·, 98. *See also* Day gods
Coffee: effect on Ixil zone, 71; in Ixil area, 83; plantations, 107-108
Cofradías: early establishment of, 54-55; increase in 18th century, 63; persecution, 66; infiltration by catechists, 82-83; ceremonies, 101, 141, 163-164; appointment of officials, 102; rural members, 105; mass for, 135, 139; of ladinos, 159
Colonialism: internal, 3; typical polity characteristics, 11, 15; Nebaj, 84
Colonos, 107
Comisionado militar, 122
Commerce: division of, 106, 133; expansion of, 131; agricultural, 172
Commercial crops, 33. *See also* Export: of goods and produce
Communication, 37; mail service, 31, telephone and telegraph, 31
Communion, 135
Commuting: cultural and social, 21
Compadrazgo, 21, 136-137, 153, 160
Compadre (diviner), 98
Competitive ethnic relations: attitudes, 148; model, 152-153; Ixil interview question concerning, 157*n*. *See also* Ethnic Relations
Concentration of early Ixil, 44, 52
Concubinage: interethnic, 161-162. *See also* Sex
Confession. *See* Church
Conflict: sociology, 4; in plural societies, 13-14; in democratic countries, 14; as stabilizing factor, 14; between Indians and ladinos, 102, 138, 155; between Catechists and traditionalists, 103, 117, 125; economic, 142
Conquest: states, 13; of Guatemala, 40-42; of Ixil, 41-42; consequences of, 44; interval between military defeat and missionary effort (six-year limbo), 51
Consensus: of values, 14; in subjective ranking, 18
Contracting: labor, 72-73, 108, 132-133; contratistas, 140
Co-parenthood, 21, 136
Corn (maize) cultivation, 29-30
Corregimiento, 47-48, 66
Corruption in government, 121, 140
Cortes y Larraz, Pedro, 65
Costumbre, 94, 145
Cotzal: altitude, 27; defeat by Spaniards, 42; depopulation of, 45; Church, 83; population in 1964,

83; school enrollment, 83; party membership, 127; fiesta, 168
Counterrevolution, 35, 77
Creation myth. *See* Myth
Crops, 32-33; cash, xi, 12, 33-34; *See also* Agriculture
Crosses, 71; integrative focus, 135
Cuchumatanes Mountains, 26
Cultivation. *See* Agriculture
Culture: as analytical unit, 2-3; change, 4, 53-54, 82, 93, 169-184; contact, 4, 22; subjective perception, 7; integration, 9; commuting (biculturalism), 21, 22-24; Marginality, 21; change theory, 22-24; dynamics, 23, 183; variations, 81; in social definition, 86-87, 87*n*, 88, 91-92; conservatism, 89; in political influence, 118; superiority, 144-145; objective vs. subjective differences, 173; psychological approach to culture change, 181
₵'iKin. *See* Day gods
Ç'iˀ. *See* Day gods

Dance, 165; drama, 71, 71*n*
Dawn ceremonies, 98
Day gods, 95-96; attributes, 98
Debt: peonage, 133-134; collection, 134
Deference, 149, 151
de la Fuente, Julio, ix
Deities, 95-99
Democracy: Herrenvolk, 11; in pluralistic societies, 11*n*, 12*n*
Demography: Guatemala, 25-27; Ixil area, 27
Dialect: intelligibility, 82, 116, 167
Diet: Indian, 30, 58, 104
Diocesan seat, 38
Disenfranchisement, 86, 126
Disputes: Indian-ladino, 155. *See also* Rebellion
Diviner, 97-98
Divorce, 68
Dominicans, 51-52, 57
Dress: Ixil. *See* Ixil, clothing
Drinking, 71, 73, 145, 163-164, 168
Dry season, 28
Durkheim, 9

Ecology of social class, 115
Economy: cohesiveness, 12; institutions and interdependence in plural societies, 12-13; well-being of early colonists, 57; self-sufficiency, 71, 130; paramountcy of Nebaj, 81; development, 84, 142; aspects of fiestas, 129, 163-164; interdependence of in urban-rural areas, 131-132; technological superiority, 156
Education: early Nebaj school, 72; in Chajul, 83; ladino domination, 85; as component of social definition, 88; as qualification for political office, 119; as related to ethnic attitudes, 154; as related to ethnic contact, 156; school enrollment, 159; Guatemalan national program, 177*n*
Egalitarian model of ethnic relations. *See* Ethnic Relations
Election: Chajul, 82; voter classification, 86; Nebaj, 123-124, 126
Elevation of Ixil towns. *See* Ixil region
El Quiché. *See* Quiche
Employment. *See* Wage labor
Encomiendas, 46-47; abolished, 61
Entertainment, 159
Epidemics, 44-45, 45*n*, 62, 64, 65
Escuela de Castellanización, 177
Estates of ladinos, 107. *See also* Fincas
Ethnic relations: in a pluralistic perspective, x-xi; group as analytical unit, 2-3, 16; parity, 14; interethnic commuting, 20, 75; culture contact, 22; relations elsewhere in Guatemala, 26; representation in government, 77, 122; identity and classification, 85-94, 182; dualism, 76, 127, 163; castes, 91, 169; barrier and stability, 87, 89-90, 168-183; affiliation in urban and rural residence, 103-105; occupational affiliation 106-108; interaction, 118, 153, 153*n*, 157, 173; in terms of three models, 147-148, 151-153, 157, 157*n;* attitudes of women, 154; division in school enrollment, 159; intermarriage, 160-161; status ambiguity, 172; in a sociological perspective, 173-183.

Ethnocentrism of ladinos, 147.
Etiquette. *See* Address forms
Evangelists, 102
Exbalamquen, 41
Execution of Ixil leaders, 155
Exploitation of Indians: colonial period, 46-49; modern period, 120, 121
Export: of goods and produce, 31, 39, 81; of labor, 73-74, 131-133

Falsehood, as an interpersonal strategy, 157*n*-158*n*
Field work and methodology, xiii, xvii, 153-4*n*
Fiesta: labor contracting during, 73, 131; allocation of municipal funds for; 129; August in Nebaj (Ixil), 101, 129, 134, 140, 141-142, 163-164; September in Nebaj (Ladino), 110, 129, 142, 165; Chajul, 94, 165-168; San Juan Cotzal, 168; economics of, 163-164
Fincas: Guatemala, 33-34; coffee, 74, 107-108; San Francisco, 83, 107, 114, 131
Fireworks, 163
Fiscal, 55. *See also* principales
Food scarcity, 109
Folk-urban dichotomy, 5
Formative period, 39
Franciscans, 51
Fuentes y Guzman, Francisco Antonio de, 60
Functional differentiation, 8-9
Functionalism, 1, 4, 9

Gage, Thomas 55-59
Garcia Granados, Miguel, 72
Golgotha, Christ of, 166
Government: national representation in Nebaj, 37; of department of El Quiché, 37-38; positions, xvi, 121-123; discrimination, 85-86; in Cotzal, 83; ethnic participation, 77, 119-121; official treatment of Ixil and Ladinos, 119-121, 129; corruption, 121; religious involvement, 123, 140-141; local development, 125*n;* service, 130; attempts at hispanization, 177
Gringo, as term used, 180
Group solidarity, 178

Herrenvolk democracy, 11, 12*n*
High priest. *See* Religion, Ixil
Hiring of labor, 132-133. *See also* Wage Labor
Hispanization, 25, 89, 91, 169-183; in ladino view of Indians, 88; in Indian view of Indians, 89
Historical interests of Ixil, 146; early descriptions of Ixil, 60, 63
Homicide, 178
Horizontal mobility, 179
Hospitality, sexual, 162
Hostility by Ixil, 82, 103, 154, 167
House type, 104; ladino, 111-112; Ixil, 58, 114
Huna·pu· *See* Day gods
Hypothetical contact, 153, 153*n*

Idioculture, 8*n*
Illiteracy, 27, 37, 71. *See also* Education
Illness: causes of, 97. *See also* Epidemics
Ilom, 40*n*, 60, 155
Imports of Ixil region, 31, 81
Income: per capita, 35-36
Independence day, 129
Indians: population concentration, 25, 89; involvement in national life and government, 36; share of wealth and power, 82-85; solidarity, 89; voting, 86; viewpoint of ethnic relations, 155-156. *See also* Ixil; Ixil region; Ethnic relations
Indianeros, 21
Individual, self-protective focus on, 178
Industry: agave fiber, 83, 130; candles and fireworks, 140; as economic stimulus, 143; textiles, 143
Inequality, social causes of, 35
In-migration: other Guatemalan departments, 171
Instituto Nacional Indigenista (of Mexico), ix, 177
Integration: social structure, 142; national, 36

Interdisciplinary approach, xiii
Intermarriage, 21, 64, 80, 160. *See also* Concubinage
Internal colonialism, 84*n*
Internal migration, 90
Intransigence of Ixil, 65
Isabella, Queen, 49
Isolation of Ixil zone, 36, 67, 69, 175; breakdown of, 142
Itzá Maya, 60
Ixil: as subjects of study, xx; population, 26-27; 42*n*, 45; social stratification, 36, 112-113; archaeology and prehistory, 39-40; defeat, 41-42; military forces, 42; names, 47; population at Conquest, 61; autonomy of zone, 67; wage labor, 73, 109, 131, 125; politics, 82, 119, 124-127; sample characteristics, 89; clothing, 93, 98, 104; theocracy, 95, 98, 143; new year, 99; internal stratification, 100; urbanism, 109; occupations, 107; proletarian status of, 109; principales, meeting of, 123; deities, 125; government viewed by ladinos, 125; economy, 130; attitudes and behavior toward ladinos, 136, 146, 151, 156, 157*n*, 178; attitudes toward own culture, 147-148; knowledge of Spanish and ladino world, 149-150, 177; xenophobia, 154; leaders executed, 155; sample results, 155-157
Ixil region, area of, ix, 27-29; altitude, 26; of Ixil towns, 27; rainfall, 28; vegetation, 28-29; Chajul, 63; boundaries redrawn, 70; boundaries, 80

Jesuits, 64
Juez de paz, 122
Juil, 40, 80-81, 102, 166
Juzgado, attitudes toward, 119-121; functions of, 105. *See also* Government

Kaqiq', 96
Kaqsučkum, 96
Kaminaljuyu, 60
Kanjobal, 60
Kuçuç, 95; Mariy, 163-164. *See also* Fiesta; August
Kumo·l, 180

Labor; contracting and recruiting, 72-73, 84, 107-109, 132, 133, 140; exportation of, 81, 131, 132; reform, 76. *See also* Migrant workers, Wage labor
Lacandons, 60
Lacantun River, 40
Ladino: change to Indian, 21; relations with Indians elsewhere in Guatemala, 26; ties to national life and government, 36, 85, 118, 129; early arrival, 69, 72; early occupations, 73; attitudes toward Ixil, 88, 125, 137, 144-145, 148, 151-153; change to ladino, 90-91; view of Indian culture, 91, 144-145; superstition, 94; use of term in Mexico, 175; estates, 107; society, 110; ethnocentricism, 110, 147; style of living, 111-112; mayors, 111, 140, in Nebaj, 84; class structure, 111, 115, in Chajul, 82, in Cotzal, 83; interview sample, 153-154; viewed by Ixil, 156; cofradías, 159; fiesta, 164-165
Ladinoization, 90-91, 125, 143, 170, 172, 177; effects of, 27
Land: ownership, 33, 34, 107-109; scarcity, 33, 108; distribution and expropriation, 34-35; tenure, 32-33; use in Guatemala, 34-35; land reform law, Decreto 900, 35, 77; reform, 15, 33-34, 125; Spanish grants, 47, 61; seizure by ladinos, 73; values in Nebaj, 115; disputes, 155
Landecho, Martinez de, 51
Language: groups in Guatemala, 25, 27*n;* dialect variation, 80, 82, 116; and ethnic classification, 88, 92-93, 118, 149-150; linguistic classification of Ixil, 185. *See also* Lingua franca
La Paz, Miguel Brito, 75
Las Casas, Bartolomé de, 45, 53
Las Casas, San Cristóbal de, 174
Leadership, Ixil, 100
Legends, 48-49, 51, 96-97, 146

Legislation, protective of Indians, 49-50
León, Diego de, 70-71
Liberation of 1954, 77
Lincoln, Jackson Steward, xiii, 112, 115
Lingua Franca, 118, 172; as cultural medium, 22-23, 176
Linguistics, model for culture study, 22-24; contact in colonial period, 63; classification of Ixil, 185. *See also* Language
Literacy: interview sample bias, xvi; and voting laws, 86; associated with ethnic group, 93-94, 94*n;* and ladinoization, 177
Livestock, 29
Lopez Cerrato, Alonso, 50
Luege, Isidoro, 67

Machismo, 162
Maestro de coro, 55
Mail flow in Nebaj, 37
Maize: cultivation, 29-30; milling, 133
Mahob'ab'al, 94
Mam (diviner), 97
Manual labor: Spanish attitude toward, 176
Manufacturing in Indian areas, 130, 143*n*
Marginality, 172; in cultural or social systems, 21
Marimba, 73, 101, 163-164, 168
Market, 74, 164, 131; days, 81
Marriage, 160-161
Marroquín, Bishop, 50
Mass: enforced attendance, 66; attendance 101, 102. *See also* Church
Mayordomo, in cofradías, 55, 100-102
Mejía, Pedro, 52
Mendez, Gonzalo, 51
Mengala, 21
Merchant-customer relations, 132-133
Mestizo, 90; in Ixil zone, 69; defined, 175*n*
Mexican anthropologists, ix
Mexico, 174-179
Migrant workers, 131-132; in Guatemala, 33; in Ixil area, 31. *See also* Labor
Migration: internal, 90; as factor in passing, 174, 171
Military confrontation in Nebaj, 155
Minifundia, 34
Miscegenation, 160
Missionaries: attempts of during early period, 51-54; modern period, 78, 82; methods, 66; efforts resisted, 67
Mobility: in class status, 21, 115. *See also* Caste
Monetary unit, 25*n*
Moneylending, 72, 133-134
Morphology: of ethnic relations, 145. *See also* Ethnic relations
Mortuary customs, 65, 68
Motivation for interethnic relations, 157
Multiple Society, 6
Municipios of Ixil territory, 26, 26*n;* administrative center, 83
Music, 70-71, 71*n;* in ceremonies, 101
Muˀs, 180
Myth, 146; creation, 96-97. *See also* Religion, Ixil

Names of early Ixil, 47
National independence celebration, 165
National society: relations of Ixil zone to, ix; defined, 6; integration of Ixil in, 36
Nebaj: altitude, 27; surrender to Spaniards, 42; change of location, 43; residences 104; salary of alcalde, 130; cemeteries, 160
New laws, 50
New year of Ixil Mayan calendar, 81, 99. *See also* Calendar

Official policies of discrimination, 85-86
Oficialistas, 86
Olaverreta, Joseph de, 63
Olmos, Pedro de, 41
Olontepeque, 52
ˀo·q'i·, 98
Orduña, Francisco de, 41

"Paganism," 94, 138, 155
Pan American Highway, 27, 38
Partido Institucional Democrático (PID), 38, 124, 126-127
Partido Revolucionario (PR), 38, 124, 126-127, 139
Passing, 21, 87, 90-92, 171-183
Paternalism, 120, 137, 147-148, 151; as tyranny, 15; as stabilizing factor, 15
Paternalistic model: of ethnic relations, 151; accepted by Ixil, 156-157; in Ixil interview schedule, 157*n*
Patron relationship, 132, 147, 149
Peasant cultures decapitated, 175
Peonage, debt, 133-134
Personality of Ixil, described by priest, 67
PID. *See* Partido Institucional Democrático
Pidgin cultures, 23
Pilgrims, 166
Plantations in Guatemala, 33; coffee, 83, 107-109, 114. *See also* Fincas
Plural society: definition, ix, 20; analytical levels in the study of, 17, 19-20
Pluralism: as analytical perspective, x-xi; analytical approaches to, 3, 16, 182; in the Americas, 5; in Asia, 5; defined, 6-8; in Africa, 4; in Europe, 9, 11; in the United States, 9; as relates to democracy and other political institutions, 11*n*, 12*n;* and economic institutions, 12, 13; and social structure, 142
Police, 47, 122
Politics: unit of study, 6-7; institutions as elements of plural societies, 10, 12*n,* 13; boundaries 11, 27; parties, 38; organization during prehispanic period, 42-43; organization during colonial period, 53; influence of ladinos, 74, 118; representation of Ixil, 77, 105; political control in Ixil area, 85; issues in 1966, 124-127; office and wealth, 112, 113, 130; urban-rural division, 127-128; influence of wealth, 140
Polygyny, 68, 162
Population: ethnic percentages, 25, 27*n,* 74, 89, 170; of Quiché, 37; prehispanic, 39; of Ixil in 1530, 42*n;* centers of Ixil in early period, 43; movements during colonial period, 44; decline, 45-46, 62; early estimates, 61-62; census of 1893, 69; 20th century growth, 74; of Chajul, 82; of Cotzal, 83; of Nebaj, 84; urban-rural, 103-108, 128. *See also* Appendix C, table 2, 194
PR. See Partido Revolucionario
Prayer-sayers, 97, 141. *See also* Religion
Preclassic period, 39
Prestige stratification, 100
Priests: Ixil, 97; Catholic, 65. *See also* Religion
Primitive isolate, 5
Principales, 43, 112-113, 122, 123, 141; fiscal, 55; in 1890's, 71; during 1940's, 74-75; meeting of, 123
Processions, 135, 163
Prostitution, 162
Protestants, 102
Puente, Francisco, 68
Puerra, Eusenio, 65
Punishment: meted by Church, 59; physical, 66; Divine, 97; by national government, 155

Q'anil, 98. *See also* Day gods
Queen of Ixil, 165
Q'esla Kub'a·l, 95
Quetzaltenango, 41, 175
Quiché: population, 26, 37, 104; Santa Cruz del, 27, 37; government of, 37-38; kings, 40; on Ixil land, 80
Quikap, 40

Rabinal Achí, 40
Raiding, 60
Rainfall. *See* Ixil region
Rapport, xv, 82
Raul, Juan, 67
Rebellion, 64, 155
Recruiting for labor, 72-73, 84, 108, 132-133. *See also* Contracting, Wage labor

Reference terms for social groupings, 147-149, 180
Refuge areas, 175-176
Regidor, 121-123; second, 127-128
Regional: integration, 5, 80; approach, ix
Religion: cohesion and conflict in plural societies, 13, 14; Chajul dominance in, 40, 82; in 19th century, 70; consumption of alcohol, 71, 145, 168; Catholic conversion, 77, 82; change, 82-83; as ethnic affiliation criterion, 94, 159; Ixil, 95-103; behavioral sanctions, 97; high priest, 97; orthodox vs. pagan, 102, 138, 155, 178; variations in, 102; and government positions, 123; as political issue, 125, 141, 143; church services, 134; social integration at cross ceremony 135; compadrazgo, 136; ritual duality, 138, 139; revitalization, 139. *See also* Church
Resistance: to orthodox Catholicism, 67-69. *See also* Rebellion, Revolt
Revolt: by Ixil, 64, 165
Revolution: in colonial situations, 15; in 1944-1954, 77, 130
Ritual: Ixil, 99; dualism, 139; role of Catholic clergy, 134-135
Rivers, 29
Roads, 65-66, 82, 83, 129; distances to major towns, 27-28, 31; new, 129*n*, colonial period, 40, 52
Rural population: Ixil area, 28; contrasted with urban, 103-108
Rural-urban areas: distinction, 83*n;* characteristics of Ixil, 103-105; dimension of political influence, 127-128, 129*n*. *See also* Economy

Sacapulas, 31, 42, 51-52; base of early missionary activities, 52, 60
Sacristans, 68
Salquilito, 115
Salvatierra, Lorenzo de, 51
Sample: characteristics, 86*n;* Ixil, 89; ladino, 153-154
Sanctions: against ladinoization, 89; religious, 97
San Cristóbal de Las Casas, 174
San Francisco plantation, 83, 107-108, 114, 131
San Juan Cotzal: *See* Cotzal
San Juan, Miguel de, 65
Santa Cruz del Quiché: departmental capital, 27, 37; in prehispanic period, 40
Santa Eulalia, 60
Scale, as dimension of social analysis, 3
School: first in Nebaj, 72; Cotzal, 83; rural, 129*n; de facto* segregation, 158-159; Cotzal and Chajul, 159. *See also* Education
Secretary, 121
Segmentary homogeneity, as component of pluralism, 8
Segregation: *de facto* in schools, 158-159; attributed to ethnicity, 158; residential, 158; school ceremonies, 159
Selectivity: in culture change, 181
Self-protective concern, 178
Servants, 112, 132, 147
Settlement: colonial pattern, 52; of Nebaj by ladinos, 72
Sex: difference in ethnic attitudes, 154; Indian-ladino relations, 160-161; sexual hospitality, 162
Sickness, 65; in colonial period, 44-45, 45*n*. *See also* Epidemics
Síndico, 121, 122, 128
Six-year limbo. *See* Conquest
Slash-and-burn cultivation, 29-30. *See also* Agriculture
Slavery, 42; Columbus' involvement in, 49; Dominican views toward, 51
Social class, 85, 115; Ixil-ladino distinction, 85, 92; objective and subjective correlates of, 17-18; achieved and ascriptive aspects, 18; stratification in Guatemala, 35; and phenotypical differences, 87; distinctions among Ixil, 100; ladino, 110-112; Ixil, 112-113; mobility among Ixil, 115. *See also* Ethnic Relations
Social criteria of ethnic membership, 86-88. *See also* Ethnic Relations

Social inequality, 35
Social mobility, 108, 112. *See also* Ethnic Relations
Social pluralism, 8-9
Social structure, 142; as analytical framework, 182
Society: as unit of analysis, 2-3, 80; arbitrariness of definition, 7; stratification, 110, 112
South Africa, 11
Spanish: army, 41; protection of Indians, 49-51; control in Guatemala, 57-59; as official language, 86; knowledge by Ixil, 149; use in process of ladinoization, 177
Specialization of production, 81
Sports, 159, 165
Standard of living, 113, 114
States, types of, and ethnic relations, 10-11
Status: objective and subjective correlates of, 17-18; systems in plural societies, 17-19; among Ixil, 55, 100, 109; and Ixil contact with ladinos, 156
Stoll, Otto, 68
Storm god, 96
Stratification: relation to pluralism, 16, 183; among Ixil, 35, 100, 112-113; among ladinos, 35-36, 110-112; of Guatemala, 35; of Ixil deities, 95, 98
Subjective view, 182; perception of cultural differences, 7, 173; perception of status, 17-18

Taboo against Indian godparents, 137
Taxes, 121; evasion of, 57. *See also* Tribute
Tecum Uman, 41
Television, 113, 159
Tepepul Ztayul, 40
Tertiary sector, 131
Theocracy, 95
Tocquevillean tradition, 7*n*, 8*n*
Torres, Juan de, 52
Totonicapán, 48, 51, 56
Tourism, 38, 145
Town Hall, attitudes toward, 119-121
Towns, during conquest period, 43; function of, 115
Trade, prehispanic, 39-40
Traditionalism: preservation of, 14, 115; in voting, 86; influence of Catholicism, 96, 134; on government, 141
Traffic, vehicular, 81-82. *See also* Roads
Transportation, 66, 83, 107, 129, 131, 167
Travel in Ixil area, 80
Tribute, 58, 60*n;* early payments by Ixil, 45; evasion of payments, 57; exoneration from, 70; exacted by principales, 71
Truth, focus on, 157*n*-158*n*
Tyranny and pluralism, 11, 11*n*
Tzintzuntzan, 175*n*
Tzeltal, Tzotzil zone, 174

Ubico, Jorge, 76
Underdevelopment, 35
United Fruit Company, 33
United States: as agent of underdevelopment and social inequality in Guatemala, 35; counterrevolution in Guatemala, 35; continued influence in Guatemala, 124
Urban: bias in interview sample, xvii; Ixil population, 27-28, 103-108; dimension in ladino politics, 128 129; dimension in ladinoization, 177
Uspantán, 41
Utatlán, 40

Values: consensus, 8, 10; as analytical perspective, 14; as explanation for culture change, 181
Vegetation. *See* Ixil region
Villages: in colonial period, 43, 60
Violence: Ixil-ladino, 155
Virgin of the Assumption, 141
Visiting patterns, 167
Voting: in Nebaj, 86; in Ixil territory, 125-127; irregularities, 126; in Chajul and Cotzal, 127

Wage labor, 31, 109, 131; colonial period, 58; export of, 73; political issue, 125. *See also* Labor, Migrant workers

Wealth: colonial period, 57; of colonial churches, 64; political office, 113; ethnic distribution of, 140
we¢ k'aol, 167
Wind god, 96
Witchcraft, 94, 98, 136, 178-179; Indian attitude toward, xvi
Worker caste, 115

Xenophobia, 154

Yucatan: regional approach in study of, 5

Zorita, 49